☆ ☆ ☆ ☆ ☆ THE ☆ ☆ ☆ ☆ ☆

AMERICAN

★ ★ ★EXPERIENCE★ ★ ★

☆ ☆ ☆ ☆ ☆ **THE** ☆ ☆ ☆ ☆ ☆

AMERICAN
EXPERIENCE

An Interpretation
of the History and Civilization
of the American People

Henry Bamford Parkes

★ ★ ★ ★ ★ ★ ★ ★ ★ ★ ★ ★

LIBRARY
BRYAN COLLEGE
DAYTON, TENN. **37321**

GREENWOOD PRESS, PUBLISHERS
WESTPORT CONNECTICUT

Library of Congress Cataloging in Publication Data

Parkes, Henry Bamford, 1904-
   The American experience.

   Reprint. Originally published: New York : Knopf,
1947.
   Includes index.
   1. United States--Civilization.   I. Title.
E169.1.P23 1982   973   82-15518
ISBN 0-313-22574-5 (lib. bdg.)

Reprinted by arrangement with Alfred A. Knopf, Inc.

Reprinted in 1982 by Greenwood Press
A division of Congressional Information Service, Inc.
88 Post Road West, Westport, Connecticut 06881

Printed in the United States of America

10 9 8 7 6 5 4 3 2 1

★ for my wife ★

Acknowledgments

*I should like to express my gratitude to the numerous peo-
ple with whom I have discussed the ideas presented in this
book and whose criticisms have assisted me in clarifying
them: particularly to the students in my seminar on American Civilization in the Graduate School of New York University during the years 1944–7; to* HERBERT WEINSTOCK
and ROGER SHUGG *of the firm of Alfred A. Knopf; to*
MARGARET SLOSS, CORINNE MARSH, EUNICE JESSUP, JOSEPH
FRANK, *and* FRANCIS FERGUSSON; *and above all to my wife.*

H. B. P.

Introduction

THE PURPOSE of this book is to present an interpretation of the character and civilization of the American people. Although it deals mainly with the American past, it is not a history of the United States. My primary object has been, not to tell the story of the American past, but to discuss its meaning and to derive from it a deeper understanding of the problems of the American present.

What does it mean to be an American? What are the special characteristics of American civilization, and in what ways does it differ from the civilization of other nations? In order to answer these questions it is necessary to turn to American history. For the character of a nation, like that of an individual, is the product of its past experience and is revealed best in its actions. In this book I have attempted to explain the historical forces that molded the American character and to show how that character has been exhibited at different periods both in thought and in behavior. This purpose has determined my selection of subject matter. I have included enough factual material to make the book intelligible to readers who know little about American history; but I have tried to include only those facts that are necessary for an understanding of American civilization or that illustrate different aspects of it. Since I did not propose to write a history of the United States, I have said relatively little about the details of political and economic development. On the other hand, I have occasionally discussed movements that have had little effect on the course of events, but that illustrate important tendencies of the American mind; and I have given considerable attention to political ideals, to religion and philosophy, and to literature.

I have written this book in the belief that American civilization has certain unique features that differentiate it from that of any European country. The culture of the United States has been the product of two main factors: of the impulses and aspirations that caused men and women to leave their European homes and cross the Atlantic; and of the influences of the American natural environment. As a result of these factors the Americans have acquired, not only certain characteristic political ideals and beliefs, but also a distinctive view of life and code of values. This view of life and code of values guide the behavior of individual Americans and are reflected in American philosophy and in American literature and art. I believe that these distinctive qualities of American culture have not been sufficiently appreciated, and that American intellectuals and political theorists have frequently been too much influenced by European concepts that have little relevance to American realities. Throughout this book I have tried to define and emphasize those qualities that are characteristically American. This emphasis explains the omission of much of the material which appears in formal histories.

I believe that once these essential tendencies of American culture have been defined, then the political and economic development of the American people, their religion and philosophy, and their literature and art can all be regarded as reflections of the same basic attitudes. The history of America can thus be interpreted as the working out of certain basic cultural drives that are exhibited both in American thought and in American action. And the problems of present-day America are due largely to certain contradictions that were always inherent in the American cultural pattern but that did not become acute until the twentieth century. These contradictions cannot be resolved unless they are understood; and they can best be understood through a study of their origin and development in the American past.

In dealing with the early political and economic development of America, I have emphasized chiefly the drive toward an agrarian democracy: toward a society, in other words, in which almost all men would be independent property owners. The product partly of the desire for independence that caused the Atlantic migration and partly of the abundance of cheap land in the American continent, the agrarian ideal took shape during the colonial period, was asserted during the Revolution, and remained a dominating factor in American politics down to the Civil War. And in spite of the growth of industrial capitalism, it has continued to have a most important influence on the attitudes of the American people down to the present day. I believe that one cannot appreciate the special qualities of American civilization unless one understands the agrarian tradition (which cannot be duplicated in the history of any important European country); yet as a result of European preconceptions (both capitalistic and Marxist), the true meaning and importance of this tradition have not been sufficiently recognized. In this book I have interpreted American political and economic history mainly in terms of the rise and decline of agrarianism, of the contradictions and limitations of the agrarian attitude, and of the conflict between American agrarianism and European doctrines of capitalism and socialism. Although the agrarian economy of eighteenth-century America has now disappeared, I believe it is only by understanding and redefining their agrarian tradition and adapting it to an industrial economy that twentieth-century Americans can create the kind of society that will fulfill their national ideals.

Those American qualities that were expressed, on the political level, by such spokesmen of agrarian democracy as Jefferson, Jackson, and Lincoln, can be traced also in the development of American religion, in the philosophy of such men as William James, and in the literature both of the pre-Civil War period and of the twentieth century. The intellectual and æsthetic manifestations of the American mind exhibit the same aspirations and the same inner contradictions as its political theory. In discussing these subjects I have tried to show what they have in common with each other and to present all of them as different manifestations of the same basic cultural tendencies. As long as the works of different American writers and thinkers are approached on the superficial level of the ideas they consciously inculcate, and are judged by their political beliefs (as in the three volumes of Parrington), they appear to be very diverse and no common pattern can be discovered. It seems to me that when they are explored more deeply and are examined for their implicit assumptions, then even intellectual creations that appear to run counter to the main stream of American development can be interpreted as significant expressions of the American spirit.

H. B. P.

Contents

☆ ☆ ☆ ☆ ☆ THE ☆ ☆ ☆ ☆ ☆

AMERICAN

★ ★ ★EXPERIENCE★ ★ ★

☆ ☆ ☆ ☆ ☆ ☆ ☆ ☆ ☆ ☆ ☆ ☆ ☆ ☆

CHAPTER I

THE NEW MAN

★ ★ ★ ★ ★ ★ ★ ★ ★ ★ ★ ★ ★ ★ ★

THE CENTRAL THEME in the history of the Americas can be stated very simply. During the four and a half centuries that have elapsed since the first voyage of Columbus, a stream of migration has been flowing from Europe westward across the Atlantic and into the two American continents. Relatively small during the first three hundred years, it increased during the nineteenth century and did not reach its peak until shortly before the First World War. In all, between fifty and sixty million persons left their European homes and established themselves in the New World. During the same period another five or ten millions were brought to the Americas by force from Africa. This is by far the largest movement of peoples in all history. There was no comparable process at any earlier epoch, and nothing like it is likely to happen again in the future. Whether one judges it by the number of individuals involved in it or by its results and implications, it is the most important single factor in the recent history of the human race.

This Atlantic migration was not the first invasion of the American hemisphere. Some twenty thousand years earlier, peoples of a different ethnic group, originating in northeastern Asia, had crossed into America by way of the Bering Strait. But it was only in Mexico and along the plateaus of the Andes that these "Indian" races succeeded in creating well-integrated societies that did not dissolve before the onset of the Europeans. In these two areas, which were among the first to pass under white control, the Indian masses, though subjugated and exploited by the newcomers, have retained their racial identity and many of their traditional characteristics. But elsewhere the hemisphere has become the undisputed property of the white man or of the Negro whom he brought with him.

In the southern continent the main lines of European settlement were marked out within fifty years of the first voyages of discovery. This rapid initial attack was followed by a long period of quiescence, during which there was relatively little new exploration or settlement. In the late nineteenth century, with a revival of energy and a new flow of migration into South America from Europe, the process was resumed. In the north the advance of the Europeans was more gradual but more consistent. Beginning more than a hundred years later than in the south, it covered only a few hundred miles from the Atlantic seacoast during the first century and a half, but gathered momentum quickly during the century that followed. The progress of white colonization reached its climax in the two continents almost simultaneously. The peoples of Argentina and Chile were imposing white rule over the hitherto unconquered Indians of the far south during the same two or three decades in which the people of the United States subjugated the Indians of the great plains and completed the settlement of the West.

That this movement of the European races into the New World should be regarded as the essential substance of American history is not difficult to understand. The explorer, the conquistador, the pioneer, and the liberator are the primary symbols of the American cultures. But the full implications, political and psychological, of this migration are not so easy to define. Establishing himself in the New World, the American repudiated a part of his European inheritance. In certain respects, though not in all, he ceased to be a European and became a new subspecies of humanity. It is only by understanding the qualities of this new man, the American, that we can interpret much that may otherwise seem puzzling or disturbing in his achievements and his behavior. We must, above all, avoid the error of regarding the civilization of America as a mere extension, without significant changes, of that of Europe. The differences between them should, in fact, be emphasized, since otherwise the American peoples will be unable either to form a sound evaluation of their own institutions or to avoid misunderstandings with those European nations with whom they must be associated.

This volume is concerned with the evolution of civilization in the United States, and here the divergence from European traditions was sharper than in the Spanish-speaking countries. Both the North and the South Americans have displayed certain common American characteristics, but these developed more fully in the north. The imprint of European institutions, of monarchy, aristocracy, and clericalism, and of the view of life and habits of thought associated with them, was much deeper and more lasting in the southern countries than it was in the United States. This was owing partly to the authoritarian policies of Spanish imperialism and partly to the presence of large Indian populations who could be reduced to a servitude resembling that of the peasants of feudal Europe. To a large degree Latin America became an extension of Latin Europe. The migration to the United States, on the other hand, created a new way of life that quickly acquired certain unique qualities.

The impulse of migration may be described, negatively, as an impulse of escape. The American fled from a Europe where he could find no satisfying fulfillment of his energies and was confronted by conflicts and dilemmas that had no easy solution. The groups who came to all parts of the New World were, in general, those who were most acutely discontented with their status in European society and who had the least hope of being able to improve it. The Hispanic colonies were settled mainly by impoverished members of the lower nobility and by adventurers from the lower classes. Unable to achieve aristocratic status at home, they hoped to win riches, land, and glory for themselves in America. Most of the early immigrants to the United States came from the petty bourgeoisie in the English cities or from the yeoman farmers; a few were motivated primarily by the desire to put into practice novel religious or political ideas, but the majority expected to improve their economic condition. The later migration from the other European countries into both North and South America was similar in character, including some religious and political refugees, but consisting mainly of ambitious younger sons of the bourgeoisie and of oppressed and land-hungry peasants from Ireland, Germany, Scandinavia, Italy, and the Austrian and Russian empires. All sought in the New World an environment where they could act more freely, without being restricted by traditional forms of authority and discipline or by a scarcity of land and natural resources.

Of the various factors that caused men to come to America, the economic was no doubt the most important. Throughout the period of the migrations, there was no free land in Europe; natural resources were limited; and the population was always in danger of increasing faster than the means of subsistence. Migration always occurred chiefly from areas of Europe where agriculture was still the chief occupation and where (owing to the growth of big estates or to genuine overcrowding) the demand for land was in excess of the supply. This was true of Spain in the sixteenth century, of England in the early seventeenth, and of Ireland, Germany, Scandinavia, Italy, and the Slavic countries of the east in the nineteenth.

An almost equally influential stimulus to migration was the European class system. This was, in fact, perhaps the chief cause of European economic privation, since the big estates of the aristocracy diminished the supply of land available for the peasants. Before the discovery of America, European society had been molded by feudalism into a tightly knit organic structure in which every individual, from the king at the top to the humblest peasant at the bottom, was expected to know his place and to perform the duties appropriate to it. These class differences had become a deeply rooted part of the European consciousness. Ambitious and enterprising members of the middle and lower classes could sometimes improve their position, either individually or in groups, but the battle against aristocratic privilege was always difficult, and never reached a conclusion. For such persons the opening of the New World beyond the Atlantic promised an easier escape from frustration and the sense of inferiority.

Privation and inequality weighed upon all underprivileged persons in Europe, but did not cause all of them to come to America. Human behavior is conditioned by economic and social factors in the sense that these establish the problems to be solved, but it is not determined by them: how particular individuals choose to act in a given situation depends upon deeper, more intangible, and more mysterious forces. Confronted by the same difficulties, some individuals preferred to submit to them or to continue struggling with them, while others, generally the more restless and adventurous, decided to come to the New World. Thus the settlement of America was a selective process that attracted those members of the European middle and lower classes who had the appropriate bent and disposition; it appealed not necessarily to the ablest or the strongest, but usually to the most enterprising. In a sense it may be said that America was from the beginning a state of mind and not merely a place.

In the New World, at least during the earlier period of colonization, this selective process continued. Those who had the requisite energy, adaptability, and capacity for endurance survived and prospered; others died of starvation or in battle with the Indians. In the course of centuries certain qualities became established as suitable to the new environment and as characteristically American. Men born in the New World were disposed, both by inheritance and by conditioning, to develop them, and later immigrant groups found it necessary to acquire them. Thus the civilizations of the New World promoted certain special psychic configurations that differentiated the American from the European.

In the Hispanic countries the presence of Indian labor and the importation of Negro slaves enabled many of the early immigrants to achieve the aristocratic status to which they aspired. But in the United States there were no Indian peoples who could be made to work for white overlords; and though the institution of Negro slavery was adopted during the colonial period, its influence was restricted to one section of the country. There were in the United States, on the other hand, enormous stretches of fertile land and vast mineral resources of all kinds. Immigrants could find, in this undeveloped and almost empty country, opportunities for self-advancement that have never been equaled in the whole of human history. The individual had to display industry, courage, and resourcefulness; but if he possessed these qualities, then security, independence, and prosperity were within his reach. This unexampled abundance of land and resources was the cardinal factor in the development of American civilization. It molded the character of the American people, and was the chief reason for the unique qualities of their way of life. It facilitated the growth of individual freedom and social equality, and it promoted attitudes of optimism and self-assurance.

The society that developed under these conditions differed from that of Europe not only in its political and economic characteristics but also in some of its animating beliefs and views of life. The American acquired new attitudes and learned to see the world in a new way. And the nationality he created became a vast experiment in new social principles and new modes of living.

The European mind had been dominated by a hierarchical sense of order. This sense was embodied most completely in the philosophical and political theory of the Middle Ages; but even after the breakdown of feudalism and the repudiation of the scholastic philosophy, it continued, in one form or another, to permeate the consciousness of most Europeans. Human society was regarded as the reflection of an ideal order derived from the will of God and fully embodied in the cosmos. And the life of the individual acquired meaning and value insofar as he conformed with the order of the society to which he belonged. Yet the Europeans believed also that the attempt to realize this ideal order in concrete forms must always be incomplete. Evil was an inherent element in human experience, and both in nature and in the human spirit there were anarchical and rebellious forces that conflicted with the ideal order and that could never be wholly controlled. This belief in the reality of evil led to the European doctrine of original sin and was the basis of the European sense of tragedy.

The first immigrants to America brought with them this sense of order, but in the American world it gradually grew weaker; it did not remain a permanent part of the American consciousness. Coming to a country where there was no elaborate social organization, and where the individual must constantly do battle with the forces of nature, the American came to see life not as an attempt to realize an ideal order, but as a struggle between the human will and the environment. And he believed that if men were victorious in this struggle, they could hope that evil might gradually be conquered and eliminated. What appeared as evil was not a fundamental and permanent element in the nature of things, but should be regarded merely as a problem to which the correct solution would one day be discovered. The American was therefore a voluntarist and an optimist. He did not believe in the devil, nor did he accept the dogma of original sin.

The most obvious result of this American attitude was the fostering of an extraordinary energy and confidence of will. The American came to believe that nothing was beyond his power to accomplish, provided that he could muster the necessary moral and material resources, and that any obstacle could be mastered by means of the appropriate methods and technology. A failure was the result either of weakness or of an incorrect technique. By contrast with the European, the American was more extroverted, quicker and more spontaneous in action, more self-confident, and psychologically simpler. His character was molded not by the complex moral and social obligations of an ordered hierarchical system, but by the struggle to achieve victory over nature.

Rejecting both the belief in a fixed social order and the belief in the depravity of human beings, the American created a society whose special characteristic was the freedom enjoyed by its individual members. Respect for the freedom of every individual and confidence that he would use his freedom wisely and constructively became the formative principles of the new American nationality. By crossing the Atlantic, the American had asserted a demand to be himself; he had repudiated the disciplines of the class hierarchy, of long-established tradition, and of authoritarian religion. And in the society that took shape in the New World it was by his natural and inherent quality that the individual was measured, rather than by rank or status or conformity to convention. To a much greater degree than elsewhere, society in America was based on the natural man rather than on man as molded by social rituals and restraints. The mores of America were less rigid and less formalized than those of any earlier community, and the individual was less inhibited. The American did not believe that men needed to be coerced, intimidated, or indoctrinated into good behavior.

By European standards this American attitude often seemed unrealistic, Utopian, and naïve. The American appeared to be deficient in the recognition of evil and in the sense of tragedy. Yet as long as he was engaged primarily in the conquest of the wilderness, he had good reasons for his optimism. His naïveté was, in fact, an expression of a genuine innocence. He was simpler than the European because his life was freer, more spontaneous, and less frustrated. In Europe, with its economic privation, its hierarchy of classes, and its traditional disciplines and rituals, emotional drives were more inhibited; and it is when aggressive energies are thrown back upon themselves and can find no satisfying outlet in action that they become evil. The European was psychologically much more complex than the American, and therefore capable of deeper and more subtle insights and of profounder spiritual and æsthetic achievements; but he was also more corrupt, with a greater propensity toward the negative emotions of fear and avarice and hatred. He believed in the depravity of human nature because he knew it in his own experience.

In social organization and in practical activity the American confidence in human nature was abundantly justified by its results. The tone of American society was more generous and hospitable, more warmhearted and more genuinely kindly, than that of other peoples. And by encouraging individuals to develop latent talents and to prefer versatility and adaptability to professional specialization, it promoted an astonishing activity and ingenuity. The genius of American life lay in its unprecedented capacity to release for constructive purposes the energies and abilities of common men and women. In consequence, the material achievements of the Americans were stupendous. And though they hated the authoritarian discipline of warfare, they displayed when they went to war an inventiveness and a resourcefulness that no other people could equal.

Yet though the civilization of the Americans had remarkable virtues, it also had grave deficiencies. The conditions that produced their material achievements did not result in any corresponding intellectual efflorescence. Their bent was toward the conquest of nature rather than toward metaphysical speculation or æsthetic creation. And though their suspicion of professional pretensions and their trust in the abilities of the common man had astonishing results in politics, technology, and warfare, the effect upon intellectual life was less desirable; for the common man has usually valued material progress above the difficult and apparently useless disciplines of abstract thought. In consequence, the more formal intellectual activities of the Americans often appeared to be timid, conventional, and derivative. They frequently used ideas that had been borrowed from Europe, and that had little relevance or vital connection with their own society. Their practice was usually bolder and more original than their theory. Outside the fields of practical activity, America developed no living system of general ideas and no continuing intellectual tradition, so that each generation of writers and thinkers had a tendency to start afresh, with little guidance or encouragement from the past.

Whether the American civilization was capable not only of rapid material growth but also of stability was, moreover, open to question. For the conditions under which it had acquired its unique qualities were transitory and not permanent. The land and the natural resources of the New World were not inexhaustible. Before the end of the nineteenth century every part of the United States had been settled; and most of its resources had become the private property of individuals. There was no longer an open frontier inviting the restless, the dissatisfied, and the ambitious. And though an expanding capitalism continued to offer opportunities for the exercise of initiative, it was only the exceptionally enterprising and the exceptionally lucky, not the average American citizen, who could take advantage of them. Under such circumstances, certain contradictions that had always been inherent in the American view of life became more manifest and more dangerous. For while the Americans had believed in a universal freedom and equality, they had also encouraged and applauded the competitive drive of individuals toward wealth and power. And in a complex industrial society this drive was directed less against nature and more against other human beings. Those individuals who succeeded in acquiring economic privileges did so by restricting the freedom of others; and the competitive struggle for power and prestige threatened to destroy the human warmth and openheartedness that had hitherto been the special virtues of American society.

How far and by what methods could the qualities of the American way of life be preserved after the conditions under which they first developed had disappeared? These questions began to confront the American people in the twentieth century. As long as they had been engaged in conquering and settling an empty continent, material conditions had in themselves promoted freedom, equality, and a spirit of co-operation. But after this process had been completed, the Americans could remain a democratic people only by conscious choice and deliberate effort. If they wished to remain American, they must now acquire a more critical understanding of their way of life, of the historical experience by which it had been shaped, and of the contradictions within it which must be eliminated or transcended. They had to establish a cultural and intellectual tradition matching their material achievements and growing out of the American experience instead of being borrowed from Europe. Otherwise the American experiment in democracy could have no happy outcome.

And upon the results of this American experiment depended, in large measure, the future not only of the Americans themselves but of the whole human race. For the movement toward individual liberation and towards the mastery of nature, which was represented in its purest and completest form in the United States, was of world-wide extent, so that the whole world seemed to be gradually becoming Americanized. During the entire period from the voyage of Columbus to the present day, while some persons sought a greater freedom by crossing the Atlantic, others fought for it at home; the same forces of social protest that caused the Atlantic migration brought about profound changes in the society, first of Europe, and afterwards of the Orient; and the rise, first of the bourgeoisie, and afterwards of the proletariat, caused a slow disintegration of traditional concepts of social hierarchy. During the nineteenth century the rapid expansion of capitalism in Europe and Asia created opportunities comparable to those existing in America, while the achievements of American democracy exerted a magnetic influence and attraction upon the peoples of other countries. Thus the civilizations of the Old World were moving in the same direction as the new civilization of America. There was no complete transformation of European society, and still less of the society of the Orient. Europe never forgot the feudal emphasis on rank, status, and authority or the belief in individual subordination to the order of the whole; nor did the European acquire the simplicity and the optimism characteristic of the American. In Europe the struggle between the principles of freedom and those of authority was unending and reached no decisive conclusion. Yet the problem that confronted the Americans—the problem of reconciling the freedom of individuals with the welfare and stability of society—had universal implications. Would the achievements of American civilization continue to attract the peoples of other countries? Or would the Ameri-

cans themselves end by abandoning American principles
and reverting to earlier traditions of authority and social
hierarchy?

For these reasons the history of America, considered as
a state of mind and not merely as a place, presented a
series of problems of immense spiritual and practical importance.

☆ ☆ ☆ ☆ ☆ ☆ ☆ ☆ ☆ ☆ ☆ ☆ ☆ ☆

CHAPTER II

THE FOUNDING
OF THE COLONIES

★ ★ ★ ★ ★ ★ ★ ★ ★ ★ ★ ★ ★ ★

IN A SYMBOLIC SENSE Columbus can appropriately be regarded as the first American. Here was a man of obscure
birth, without influential family connections or financial
resources, who had the audacity to plan an enterprise
without precedent in recorded history. He was a skillful
seaman, and his project was supported by the best geographical learning of his time; yet it was not primarily by
his ability or his knowledge of navigation that he earned
his immortality, but by the quality of his will. To discover
America required the courage to sail westward across the
ocean for as long as might be necessary, not knowing where
one was going or whether one would ever return. Other
men had believed that there might be land on the other side
of the Atlantic; but nobody else had dared to put this
hypothesis to a conclusive test. This kind of enterprise
and audacity, and this energy and confidence of the will,
were to be the primary characteristics of the settlers and
builders of America as well as of its first discoverer.

A similarly American quality was displayed by the
Spanish conquistadors. After Columbus had discovered
the West Indies, enterprising young men from the lesser
nobility and from the lower classes in Spain began to cross
the Atlantic in search of gold and glory in the New
World. Small groups of free-lance adventurers, with little

official assistance, explored and conquered first the islands and the Isthmus of Panama, then the mainland of Mexico, and afterwards all of the southern continent except Brazil and the plains of the far south. Within two generations after the first voyage of Columbus, the conquistadors had established Spanish authority over an immense territory extending northwards to California and Florida and south as far as Chile and La Plata.

But in Hispanic America this outburst of individual energy and self-confidence lasted only during the period of discovery and conquest. After a territory had been taken by the conquistadors, it was quickly transferred to royal authority, and royal officials from the Spanish peninsula were sent to govern it. The peoples of Mexico and South America became accustomed to despotic rule, to an authoritarian church, and to an aristocratic social structure. It was not until 1810 that they began to throw off the yoke of Europe, or that there was any revival of the exuberant enterprise and audacity that had been displayed by the conquistadors.

The early English colonization in America was much less dramatic, and did not promise any such easy road to fame and fortune. It did not begin until long after the Spaniards had conquered and settled their part of America; Mexico and Peru contained flourishing cities, with all the institutions of a developed civilization, at a time when the territories north of Florida were still covered with immense forests and inhabited only by a few tribes of Indians. This region had been ignored by Spain because it did not offer any easy acquisition of wealth, and it was occupied by the English only because more attractive areas of America were closed to them. The handful of struggling colonies, beginning with Virginia in 1607, Plymouth in 1620, and Massachusetts in 1630, which were planted by the English along the Atlantic coastline in the course of the seventeenth century, seemed for a long time to be humble and unpretentious enterprises when contrasted with the achievements of Spanish imperialism. But since the English colonies were not governed despotically, and were allowed freedom to develop their own way of life, they had much greater potentialities for growth.

With few exceptions, the English colonies were originally founded by men of the aristocratic and upper bourgeois classes who acquired ownership of American lands from the King of England and then set about peopling them and developing them. In most instances, however, they derived few profits from their colonizing enterprises and did not retain permanent control. Most of the colonies eventually passed under the direct authority of the crown. Some colonies (such as Maryland and the Carolinas) were planned as feudal principalities, the proprietors of which would receive rents and enjoy the prestige associated with landownership. Others (such as Virgina) were established by companies of merchants who were willing to invest money in colonization in the hope of earning commercial profits. In the New England colonies, pecuniary motives were of secondary importance, and the main purpose of the founders was to establish a society in which Puritan religious ideals could be put into practice. A similar religious idealism led, later in the century, to the colonization of Pennsylvania under the leadership of the Quaker William Penn. But most of the founders of the colonies did not settle permanently in America themselves. The men and women who actually crossed the Atlantic belonged predominantly to the poorer classes, both rural and urban. Although the early migrations brought a few English gentlemen to America, the vast majority of the settlers were small farmers, city craftsmen and traders, and servants. Accepting the inducements offered them by the founders of the colonies, they came to the New World in quest of opportunities for advancement that they could not find at home.

The early history of America was largely the story of how these English colonists were gradually transformed into Americans. This process began when they made the Atlantic crossing and started to make new lives for themselves in the New World. In order to understand it, it is necessary to know what English institutions and ways of thinking they brought with them across the Atlantic. The first Americans were also Englishmen, and when they reached America their initial tendency was to reproduce, in its essential features, the English social organization to which they were accustomed. In the American environment some elements of this English inheritance afterwards disappeared or underwent a slow modification, while others persisted and were ultimately incorporated into the new civilization of the United States.

The English society of the seventeenth century, like that of all European countries, was pervaded by the consciousness of class distinctions. In fact, the sense of class, which judges the individual by his role and status in the social organism rather than by his intrinsic quality as a human being, was perhaps more deeply ingrained among the English than among other European peoples. There was more social mobility in England than elsewhere, so that it was possible for the peasant to become a bourgeois and for the bourgeois to climb into the ranks of the aristocracy, but the class lines themselves were always clearly defined. This class sense was the cultural reflection of wide economic inequalities. The English ruling class consisted of the great landowning families, many of whom were originally of bourgeois descent, but who had adopted the aristocratic attitudes of their feudal predecessors. With their palatial country houses and broad estates, they dominated the small farmers who composed the bulk of the rural population; and since landlordship meant both prestige and leisure, they were the political leaders of the whole country. Meanwhile, similar class divisions were developing in the cities among the growing bourgeoisie. There were wide economic and social differences between the wealthy merchants and financiers, who aspired to aristocratic status and who could often obtain special privileges from the crown, and the small shopkeepers and artisans.

This English class structure was transmitted to the American colonies. Although most of the early settlers wished to escape from a society in which they had little social and economic opportunity, they had no conscious desire to create an egalitarian society in the New World. They still took it for granted that leadership belonged to a ruling class of the rich and wellborn. The English gentlemen who came to America brought with them their rights to political leadership and social privilege, thus laying the foundations of an embryo American aristocracy. When colonial families acquired wealth, they assumed that they should also enjoy social prestige and political power; and poorer and more humble citizens were usually willing to allow decisions to be made by those who were qualified for responsibility by birth, wealth, and education.

Virginia, Maryland, and the Carolinas remained almost wholly agricultural, adopting tobacco and rice as their chief commercial crops; and their social organization soon became a reflection of that of rural England. Some of the early settlers, though mostly of middle-class and yeoman-farmer descent, acquired ownership of large plantations and began to develop the attitudes of a landed aristocracy. Through the seventeenth century the laborers on the plantations consisted chiefly of indentured servants shipped out from England. Under the terms of their contracts the servants were set free after from four to seven years, and could then become independent landholders, beginning as small farmers and occasionally ending their lives as wealthy planters. The planters claimed the powers of a ruling class in the Southern colonies in the same way that the big landowners governed rural England; they usually worked in co-operation with the British governors and with the state-supported Anglican Church.

In the New England colonies, on the other hand, land was distributed in small lots, and no landowning aristocracy emerged. Most of the settlers became small farmers, but the soil was stony and not very fertile, so the more enterprising quickly turned to the sea for livelihood by the development first of fishing and afterwards of foreign commerce. Trade and shipping became the chief avenues to wealth and prestige, and Boston and other seaport towns grew into important mercantile centers. A class of wealthy merchants soon rose to leadership, modeling themselves on the merchants of the English cities. The bourgeois character of the New England colonies was confirmed by their Puritan theology and system of church government.

In the long run, however, the English class structure could not be maintained in the New World. Aristocratic

principles were incompatible with the conditions of American life; and as the colonies expanded and European attitudes began to recede into the background, the masses of
the people, who had acquired independence and self-
assurance by struggling with the wilderness, became increasingly unwilling to accept the domination of a new
American ruling class. Conflict between the principles of
aristocracy and those of democracy was perhaps the main
theme in the early political history of the United States.
Eventually the English class feeling vanished from the
political consciousness of America. The United States became a country without a ruling aristocracy; wealth no
longer entitled its owners, with the assent of the masses, to
political leadership and social domination. It was in this
respect that the civilization of the United States diverged
most sharply from that of England.

Other elements in the English inheritance, however,
proved to be suited to American conditions. The first
colonists brought with them not only hierarchical social
attitudes, but also well-established political habits and ways
of thinking that became, with few important modifications,
a permanent part of American civilization.

Although the English were not a democratic people, they
prided themselves on being a free people, and had acquired
a deep-rooted hostility toward any form of arbitrary power.
Long before the colonization of America they had become accustomed to the election of a legislative body that
limited the powers of the monarchy, and they believed that
every individual had certain rights and immunities which
should be maintained by written laws and by an independent judiciary. The typical Englishman was an individualist
jealous of any restriction upon his right to do and say as
he pleased; and while he accepted his status in the social
organism and the duties and obligations that belonged to it,
he believed also that certain areas of life were his own
private concern and should be protected against political
and social interference.

Yet the individualism of the English was not incompatible
with political co-operation. Certain other characteristics of
English culture made it possible for them to reconcile free-

dom with order and gradually to develop a system of government in which executive authority was responsible to the will of the people. The English displayed little of that propensity toward intolerance and fanaticism which makes political differences irreconcilable; they were usually willing to recognize that all points of view might contain some aspects of the truth and to believe that conflicts should be settled by mutual concessions and adjustments rather than by violence or coercion. The Englishman did not believe too firmly that his own ideas were right and that the ideas of his opponents were wrong. This spirit of tolerance and compromise was connected with the empirical tendencies of English philosophy and English ways of thinking. The English distrusted long-range plans and elaborate intellectual systems; they were in the habit of judging ideas and institutions in pragmatic terms and of being guided by practical expediency rather than by logical coherence and consistency. They were inclined to regard reality itself as disorderly, many-sided, illogical, and unpredictable, and for this reason they did not take any system of ideas too seriously. It was this mental attitude that made it possible for the English and their American descendants to work out a system of government in which the majority had the right to rule, while the minority had the right to criticize. For it is only when conflicts are concerned with questions of immediate practical expediency that men are willing to accept compromises, and, if defeated in an election, to obey the decisions of their victorious opponents. Conflicts between opposing intellectual systems are always irreconcilable, and can be settled only by civil war.[1]

[1] *The Latin peoples (presumably because of the influence of the Catholic Church, with its elaborate structure of dogmas) have been particularly prone to see political conflicts in terms not of concrete practical differences but of irreconcilable intellectual systems. Since 1789 there have been two Frances: the royalist and authoritarian France of the old regime, and the democratic and secular France of the Revolution. The same kind of division, in an even more intensified form, has existed in Spain and throughout most of Spanish America. This has been one of the main impediments to the development of peaceful constitutional government in the Latin countries. In recent*

These English political and intellectual habits were brought to the American colonies. Although the first colonists were willing to accept aristocratic leadership, they also believed that government should not be arbitrary. Attempts by some of the founders of the colonies to retain absolute power in their own hands quickly provoked complaints of tyranny. Both the founders and the British government were compelled to agree that, in crossing the Atlantic, the colonists had not forfeited any of the rights and immunities they had enjoyed in England. The commercial company that settled Virginia found it advisable to establish a legislature as early as 1619. The group of merchants, ministers, and country gentlemen who founded Massachusetts tried at first to set up an authoritarian government that would interpret and enforce the will of God and the principles of their Puritan religion; but after 1634 they were compelled to share their power with an elected assembly, though the restriction of voting to church members maintained the Puritan character of the colony. That every colony had a right to a legislature that would check the authority of the governor and the council was soon generally admitted, though, as in England, the franchise was everywhere limited by property and religious qualifications. And in every colony the rights of individuals were guaranteed by written codes of laws, by an independent judiciary, and by such institutions as trial by jury. Throughout the colonial period the British government continued to regard the colonies as subordinate to the mother country and to supervise their economic development in order that American trade might provide profits for British merchants; but it made few attempts to restrict their political liberties.

Transplanted into the American world, the political and legal institutions that had been brought from England gradually diverged from those of the mother country; but the Americans retained, with some modifications, the essen-

---

years the maintenance of constitutional government in other countries also has been threatened by the growth of a new intellectual system incapable of compromise: revolutionary Marxism.

tial political habits and attitudes of their English ancestors. They became a more gregarious people than the English, but they were equally insistent on their right to individual freedom and independence, and they were even more inclined towards pragmatic and empirical ways of thinking. Retaining the English capacity for tolerance and for compromise, they were able to work out a system of representative government that differed in detail from that of England but was based on the same fundamental principles. Unlike the Hispanic Americans, who were compelled when they became independent of Spain to adopt alien institutions to which they could not quickly become habituated, the people of the United States were able to build their own form of government on European foundations and to work out their own political practices by a slow and mainly peaceful evolution.

2

In spite of the strength and persistence of this English inheritance, the men and women who crossed the Atlantic quickly became differentiated from those who had remained at home. From the very foundation of the colonies they began to acquire new characteristics that were distinctively American. In order to appreciate this transformation, we must visualize the colonizing process in concrete terms. What sort of people made the Atlantic crossing, what experiences did they undergo, and how were they affected by them? History is about human beings, not merely about general trends; and if we concentrate on economic pressures and political ideologies, and forget the living individuals who responded to them, its ultimate meaning may elude us. It is easy to elaborate economic interpretations of the beginning of the United States: to ascribe it to scarcity of land and overpopulation in England and to the emergence of a capitalist economy in which merchants owned fluid capital and wanted profitable investments. But such factors are not the only determinants of historical processes. The course of events is affected also by the character of individuals, by their anxieties and aspirations, and by their capacity for courage, intelligence, and self-sacrifice.

Most of the early colonists were very ordinary men and women in no way outstanding in ability or moral quality and with no special training or aptitude for discovery and colonization. Probably most of them had never previously traveled more than a few miles from their homes. The America to which they came consisted mostly of an immense forest, stretching inland from the seacoast for hundreds of miles, inhabited only by savage Indians and filled with unknown dangers of all kinds. After being confined for two months or more in the tiny vessels that carried them across the Atlantic, they found themselves alone in this wilderness where they must build themselves houses and set about clearing farmland and raising crops. Most of the early colonies, being poorly planned and inadequately financed, endured "starving times" during the first winters; the settlers were decimated by famine and disease, and only the strongest and most tenacious survived. Some groups of settlers perished miserably or fled back to the security of Europe. The colonies that survived did so because a sufficient number of their members had the elemental qualities of courage, resourcefulness, and co-operativeness. The United States was founded on the moral fiber of these very ordinary people.

If the plantings of the first colonies were isolated episodes, there would be no need to insist on these facts. But the whole of the United States was settled in a similar manner. The experiences of the first Virginians and the first New Englanders were repeated again and again, with minor variations, in the expansion of the United States across the continent to the Pacific Coast; and down to the end of the nineteenth century this western expansion was the primary element in the development of the American people. The character of the Americans was molded more by the conquest of the continent than by any other factor in their history. The story of this expansion is essentially an epic; but unlike other epics, written or enacted, it had as its protagonists not heroes or demigods but plain average citizens.

Obviously the colonizing process brought about certain psychological changes in those who participated in it; and some of these changes were important. Picture a group of Englishmen from a petty bourgeois or yeoman-farmer background, accustomed to a settled and traditional way of life, who, usually without any real foreknowledge of what confronted them, found themselves suddenly ejected upon the desolate shores of the New World. In America they were thrown wholly upon their own resources; in order to survive they had to find within themselves a moral strength that they had previously had little occasion to develop. Under such circumstances physical strength, tenacity, adaptability, and resourcefulness assumed a new importance, whereas talents and capacities of no immediate practical utility, however valuable in an advanced civilization, became positive encumbrances. Human nature in America became elemental and lost its sophistication. This emphasis on the physical and the practical did not mean any loosening of moral ties. On the contrary, it was only by willing co-operation that any colony could hope to survive; the wilderness enforced neighborliness and mutual aid, and men had to rely on each other as well as on themselves. But in proportion as they succeeded in overcoming their environment they discovered their own powers and learned a new self-confidence and spirit of independence. The class distinctions they had brought from Europe began to weaken: leadership had to justify itself by superior capacity and moral quality; men could not claim superiority by virtue of rank and birth alone. Nor were colonists who had discovered by their own efforts the secret of survival likely to accept meekly the domination of entrepreneurs and officials on the other side of the Atlantic. Proud of their own achievements, they felt little sense of obligation to men who, having taken no part in the actual labors and dangers of colonization, were expecting to share in the profits.

Strength of will, self-reliance, adaptability, neighborliness, respect for talents with practical value, disregard for artificial distinctions, the drive towards independence—these traits, which were stimulated first at Jamestown and

Plymouth and Boston, were reinforced again and again as the tide of migration moved westwards. The qualities that made it possible for men to survive in the wilderness, and that eventually enabled them to win prosperity, became, in fact, the most important aspects of the new American personality. In America it was chiefly by these that the value of a man was measured. And though the new man did not fully assert himself until the nineteenth century, he began his existence when the first boatload of immigrants landed on the shores of Virginia.

As a concrete example, let us consider the story of the Pilgrim Fathers who founded Plymouth. In itself the Plymouth colony was of small importance, but as a specimen of the American spirit it deserves some detailed consideration. In spite of its insignificance, twentieth-century Americans like to remember Plymouth with special affection; more than any other of the early colonies it has become a part of the national mythology. This preference has a reason that should not be overlooked. Plymouth was the most American of the early colonies because it was founded, not by an English proprietor or commercial company, but by a very humble group of actual colonists. It was the creation of plain citizens who lacked both experience and resources, but who had the audacity to believe that they could survive in America on their own. Inevitably they made almost every possible mistake and suffered almost every possible misfortune; yet the enterprise succeeded.

The story began at Leyden in Holland, where a group of English people of the lower middle class, who belonged to an obscure and despised religious sect, had taken refuge from intolerance. Since they found it difficult to support themselves at Leyden, it occurred to some of them that they might make a better livelihood by migrating to Virginia. This suggestion provoked long debates. It was pointed out that they had no financial resources, that the voyage across the ocean was long and perilous, that if they ever reached the New World they would probably die of famine and disease, and that if they survived these dangers they might be captured by savage Indians who delighted not only in killing their victims but also in torturing them. All these statements were undeniably true. Nevertheless, thirty-five persons decided to make the attempt.

Having obtained permission to settle in Virginia, they started negotiations with a group of London merchants who wished to invest money in a colonizing enterprise. Two members of the group went to London, accepted the terms put forward by the merchants, and began buying supplies in a very reckless and indiscriminate fashion and making preparations for the voyage. The remainder of the party used part of their scanty resources to buy a ship, the *Speedwell,* and then crossed from Holland to the English seaport of Southampton. Here the *Mayflower,* which had been chartered for the Atlantic crossing, was awaiting them; and they were joined by a number of other colonists—servants, craftsmen, and others—who had been gathered by the merchants and who did not belong to the same religious persuasion.

It was at Southampton that their troubles began. The merchants had insisted that for seven years the colonists should work as a community, devoting all their time, beyond what was needed for keeping themselves alive, to the production of commercial commodities for shipment to England. Since the merchants were making a heavy investment in the hope of profits, this was no doubt a justifiable demand; but the Pilgrims had counted on being free for part of their time to work on their own houses and farms, and when they heard the terms of the contract, they were so disgusted that they refused to sign it. Unfortunately, their money was all spent; and since they could get no further advance from the merchants, they had, in order to meet immediate expenses, to sell sixty pounds' worth of the precious supplies that had been bought for the voyage. Thus they found themselves about to embark for America without a number of the articles considered essential for colonization, "scarce having any butter, or oil, not a sole to mend a shoe, not every man a sword to his side, wanting many muskets, much armor, etc." (according to their

own historian, William Bradford). Under the circumstances they could only "trust to the good providence of
God." [2]

For the next few months the story of the Pilgrims, as
might have been predicted, was chiefly a catalogue of disasters. They set sail from Southampton on August 5, 1620,
in their two vessels, the *Speedwell,* which they had bought
for permanent use in America, and the *Mayflower,* which
had been chartered for this voyage only. Presumably they
were still proposing to go to Virginia, and were expecting to
arrive there before the end of the summer. After a few
days at sea, the *Speedwell* developed a leak, so they turned
back to Dartmouth to have her repaired. They sailed a
second time, and had gone more than three hundred miles
into the Atlantic when the *Speedwell* again began leaking,
and again both vessels had to return to England. It was
decided finally that the *Speedwell* must be abandoned, and
that the *Mayflower,* with those members of the party who
were still willing to proceed, should make the crossing
alone. The *Mayflower* left England for the third and last
time on September 6. Measuring not more than one
hundred feet in length and about twenty at her greatest
width, she was carrying exactly one hundred passengers,
of whom twenty-eight were children. Two more children
were born during the voyage.

The Atlantic crossing took nine weeks. The voyage was
stormy, and at one period, with the vessel leaking and one
of the masts bending dangerously under the wind, there
were consultations about the advisability of returning to
England. But the Pilgrims decided to proceed, and on
November 10 they reached land, not Virginia, as had originally been planned, but the desolate shores of Cape Cod.
For half a day they turned southwards, hoping to reach the
Hudson River; but after encountering heavy breakers and
adverse winds, they returned to Cape Cod and anchored
there. According to Bradford, the crew of the *Mayflower*
was impatient to return home and threatened to deposit

[2] *William Bradford:* History of Plymouth Plantation (*printed
1923*), *p. 82.*

them and their goods on shore and abandon them; so the colonists had to find a location for their permanent settlement in the immediate neighborhood as quickly as possible.

The situation in which the Pilgrims now found themselves was gloomy and desperate in the extreme. They had reached their promised land, but as a result of all the delays they had arrived at the worst possible time of year. And instead of landing in Virginia, where they might have turned to other colonists for assistance, they were in a bleak, desolate, and almost unknown country where they must be dependent entirely upon their own scanty supplies for protection against the winter and the Indians. Whether they would receive any help from England was doubtful; their friends at Leyden had no resources; and after their refusal to sign the contract, they could not count on further assistance from the merchants.

Under such circumstances the chief need was to maintain the unity of the party and prevent demoralization. It must be remembered that only a minority had belonged to the Leyden congregation, the remainder having been strangers to them prior to their meeting on shipboard. Now that they had arrived at a place where there was no settled authority, some of the strangers—servants and others—began to say that "when they came ashore, they would use their own liberty, for none had power to command them." In order to put a stop to the "discontents and murmurings amongst some, and mutinous speeches and carriages in others," it was necessary to improvise a government, and such a government could only be based on the principle of majority rule. It was to meet this crisis that the famous Mayflower Compact was drawn up. The Leyden group induced most of the party to sign an agreement by which they combined into a "civic body politic" with power to make laws and elect officials whom everybody must obey.[3]

They chose Plymouth as the best site for a permanent settlement, and landed there on December 16, just as the most severe period of the winter was beginning. The horrors

[3] *Ibid., pp. 106–7.*

of the next three months were almost beyond human endurance. They were already weakened by scurvy, lack of food, and the long confinement on shipboard, and now they had to take shelter from the cold in a few hastily constructed huts. Almost the whole party fell ill. No less than fifty of them died, and only six or seven remained uninfected. This was the period of crisis, during which the conventions of civilized society could no longer protect them and the essential quality of every individual was fully revealed. Alone in an unknown wilderness, during a winter longer and colder than any of them had known before, with savages lurking in the woods outside, and famine and pestilence among themselves, they could rely only upon their own courage and their willingess to help each other.

They earned their place in history by the manner in which they came through this ordeal. The party did not disintegrate or give up hope. Through the winter those who were well continued to help the sick, doing "all the homely and necessary offices for them which dainty and queasy stomachs cannot endure to hear named, and all this willingly and cheerfully, without any grudging in the least." [4] When spring came, the epidemic ended; and the survivors, weak as they were, could feel that the worst was over.

Their first piece of good fortune was to find a friendly Indian willing to show them how to plant corn (kernels of which they had found in an abandoned Indian settlement) and catch fish. Without his assistance they would probably have died of starvation. These artisans and craftsmen were accustomed to urban life and had little knowledge of farming or of hunting and fishing; and the seeds they had brought from England, and which they planted when they were able, "came not to good, either by the badness of the seed, or lateness of the season, or both, or some other defect." [5] But with help from the Indians, they were able to support themselves through the summer of 1621 chiefly on fish, and in the autumn they could catch deer and turkeys.

[4] Ibid., p. 108.
[5] Ibid., p. 116.

Their troubles were by no means ended. It was several years before they were able to raise harvests large enough so that they were no longer hungry. They had to support several parties of new colonists, some of them friends and relatives of the original group, who "when they saw their low and poor condition ashore, were much daunted and dismayed," [6] and others sent by the London merchants. Thirty-five came in the autumn of 1621, sixty-seven in the following year, and another large party in 1623. These had to be fed, and each time a fresh contingent arrived the whole colony had to go on half rations until the next harvest. In the summer of 1622 several members of the colony were publicly whipped because, driven by hunger, they had taken and eaten corn before it was ripe.

Their relations with the London merchants, moreover, continued to be difficult. The ship that brought the new colonists in 1621 brought also an angry letter, complaining because the *Mayflower* had been sent back to England empty, and suggesting that the Pilgrims must have spent their time "discoursing, arguing and consulting" instead of gathering a cargo.[7] Required to change their minds and sign the contract they had rejected the previous year, if they wished for any further help from England, the Pilgrims decided to give way. Yet in spite of this surrender they received only more complaints and more new mouths to feed, and no effective help. The merchants seemed to be incapable of appreciating the difficulties of life in the American wilderness. Finally the Pilgrims decided to take matters into their own hands. One of the Leyden party was sent back to England to negotiate a new contract under which they were to be their own masters; nearly three quarters of the original investment of the merchants was canceled, and the remainder (amounting to eighteen hundred pounds) was to be paid off at the rate of two hundred pounds a year. They then borrowed money from other London financiers (at rates varying from thirty to seventy per cent) in order to buy the supplies that they

[6] *Ibid.*, p. 156.
[7] *Ibid.*, p. 122.

needed. The Pilgrims continued to have financial troubles
for a number of years, as a result either of dishonesty or of
extreme incompetence on the part of the representative
whom they had sent to London; but by trading in beaver
skins with the Indians, they were able eventually to free
themselves from debt. Thenceforth they were legally free
from external control, as they had been in actuality from
the time of their landing. Entirely by their own labors,
they had discovered how to survive.

This story contains, in embryo, much of the early history
of the United States. In the traditional versions, however,
its full significance is not always made clear. Too much
emphasis, for example, has been given to the influence of
religion. But only a minority of the Plymouth colonists had
belonged to the Leyden congregation (though it is true
that these supplied most of the leadership); and even the
Leyden group (according to their own historian, William
Bradford) came to America primarily in the hope of
making a better livelihood. Essentially the Pilgrims were
moved by the same hopes that had moved all the other
men and women who have made the Atlantic crossing.
They differed from the other early colonists chiefly in
that they had no wealthy proprietor or commercial company to guide and assist them. And this independence of
Europe made Plymouth a better example of the American
spirit. Here was a group of plain citizens who set out on
an extremely rash adventure for which they were very
badly prepared, but who came through to ultimate success.

Their lack of any special distinction is, in fact, the most
significant feature of the *Mayflower* passengers. It is true
that the Leyden party belonged to a heretical religious
congregation, as a result of which they had suffered from
persecution, and that their moral standards were relatively
high. But in other respects they were in no way unusual,
either in ability or in character. Their preparations for
founding a colony were altogether inadequate, and from
start to finish they mismanaged their financial affairs in a
most extraordinary way. In their dealings with the Indians

and with certain rival groups of colonists who attempted
to settle in New England a few years later, they showed
themselves suspicious, self-righteous, and capable on occasion of acting with real cruelty. As Bradford's narrative
shows, they believed that everybody who had any dealings
with them was trying to take advantage of them. They felt
particularly resentful, for example, toward the London
merchants who had financed them. Perhaps one could
hardly expect the men who starved at Plymouth to appreciate the viewpoint of entrepreneurs who stayed in the
security of their London countinghouses, venturing only
their money and not their lives. Yet in reality the demands
of the merchants, who had invested money in a very risky
enterprise, and who did actually lose most of their investment, were by no means unfair or exorbitant.

It is only by recognizing the very human weaknesses of
the men of the *Mayflower* that one can properly evaluate
their achievement. By displaying the elemental qualities of
courage, industry, and co-operativeness they succeeded in
conquering the wilderness in which they had chosen to
settle. And as a result of the process of colonization they
began to become Americanized. Almost their first action
after reaching the New World was to adopt the essential
institutions of democracy, not only because some of them
believed in popular government but also—and chiefly—
because otherwise they could not hope to maintain order
and unity among themselves. They had to improvise a
government, and under pioneer conditions no other kind
of government could win assent. By adapting themselves to
new conditions, moreover, and winning prosperity for
themselves, they discovered their own latent powers and
acquired a new self-confidence. Bradford's history is a
significant document for the study of the American spirit,
not only because of the admirable honesty and simplicity
with which it is written, but also because it illustrates a
process of psychological growth. The self-assured statesmen, merchants, and farmers of Plymouth Plantation were
very different from the humble and poverty-stricken artisans
and shopkeepers who had set out from Southampton. The

history of Plymouth exemplified that confidence in the essential capacity and integrity of the average citizen which became the basic principle of American civilization.

3

Once the first colonies had been established, the flow of population across the Atlantic continued with a slowly increasing momentum. More men and women came to America in the eighteenth century than in the seventeenth; more came in the nineteenth than in the eighteenth. There are no exact statistics of colonial immigration, but it is probable that the total population amounted to about a quarter of a million by 1690, and that by 1775 it approached two million and a half.

Throughout the colonial period many immigrants came of their own volition, drawn to America by the magnet of cheap and abundant land; others were transported as a punishment for minor crimes or were enticed to make the crossing by sea captains engaged in the business of shipping servants to the colonies. But a considerable proportion even of the voluntary immigrants had to sell themselves into service in order to obtain passage across the Atlantic. The immigrant ships were packed with the most precious of the commodities needed in America—human labor in the form of indentured servants who would work for colonial planters or merchants. For two months or more they were imprisoned on shipboard, in danger of pestilence and starvation; when they reached the promised land, they had to work out their period of service in a status little better than chattel slavery. But the survivors finally became free men, with the right to acquire land for themselves. Many prosperous and dignified families were founded by men and women who first reached America in this humble capacity.

Although England was the chief source of the migration, the racial composition of the colonies was never wholly English. News of the land of opportunity across the Atlantic soon began to spread to oppressed groups in other parts of Europe. The Dutch had been the first settlers in

parts of New York and New Jersey. Before the end of the
seventeenth century, French Huguenots had established
themselves in several of the seaboard cities. In the early
eighteenth century came a mass migration of German
farmers from the Rhineland, followed by an even larger
movement of Scotch-Irish from Ulster. Representatives of
a dozen other races came to the colonies in smaller numbers. The America of the eighteenth century was already
Scotch, Welsh, Irish, French, Dutch, German, Swedish,
Italian, and Jewish, as well as English; and the process of
intermingling and intermarriage had begun. Before the
Revolution, the French writer Crèvecœur, who spent fifteen
years in the colonies, commented on "that strange mixture
of blood, which you will find in no other country." "Here,"
he declared, "individuals of all nations are melted into a
new race of men. . . . I could point out to you a family
whose grandfather was an Englishman, whose wife was
Dutch, whose son married a French wife, and whose present four sons have now four wives of different nations." [8]
In 1776, Paine could truthfully declare that all Europe, and
not England alone, was the real "parent country" of America.[9]

In the Amercian environment, all these different racial
groups multiplied with astonishing rapidity. Under pioneer
conditions, where land was abundant and labor was scarce,
children were economic assets; and once the hardships of
the initial settlement had been overcome, food was plenti-
ful and there was no danger of famine. Many colonial
parents had a child every two years with almost mathematical regularity. Families of ten were frequent; families
of fifteen or twenty were by no means unusual. Even without new immigration the population of the colonies appears to have been capable of doubling itself within thirty
years. There have been few comparable examples in all
history of such a capacity for rapid multiplication.

As the population increased, the areas of white settlement slowly grew larger. There was little planning or par-

[8] *J. Hector St. John de Crèvecœur:* Letters from an American
Farmer, *III* (*Everyman's Library edition*), *p. 43.*
[9] Writings of Thomas Paine (*1894*), *Vol. I, p. 87.*

ticipation by any political authority. Governments normally intervened only in order to negotiate or wage war
with Indian tribes and to grant titles of landownership.
There were no outstanding leaders, like the conquistadors
who carried Spanish civilization into the mountains and
jungles of South America or the great French explorers of
the St. Lawrence and the Mississippi. The expansion of the
colonies was a spontaneous movement of private citizens;
generation after generation, they were drawn farther into
the West by some impulse of restlessness or adventure,
and by the hope of a better livelihood and greater independence. Like all democratic processes, this appears un-
dramatic when it is viewed only in its main outlines; it
must be visualized in detail, in terms of those who participated in it, if its meaning is to be appreciated. But since
the average American generally lacked the capacity for
self-expression and the inclination to dramatize and reflect
upon his own activities, we cannot often watch the movement in operation.

From their initial settlements near the seacoast the
Americans pushed up the rivers which led into the interior
of the continent, establishing themselves along the banks
of the Connecticut, the Hudson, the Delaware, the Susquehanna, the Potomac, the James, and the Savannah. Almost
everywhere they found immense forests, which had to be
cleared and transformed into open farmland; almost everywhere they encountered wandering tribes of Indians, with
whom they fought an unceasing warfare. But the forests
were gradually explored, as hunters, fur trappers, and prospectors made their way along the Indian trails between one
river and the next; and the areas of cultivated farmland
slowly expanded. Sometimes an individual family moved
a few miles farther into the wilderness and carved a farm
out of the forest. Sometimes a group of families, having
agreed with each other to migrate and decided upon a
destination, packed their goods into wagons and set out
together on a march into the west. The advance guard
of the white invasion usually consisted of rough frontiersmen who were peculiarly restless or shiftless, and who
brought with them few of the habits of civilization; but

within ten years or a generation after they had opened up
a new territory, they were usually followed by groups of
more respectable and industrious citizens who established
the institutions of a settled society.

The conquest of the wilderness was always an arduous
and perilous process that required the utmost adaptability
and capacity for endurance; but its promises were propor-
tionately tempting. To immigrants from Europe, with its
overcrowded villages, its big private estates, and its limited
natural resources that imposed a constant prudence and
economy, the riches of America seemed to be infinite.
Here were forests abounding in all kinds of birds and
animals, rivers filled with fish, strange trees and plants,
and in many places a topsoil so deep that the farmer could
scarcely reach the bottom of it. Once a company of pioneers
had succeeded in taking possession of a new area, they had
farmlands much broader and more fertile than any their
ancestors had ever known; they could produce what they
needed in a profusion and a variety sufficient not merely
for subsistence but for luxury; and in all essential respects
they were their own masters. It is not surprising that a
lavish generosity and a reckless consumption of natural
resources became characteristic of the American, and
that his farming techniques were more wasteful and less
efficient than those of his European ancestors. In a continent whose wealth seemed so inexhaustible, why should
one stint oneself for the sake of future generations?

In this manner the frontier line, which divided the settled
area from the wilderness, moved slowly westwards until,
by the middle of the eighteenth century, it ran down the
main ranges of the Appalachians, most of the coastal plain
from New England to the Carolinas having been brought
under white control. In a century and a half, the Americans effectively colonized an area of about two hundred
thousand square miles, more than twice as large as the
whole of Great Britain.

In New England the first areas of colonization were
along the seacoast and in the valley of the Connecticut
River. Most of southern New England was settled during
the first hundred years; and the movement then turned

northward into the mountains of New Hampshire and Vermont and westward towards the Berkshire Hills and the Hudson River. This westerly migration was eventually to make large areas of the Mississippi Valley and the Far West into extensions of Massachusetts and Connecticut. Relatively few immigrants came to New England after 1640; and its expansion was more orderly and less individualistic than that of other sections. Caravans of New England farmers marched together into the wilderness to found new townships, often under the leadership of a minister who gave them religious guidance and encouragement. Wherever they settled, they brought with them their characteristic religious institutions, their puritan morality, and their democratic practice of dividing the land into small farms.

New York was the least American in its institutions of any of the colonies, since the Dutch had divided the land into big feudal estates, and this practice was continued by the early British governors. Most of the land became the property of a few big families who collected rents from dependent tenant farmers. Expansion was checked both by the property system and by the powerful Iroquois Indians in the western part of the. colony. In Pennsylvania, on the other hand, where there were liberal institutions and no religious discrimination, the flow of migration was particularly rapid. After English Quakers under the leadership of William Penn founded Philadelphia and settled the southeastern part of the colony, there came many thousands of Germans, who took possession of the fertile lands along the Delaware, Schuylkill, and Lehigh rivers. Continuing to speak their own language and to preserve their own religious institutions, the German communities remained for generations almost isolated from the American life around them. After the Germans came the Scotch-Irish, a most vigorous, aggressive, and disputatious race of Calvinists. Through the middle decades of the eighteenth century a stream of Scotch-Irish caravans was flowing westward across the first mountain ranges into the valleys of central Pennsylvania. Here many of them swung their wagons and pack horses southward, and began to move down the valleys into the back country of Virginia and the Carolinas, so

that finally almost the whole of the southern frontier line
was held by families of Scotch-Irish descent. Settling where
they chose, without regard either for the claims of the
Indians or for legal titles of landownership, and submitting
to no authority except that of their Calvinist Jehovah, they
became the dominant breed in vast areas of western
America.

In the Southern colonies, the "tidewater" lands close to
the seacoast were the first to be settled. In these regions,
particularly in Virginia and South Carolina, a small number of families gradually acquired ownership of most of the
land, and created large plantations for the production of
tobacco and rice. Former servants and new immigrants
moved up-country or into North Carolina, establishing
small farms in areas not yet dominated by the plantation
system. Thus two different economies prevailed throughout
the South: that of the planter in the rich seacoast and valley
lands, raising commercial crops for shipment to Europe,
and that of the self-sufficient small farmer in the forests
and hill country of the interior. Before the middle of the
eighteenth century, the rising tide of westerly migration had
reached the first mountain ranges and was beginning to
mingle with the movement of the Scotch-Irish coming south
from Pennsylvania.

The whole process was not merely a geographical expansion; it was also a psychological development by which
Europeans were transformed into Americans. In the American world the individual was the master of his own destiny.
He could succeed by his own efforts; and if he failed, he
had only himself to blame. This was the lesson taught by
innumerable examples and remembered in countless families. According to Crèvecœur, whose *Letters from an
American Farmer* (in spite of idyllic exaggerations) offers
perhaps the most penetrating interpretation of colonial
life, it was the growth of this sense of freedom and opportunity that made the American. "An European, when he
first arrives, seems limited in his intentions, as well as in
his views; but he very suddenly alters his scale. . . . He
no sooner breathes our air than he forms new schemes,
and embarks in designs he never would have thought of

in his own country. . . . He begins to feel the effects of a sort of resurrection; hitherto he had not lived, but simply vegetated; he now feels himself a man, because he is treated as such. . . . Judge what an alteration there must arise in the mind and thoughts of this man; he begins to forget his former servitude and dependence, his heart involuntarily swells and glows; this first swell inspires him with those new thoughts which constitute an American. . . . The American is a new man, who acts upon new principles; he must therefore entertain new ideas, and form new opinions. From involuntary idleness, servile dependency, penury, and useless labor, he has passed to toils of a very different nature, rewarded by ample subsistence." [1]

Imagine a typical case history. Picture some young man, born to a family of yeomen or artisans in an English village, growing up in a small traditional community in which the poor were expected to know their place and the will of the local squire was law, impelled by some misfortune or some offense against the local laws or mores to seek his fortune elsewhere, wandering to a seaport city, enticed by a sea captain to sign up for transportation to the colonies, set ashore at Philadelphia or Baltimore, sold into service as a domestic servant or a laborer on a Southern plantation, and free finally to find his own livelihood and follow the bent of his nature in the wilderness. If he preferred to be lazy and improvident, he might become one of that lawless and nomadic breed, more savage than the Indians around them, which inhabited the outermost limits of the frontier; or he might spend his mature years scraping a meager living in some forest clearing on the fringes of a white settlement, shooting birds and squirrels and drinking corn liquor and enjoying his leisure while supported mainly by the labor of a wife and children. But if he had physical vigor and the will to succeed, he could end his life as the owner of a substantial farm and the patriarch of a rapidly growing tribe of descendants, somewhere perhaps on the banks of the Susquehanna or in the Great Valley of Virginia. Such

[1] Letters from an American Farmer, *III* (*Everyman's Library* edition, pp. 44, 58, 59).

a transformation, repeated many thousands of times, was the essential substance of colonial history. And the moral of the story was always the same: the capacity and adaptability of the common man, provided he was free from traditional social restrictions and had the necessary initiative, energy, and determination.

☆ ☆ ☆ ☆ ☆ ☆ ☆ ☆ ☆ ☆ ☆ ☆ ☆ ☆

CHAPTER III

COLONIAL SOCIETY

★ ★ ★ ★ ★ ★ ★ ★ ★ ★ ★ ★ ★ ★ ★

As THE COLONIES EXPANDED, American society began to assume a definite configuration. By the middle of the eighteenth century it was becoming evident both to European observers and to the more discerning and widely experienced of the Americans themselves that the emerging civilization of the thirteen colonies could not be regarded as a mere extension of that of Great Britain, or even of Europe. It had certain unique qualities that could not be paralleled in any other country at that period, and perhaps not even in history.

The primary characteristic of American society was its freedom from extreme economic inequalities. Its egalitarianism was by no means absolute. There were considerable economic differences between the ambitious merchants and landowners of the seaboard and the small farmers. There were sectional differences between East and West, due largely to the tendency of seaboard speculators to acquire ownership of Western lands and to collect rents from the farmers who settled on them. Yet though some families were rich and some were poor, the gulf between them was smaller than anywhere else in the world; and the vast majority of the white population occupied a middle position in which they enjoyed economic security and independence and were neither exploiters of other men's labor nor themselves the victims of exploitation. In no other country did the common man have such opportunities; in no other country were the masses of the people so free from poverty and oppression. This was the verdict both of sympathetic Europeans, such as Paine and Crèvecœur, and of those Americans who had the best opportunities of contrasting America with Europe. In America, said Benjamin Franklin, there were "few people so miserable as the poor of Europe," and "very few that in Europe could be called rich. . . . It is rather a general happy mediocrity that prevails." [1]

The two most widely cultured and talented Americans of the eighteenth century were Franklin and Jefferson. Each of them knew European society intimately by personal experience; and each of them had a strong appreciation of all that Europe could offer in the way of intellectual, scientific, and æsthetic achievement. Yet for both of them the difference between America and Europe was almost a difference between heaven and hell. "Had I never been in the American colonies," said Franklin in 1770, after a tour of the British Isles, "but was to form my judgment of civil society by what I have lately seen, I should never advise a nation of savages to admit of civilization; for I assure you that in the possession and enjoyment of the various comforts of life, compared to these people every Indian is a gentleman; and the effect of this kind of civil society seems only to be the depressing multitudes below the savage state that a few may be raised above it." [2] Jefferson, writing from France some years later, was even more emphatic. "Of twenty millions of people supposed to be in France," he declared, "I am of opinion there are nineteen millions more wretched, more accursed in every circumstance of human existence than the most conspicuously wretched individual of the whole United States. . . . The truth of Voltaire's observation offers itself perpetually, that every man here must be either the hammer or the anvil. It is a true picture of that country to which they say we shall pass hereafter, and where we are to see

[1] Information to those who would remove to America (*1782*).
[2] *Carl Van Doren:* Benjamin Franklin (*1938*), p. 393.

God and his angels in splendor and crowds of the damned trampled under their feet." [3]

The representative citizen of eighteenth-century America was the farmer. At the time of the Revolution, at least nine tenths of the white population made their living from the land, and in all the colonies from New Hampshire down to Georgia the vast majority of them were independent small proprietors. There was one other class that also exemplified the "general happy mediocrity" characteristic of American society: namely, the artisans and mechanics who performed whatever manufacturing was done in colonial America. Since industry had not yet been mechanized, they were skilled craftsmen and not factory workers; and though some of them were journeymen working for wages, there was no sharp class distinction between employer and employee. In accordance with the old guild tradition, most journeymen expected sooner or later to become economically independent; and as Franklin and others argued, no large or ill-paid working class could develop as long as there was vacant land in the West and men were free to go there. But it was the small farmer who especially typified the emergent American society and who embodied its unique qualities. Many of the enduring characteristics of the American creed and the American national character originated in the way of life of the colonial farmer. And many of the internal stresses that appeared in American society at later periods were due to the incompatibility of eighteenth-century agrarian attitudes with a nineteenth-century industrial environment.

If the colonial farmer was prudent and industrious, he could hope to enjoy an economic independence of a kind that it is difficult for the men of the twentieth century even to visualize. Eighteenth-century farming was primarily for subsistence, not for the market. A farm family produced almost all its own food, its own clothing, and its own tools and utensils. The farmer needed to sell a small surplus only in order to earn money for the payment of

[3] *Letters to Mrs. Trist, Aug. 18, 1785. Letter to Charles Bellini, Sept. 30, 1785.*

taxes and the purchase of salt, gunpowder, metal, and a few luxuries. As long as there was an open West, he could raise a large family to assist him, in the confidence that when his sons were of age they could provide for themselves by migrating to unsettled country. This degree of independence was not always achieved: a number of eighteenth-century farmers had to borrow money in order to establish themselves, and as a result of improvidence or bad luck never succeeded in paying off. But as long as the farmer avoided debt and could meet his small expenses by selling his surplus products, he need be afraid of nothing except some major natural catastrophe or act of God.

The price of independence was constant labor by every member of the family, from the small children up; the farmer had always to be hard-working, versatile, and adaptable; but the rewards, material as well as psychological, were substantial. "I know no condition happier than that of a Virginia farmer might be . ." declared Jefferson, after he had seen Europe. "His estate supplies a good table, clothes himself and his family with their ordinary apparel, furnishes a small surplus to buy salt, sugar and coffee, and a little finery for his wife and daughters, enables him to receive and visit his friends, and furnishes him with pleasing and healthy occupation." [4] The prosperous farmer of New England or Pennsylvania or the Shenandoah Valley was no European peasant. And there was plenty of gaiety, even among the dour New Englanders and Pennsylvania Scotch-Irish. There were religious and family festivals, where the tables groaned under an immense variety of foods, and the flow of whisky or rum was unlimited; the communal songs and dances that had been brought across from Europe; "frolicks" and entertainments to celebrate a harvest or the raising of a new barn or the clearing of a stretch of forest.

Such a life was remarkably free from serious psychological stresses and frustrations. As long as the farmer remained his own master he was not likely to feel that he was the victim of unjust social forces. This was not be-

---

[4] *Letter to James Currie, Aug. 4, 1787.*

cause he was exempt from a normal human competitiveness. His drive towards greater physical comfort and higher
social status was, in fact, frequently sharpened by memories of poverty and oppression in Europe. Some farmers
acquired greater wealth and prestige than their neighbors,
and when a new territory was settled, there was likely to
be a scramble to pre-empt the most desirable lands, sometimes by dishonest methods. Most farmers probably regarded wealth and prestige as desirable goals, and had no
desire to see competition limited or equality institutionalized. But in colonial America, where land and resources
were abundant and labor was scarce, competitiveness could
never become acute or inequality excessive. The aggressive
energies of the American farmer were directed primarily
against nature, not against other human beings; and the
fulfillment of his ambitions was to be sought not by
struggling with complex social forces but by mastering the
wilderness. And if he was exempt from natural catastrophes,
his success depended, in a most unusual degree, on his
own physical and moral qualities. In the agrarian society of
colonial America (except insofar as sharp practices were
employed in pre-empting Western lands) industry, honesty,
and sobriety were normally rewarded, and poverty was
normally the result of idleness and improvidence. There was
therefore a clear correlation between material success and
those qualities which Americans had been taught to regard
as virtuous. This harmony between the material and the
moral standards of the community (which never exists to
the same degree in any complex or sophisticated social
system) was of immense importance in promoting the
American qualities of optimism, self-assurance, and confidence in human nature. The American farmer lived in a
rational world in which he could plan for the future and
could assume that his rewards would not be seriously out
of proportion to his merits.

In such a society men felt little need for any organized
government. The repressive power of the state must be
invoked most often where there is scarcity and the haves
must be protected from the indignation of the have-nots;
but colonial America was a land of plenty, and (except

on the Southern plantations) there was no class of have-nots. Agrarian communities could deal, extralegally, with their own offenders, and not infrequently did so by rough but effective methods: troublemakers might be beaten, stripped naked, dragged on rails, tarred and feathered, or ridden out of town. Deliberate crime was rare, since there was little motive for it. Along the Western frontiers, to which the more lawless and improvident individuals were likely to gravitate, there was more disorder, but most frontiersmen were accustomed to defend themselves by rough-and-tumble fighting, and sometimes by shooting, and preferred to dispense with the forces of organized law and order. Many parts of America resembled the back country of North Carolina as described by Colonel William Byrd. "The government there is so loose," he declared, "and the laws so feebly executed, that, like those in the neighborhood of Sydon formerly, every one does just what seems good in his own eyes. . . . Besides, there might have been some danger, perhaps, in venturing to be so rigorous, for fear of undergoing the fate of an honest justice in Corotuck Precinct. This bold magistrate, it seems, taking upon to order a fellow to the stocks, for being disorderly in his drink, was, for his intemperate zeal, carried thither himself, and narrowly escaped being whipped by the rabble into the bargain." [5]

For many colonial farmers, in fact, particularly those in the West, the state was distinctly an alien institution. It collected taxes from them, but it gave them little service or protection in return. The settlement of the West was mainly a movement of individuals, with little government planning or support. Located on the seacoast and dominated by seaboard interests, the colonial governments frequently failed to assist the Westerners even when assistance was most needed and might most reasonably have been expected: when there were Indian raids. And insofar as the seaboard families used their political power to acquire legal title to unsettled Western lands, the state was actually

[5] *Quoted by V. L. Parrington:* Main Currents in American Thought (1927), *Vol. I, p. 140.*

the enemy of the Western farmer. Settlers did not wish
to be coerced into paying rents to some absentee owner.
The American farmer was, in fact, a natural anarchist who
saw no reason why he should obey laws that he disliked,
and who felt instinctively that the best government was
the government that governed least. And since his chief
desire was to be free from interference, he did not arrive
easily at the idea that he might himself aspire to political
power and use it for his own advantage. When he found
himself in difficulties, he occasionally resorted to political
action, but his general tendency was to think of the state
as always an instrument of oppression, and at best a necessary evil.

Under such conditions some English characteristics persisted or grew stronger, while others disappeared or underwent a slow transmutation. At the time of the Revolution,
a majority of all white Americans were still of English
descent, and the immigrants from other European countries
had not essentially modified the American character or
American institutions. They made some incidental contri-
butions to the American way of life (non-English influences
can be traced occasionally in architecture, in speech and
vocabulary, in domestic manners and customs), but they
did not affect it fundamentally. After reaching America
the non-English immigrants were educated and conditioned
into a culture that had first been established by colonists of
English descent and afterwards changed by the American
environment.

Most American farmers displayed an empirical and pragmatic cast of mind similar to that of the English. This
English characteristic was, in fact, developed further among
the Americans. The conditions of American life imposed a
severely practical and utilitarian attitude. Since the farmers
who composed the bulk of the population had to earn
their own living by their own labor, and since there was
no well-established leisure class, every activity was likely
to be judged by its consequences in promoting human
welfare. Purely intellectual and æsthetic pursuits were not
generally esteemed or encouraged; and as Franklin remarked, in a paper written in the year 1782, "the natural

geniuses that have arisen in America with such talents have uniformly quitted that country for Europe, where they can be more suitably rewarded." [6]

The English sense of class, on the other hand, gradually grew weaker. Through the colonial period, merchants and planters continued to regard themselves as a ruling class, and for a long time their claims to leadership were accepted by the farmers. But the general tendency of American agrarian life was to cause men to regard inherent quality rather than family inheritance as the only criterion for judging one man to be superior to another. Under pioneer conditions it was easy to reach the conclusion that all men had been born equal. Franklin warned any European "who has no other quality to recommend him but his birth" not to go to America. "In Europe it has indeed its value; but it is a commodity that cannot be carried to a worse market than that of America, where people do not inquire concerning a stranger: *What is he?* but: *What can he do?* If he has any useful art, he is welcome; and if he exercises it, and behaves well, he will be respected by all who know him; but a mere man of quality, who on that account wants to live upon the public, by some office or salary, will be despised and disregarded. The husbandman is in honor there, and even the mechanic, because their employments are useful. The people have a saying that God Almighty is himself a mechanic, the greatest in the universe; and he is respected and admired more for the variety, ingenuity, and utility of his handiwork than for the antiquity of his family." [7]

Meanwhile the individualism of the English was considerably modified. The American farmer liked to do as he pleased; he was, in fact, bolder and quicker in action than his English ancestor, and more ready to resort to violence and to defy the forces of organized government in defense of what he regarded as his individual rights. But in the open spaces of America, where everybody had elbowroom, privacy was no longer a closely guarded possession. Pio-

[6] Information to those who would remove to America.
[7] *Ibid.*

neer conditions made men gregarious. In every farming community it was customary for neighbors to assist each other in clearing land or building a new house; and a generous and unsuspicious hospitality to friend and stranger alike became a part of the mores of the new society. The individualism of the farmer was never rugged. This growth of the co-operative impulses was not an unmixed advantage, however, since it was inevitably accompanied by a greater pressure toward social conformity. While the American was less eager to protect his own privacy than was his English ancestor, he was also more prone to interfere with that of others. He could welcome strangers with an open-hearted warmth without first inquiring into their antecedents and family histories, but he expected a similar gregariousness in return. The society of agrarian America was a society of average men and women. They were not always willing to tolerate neighbors who might be guilty of eccentricity, non-conformity, or heresy.

2

Yet though democratic principles were inherent both in the pioneering activity itself and in the conditions of colonial agrarian society, their full realization was a slow process requiring both a development of explicitly democratic ideals among the farmers and mechanics and a struggle with those mercantile and landowning groups who were opposed to democracy. The first settlers brought with them European ideas of class privilege and theocratic discipline, and colonial society had initially been organized among class lines. Families that had enjoyed a higher status in England before the migration continued to claim social distinction and political leadership in America, and the hereditary differences between the gentleman and the plain citizen did not quickly disappear.

This class system was at first generally accepted by most of the rank and file of the colonists. They were seeking to escape from oppressive social restrictions, and to find greater independence and wider economic opportunities; but they were not capable of visualizing a new kind of society in which equality had been institutionalized. Ambitious colonists aimed not at destroying aristocratic institutions but at becoming aristocrats themselves. Men's ways of thinking always change more slowly than the material conditions of their existence; and immigrants continued to think as Europeans even after they had begun to act as Americans. Their conscious attitudes were still conditioned by the European ideas they had acquired during their formative early years. Throughout the colonial period the English class system continued to exercise a magnetic influence on American society. The "happy mediocrity" of America was caused not by deliberate planning but by the abundance of land and resources and the scarcity of labor; it came about not because of, but in spite of, the conscious ideas of most early Americans.

For these reasons every colony quickly acquired an embryo aristocracy, which modeled itself on that of England. This consisted partly of families whose claims to superiority ante-dated the migration, and partly of other families of more humble origin, who were able to work their way to the top of the social ladder by industry, shrewdness, and good fortune after their arrival in America. In general, these embryo aristocracies were most strongly entrenched along the Atlantic seaboard, in the regions that had been settled earliest. Regions geographically more distant from Europe were also further removed in their political attitudes; in the West few families made aristocratic claims and even fewer were willing to assent to them. Throughout the colonial period there was a growing spirit of revolt against the aristocratic principle, marked by occasional outbreaks of violence; but it was not until the Revolution that it was generally challenged and not until the nineteenth century that it was overthrown.

The colonies were not governed democratically. In most of them a large proportion of the inhabitants were excluded from the franchise, usually by property qualifications, and the distribution of seats in the legislature favored the more aristocratic seaboard localities. Even more important than these legal discriminations was the continued prevalence of class attitudes of mind, both among the ruling families and among the farmers and mechanics. It was assumed that political affairs should be handled only by those who were specially qualified by birth, wealth, and education, and that small farmers, artisans, tradesmen, and servants should not presume to meddle with them. Many rural communities, both in New England and in the South, were in the habit of following the leadership of some individual of superior wealth and family distinction, accepting him as their permanent representative in the legislature, the colonel of the local regiment of militia, and the judge of the local court of justice, and allowing him the prerogatives and sometimes the title of squire.

The tradition of class rule was accompanied by a belief in ecclesiastical establishments. Underlying both these attitudes was the assumption that the natural man was weak, fallible, and sinful, and must submit to external discipline and authority, to be exercised by men with the appropriate training and qualifications. A privileged clergy, supported and protected by the state, must therefore give religious and moral guidance. The Congregationalist Church in Massachusetts and Connecticut and the Anglican Church in parts of New York and in the South were authoritarian tax-supported institutions, claiming a monopoly of religious truth and usually working in co-operation with the secular ruling classes. Only in Rhode Island and in the Quaker colonies was there religious freedom. Elsewhere it was assumed that religious discipline and conformity were necessary for social order; if individuals presumed to think for themselves in religious matters, the result would be moral and political anarchy.

Like all ruling classes, the aristocratic groups had a tendency to identify their own welfare with that of the whole community; and without being consciously grasping or self-interested, they were inclined to use their power for economic ends. Two expressions of this propensity were of special importance. In almost all the colonies the wealthier families sought titles of ownership to Western lands by buying them at low prices from royal officials or from colonial legislatures; this caused conflicts with farmers who wished to settle on those lands and who saw no good reason why they should pay rents for them. And in those colonies where political power belonged to mercantile oligarchies interested in lending rather than in borrowing money, there were disputes about the currency. The creditor groups wished to maintain a stable currency, whereas debtor interests, consisting of some of the farmers and some of the more enterprising of the merchants, advocated some form of inflation. Both in their attempts to enforce payment of rents from Western lands and in their fight to prevent inflation the colonial aristocracies were supported by the royal governors and by the British Parliament. The struggle for American democracy had therefore to become also a struggle for American self-government; the aristocratic principle could not be overthrown as long as the British authorities had a right to interfere with American affairs.

During the seventeenth century, Massachusetts and Connecticut were governed by a combination of Puritan clergymen and secular ruling families, who claimed that they alone could interpret the will of God. Any who ventured to doubt that religious truth was known to the ruling oligarchy, or who asserted that there was some alternative access to the divine will, were condemned as heretics and punished or expelled. This leadership was accepted, however, by the large majority of the rank and file of the colonists, nor did the members of the oligarchy abuse their powers for personal advantage. Displaying the virtues as well as the vices of the Puritan temperament, they were hard-working, sober, conscientious, and public-spirited. By modern standards their rule was stern (though it was decidedly more enlightened and humane than that of any European government at the same period), but it was not arbitrary or consciously unjust.

In the eighteenth century there was a change of character in the Massachusetts ruling class, and to a smaller degree in that of Connecticut. The government became more secular and less severe. In Massachusetts, political leadership was assumed by mercantile and shipowning families who had made fortunes out of trade with Great Britain and the West Indies. The Congregationalist clergy lost most of

their political influence in spite of the efforts of such men
as Increase and Cotton Mather to maintain the old theocratic regime. As a result of intervention by the British
government, wealth rather than church membership became the basis of the franchise qualifications, and a
limited degree of religious toleration was established. The
new ruling class continued to display a Puritan industry
and sobriety, but few of them retained any vital belief
in the religious doctrines of their ancestors. With increasing
wealth and self-assurance they acquired instead the eighteenth-century creed of reason, respectability, and decorum.
They built themselves substantial houses on Beacon Hill in
Boston or on the outskirts of Salem or Newburyport,
equipped them with furnishings imported from England,
lived in a style of dignified luxury, and sometimes took
an interest in learning and scholarship. Frequently working in close co-operation with the royal governors and
monopolizing the higher administrative and judicial positions in the Massachusetts government, the mercantile
families provided a leadership that was able and generally
honest, but somewhat conservative and undemocratic. They
assumed that government belonged to "gentlemen of principle and property" and to "the wise, the rich and the
well-born," and that a transfer of political power to the
farmers of the back country or to the mechanics of the
cities would mean anarchy and barbarism.

Similar mercantile oligarchies dominated the cities of
New York and Philadelphia; but elsewhere the aristocratic
principle was associated with the ownership of land rather
with trade. As in Europe, the big landowning families
hoped to perpetuate their authority through the generations
to come by means of the feudal principles of entail and
primogeniture.

The colony of New York was controlled by a few big
families—Van Rensselaers, Livingstons, Van Cortlandts,
Beekmans, Schuylers, Morrises, and others—who owned
princely estates and competed with each other for political
power and office. But it was in the Southern colonies, and
particularly in Virginia, that the influence of the English

class tradition was most conspicuous. The Virginia planter
of the tobacco country, with his large plantation house,
his broad acres, his horde of dependent slaves, and his
assumptions of political privilege and leadership, consciously modeled his way of life on that of the great lords
who ruled rural England.

The Virginian was much closer to the soil than was his
English exemplar; less of a privileged aristocrat and more
of a business man, he was more vitally concerned with the
material basis of his existence. His wealth came not from
the collection of rents from tenant farmers, but from the
management of slaves and the production and marketing
of tobacco. He also had more of a middle-class ambition
to enlarge his estate and to increase his fortune by land
speculation. And since he was usually in debt to the London
merchants to whom his tobacco was sold, his economic
status was often decidedly precarious. Yet by the late
eighteenth century, after Virginia plantation society had
had time to become stabilized, it had acquired much of the
grace and leisureliness and the sense of *noblesse oblige* that
are the characteristic virtues of aristocracy, while at the
same time its system of privilege was tempered by the
essentially democratic environment in which it had grown
up. It had developed a code of values and an accepted
style of living in which there was a place for the pleasures
of physical activity and social intercourse, for the cultiva-
tion of the mind, and for disinterested political activity.
The Virginia planter was addicted to a wide and generous
hospitality, and he enjoyed hunting, horse racing, dancing,
drinking, and making love. Not infrequently he also gathered a library, engaged in political and philosophical
speculation, planned his house and gardens with a view
to æsthetic effect, attended seriously to his duties as a
legislator, and was capable of liberal and humanitarian
ideals. The society that produced Washington and Jefferson had a charm, a sanity and sense of balance, and a
broad humaneness that have not been equaled elsewhere
in Anglo-Saxon America. Being based on the aristocratic
principle, it could not endure; its continued existence

could not be reconciled with the main trends of American development. Yet life in America was impoverished by its inevitable disappearance.

The greatest blemish of the plantation system was the institution of Negro slavery. Although the first cargo of Negroes had been brought to Virginia by a Dutch ship as early as 1619, the labor supply on the Southern plantations continued to be mainly white for several generations. But near the end of the seventeenth century, merchants in Great Britian and New England began to discover the profitable potentialities of the slave trade. During the next half-century the seaports of the Southern colonies were flooded with shipments of Negroes kidnapped and transported from the western coastline of Africa; and slaves replaced white indentured servants in the whole plantation region from Maryland down to Georgia. In 1700 there were only about twenty thousand Negroes in the colonies; but by 1775 the number had risen to more than half a million, so that Negroes comprised one-fifth of the total population, the vast majority of them being laborers on Southern tobacco and rice plantations. Slavery existed in every American colony, but it was only in the South that it became an integral part of the economic system and exercised a pervasive influence upon the whole social structure.

Liberal-minded Americans, both Northern and Southern, deplored the slave trade, and some of them felt that it was a crime for which a bloody reparation might be exacted from posterity. But the profits to be made out of slave labor, and the social prestige to be acquired from the ownership of slaves, were arguments that could not be resisted by the planter class or by those who aspired to belong to it. And even those Americans who regarded the eventual abolition of slavery as just and necessary could not accept with equanimity the idea that white and black might one day live alongside each other and mingle with each other on terms of complete equality. The strange and sinister phenomenon of race prejudice had already established deep roots in American society for reasons which are somewhat obscure. It never became important

in Brazil, where Negro slavery was established over a
longer period than in the United States; and even among
the English colonists it does not appear to have shown itself
immediately. In early Virginia there was not at first any
clear differentiation between the Negro slave and the white
indentured servant. But by the eighteenth century most
white Americans had learned to regard all Negroes, no
matter what their personal qualities might be, as belonging
to a race that must forever remain inferior. For a long
time American democracy was to be limited by a color
line. This was to be one of its greatest failures, and was
to cause conflicts and maladjustments that had a lasting
and far-reaching effect on American political and social
life.

3

The conflict between the aristocratic principle and the
rising spirit of democracy may be considered as the main
theme in the early political history of the Americans. Yet
it should not be forgotten that even before the Revolution,
American society was less deeply divided than that of
any other country, and that by European standards it was
already democratic in spirit. Merchants and landowners
might speak of the dangers of mob rule in tones of the
greatest alarm, and farmers might be very ready to get
down their guns in order to drive rent collectors away.
Yet by contrast with Europe the division between rich
and poor was relatively narrow, and the vast majority of
the population were neither one nor the other, but were
independent property owners. The richer families, in spite
of their fondness for European aristocratic pretensions and
ways of thinking, were not really comparable to the leisured
landowning nobility of England and France; even the
Southern planters were essentially middle class. And the
farmers and mechanics who championed democracy were
very different from the degraded proletariat of the European cities.

Nor were there any deep ideological divisions in
America. All Americans of all classes had similar ambitions

for economic advancement and similar social ideals; and all of them were in agreement about certain basic principles, disagreeing only in the deductions to be drawn from them. The internal conflicts in American society were rarely fought on any clear-cut lines either of class or of ideological difference. They were conflicts between those who had acquired special privileges, either political or economic, and those who had not. In such conflicts the more enterprising of the merchants and landowners were often to be found on the progressive side. The achievement of democracy, with its slogan of equal rights for all and special privileges for none, was a by-product of these struggles.

The most fundamental of political divisions is between those who regard individuals as existing for the sake of the state and those who believe that the state exists for the sake of individuals. The former viewpoint has constituted the philosophical basis of European conservatism, and has served to justify the preservation of traditional forms of class rule and the regimentation of opinion. But neither in the eighteenth century nor at any later period did this attitude win any support among Americans. The methods by which America had been settled and the freedom and fluidity of American life made it obvious that the state had no reality apart from the individuals of which it was composed and that it should be regarded as an instrument for the service of its citizens and not as an end in itself. Almost all Americans regarded it as self-evident that individuals had rights with which the state could not legitimately interfere. In this sense almost all Americans, whether rich or poor, aristocratic or democratic, were liberals. There has never been any conservative tradition, in the European sense, in American political thinking.

The American belief in individual rights was initially derived from the liberal tradition of England, and was strengthened by the colonizing and pioneering experience; but its more specific formulation was provided by European theorists of the social-contract school, and particularly by John Locke. That men were endowed by nature with rights to life, liberty, and private property; that the state was based on a contract freely entered into by its citizens; that the only true function of government was to protect the rights of the citizens; and that a government might be changed or overthrown whenever it ceased to maintain these rights—these doctrines were in harmony with American attitudes and were corroborated to a remarkable degree by actual American experience. Before the Revolution almost every literate American had learned the vocabulary of the natural-rights philosophy, and almost every American accepted its truth as self-evident. Although it had originated in Europe, the Americans assimilated it so thoroughly that they made it their own. It became the American creed and the formative principle of the new American nationality.

Judged by European standards, this new American society had obvious deficiencies. If it surpassed Europe in the opportunities it offered to the common man, it was inferior in intellectual and æsthetic achievements. In a society where most men supported themselves by their own labor, and where there was no leisure class interested in patronizing the arts, there was no room for an intelligentsia. The only class of men who could devote themselves primarily to intellectual pursuits was the clergy. In consequence colonial America produced no important speculative thinking (except in theology) and no great works of art. In these respects it was inferior not only to Europe, but also to the Spanish colonies of Mexico and Peru. The highest creations of the human mind are necessarily the work of professionals, and professionalism was both incompatible with the conditions of American life and contrary to the American spirit. The American was distinguished for breadth and versatility rather than for intensive concentration; he was inclined to try his hand at a dozen different occupations and to indulge a great variety of different interests.

Yet though culture in America was thinner than in Europe, it was also spread more widely. The proportion of the population, especially in New England, who could be considered literate, and who had some knowledge of the classics and of the more important contemporary

European writers, was probably larger than in any other country. Jefferson once remarked that the modern wagon wheel, with the circumference made from a single piece of wood, had been invented by a New Jersey farmer who had found it described in Homer. American farmers, he added, were the only farmers who could read Homer. It would be an exaggeration to maintain that many Americans could read Greek, or that a majority of them read books at all. But the farmer with serious intellectual interests was not an infrequent figure.

And though colonial America had no room for an art that did not serve utilitarian purposes, it could produce useful objects that were also beautiful. The thirty years preceding the Revolution were the great age of colonial architecture, marked by the construction of churches, government buildings, Southern plantation houses, and private homes that had an admirable strength, simplicity, and harmony. The English Georgian style supplied the model, but this was simplified and adapted to American needs and building materials by the colonial craftsmen. It would be easy to argue that their work has never been surpassed by later American architects. A similar good taste was displayed in the making of chairs and cabinets, silver and pewter ware, and decorated pottery—the good taste of men who concentrate upon achieving some useful purpose rather than upon attracting attention by the virtuosity with which they handle their medium of expression.

The same quality was to be found in the New England school of portrait-painting. Colonial painting was strictly functional; its purpose was to record a likeness, not to achieve some æsthetic effect. But those painters who mastered their medium could achieve a realistic fidelity to fact and convey a sense of life and of individual personality that a too self-conscious artistry might have destroyed. This, in fact, is precisely what happened in the case of the most gifted of the colonial painters, John Singleton Copley. During the first twenty years of his career, Copley remained in Boston and painted portraits that have rarely been surpassed by any later American. During this period his work was not only of the highest quality; in its capacity to portray men and women as individuals, and not merely as specimens of social types and classes, it was also profoundly true to the spirit of American society. Unfortunately, Copley was not content to be merely a hired craftsman; he aspired to be an artist; and at the age of thirty-seven he left for Europe in order to learn how great works of art were created. But the elaborate battle pieces and historical episodes to which he devoted the forty years he spent in London were inferior to his Boston portraits. He lost the qualities of an honest craftsmanship without acquiring those of the creative imagination.

The merits of the colonial way of life were most fully exemplified in its representative man, Benjamin Franklin. Franklin was one of those men who achieve distinction by embodying completely the spirit of the society in which they live, rather than by deviating from it or going beyond it. He was the ideal common man of the American world, bold enough to try his hand at everything and unintimidated by professional pretensions of any kind, whether in politics or in science and literature. A human being with certain obvious limitations, having little sense of poetry and no taste for mysticism, endowed with a cool, uncomplicated, and somewhat calculating temperament, he cannot be accounted great by virtue of his concrete achievements in any field; he did not belong to the first rank as a writer or as a scientist or as a statesman. But he applied himself to an astonishing variety of different occupations; and to everything he brought the same refreshing qualities of sanity, realism, tolerance, resourcefulness, and human understanding. He was a great man because of what he was in himself rather than because of any specific accomplishment. This kind of greatness was possible in colonial America not only because of its democratic spirit but also because of the consistency of its intellectual and moral attitudes with its economic and social organization. The individual was able to achieve an integrated personality because he lived in a harmonious society. In his *Poor Richard* aphorisms Franklin could formulate the folk morality of his society without criticism or cynicism; his approval of

those bourgeois virtues which brought economic success
was only one aspect of his many-sided character, but it
was not out of keeping with his other qualities. And it was
because Franklin was so completely an American that he
could represent America so successfully over a period of
more than twenty-five years in European countries. Enjoying European society, and valuing all its qualities of charm
and intellectual attainment, Franklin never lost contact
with his American background or ceased to appreciate its
unique virtues. As a result of his deep-rooted Americanism,
this Philadelphia printer and son of a Boston tallow-chan-
dler was able to mingle with European aristocracies and to
defend American interests at the British and French courts
with a complete self-assurance and sense of equality. He
was neither intimidated by Europe nor impelled to depre-
ciate it and attack it.

Many-sided humanity rather than specific accomplishment was, in fact, what characterized the eighteenth-century
American in general. The leading figures of America were
inferior to Europeans as artists or scientists or philosophers;
but they were more successful as human beings. The men
who made the Revolution were by no means geniuses, and
they did little original thinking. But with few exceptions
they had the sanity, the integrity, and the self-confidence
that are the fruits of a well-balanced way of life and a
healthy social organization.

The impact of this new American man upon Europe was
of the greatest importance. What impressed liberal-minded
Europeans was not merely the political maturity of the
Americans: their respect for individual freedom, their
ability to govern themselves, the high intellectual level of
their political debates. It was the advent of a society in
which almost all men were property owners, and in which
there were no parasitical aristocracy, no privileged bureaucracy, no proletariat, and no beggars. Here for the first
time in history was a society that (except in the one great
matter of slavery) appeared to have organized itself on
principles of reason, justice, and humanity. Such a spectacle
was in harmony with the main tendencies of eighteenth-
century European thought, which looked for salvation from

a corrupt social system in the simplicity of a more natural existence. A figure like Franklin was a living confirmation of the dreams of the Enlightenment. If eighteenth-century America borrowed its political theories from Europe, it more than repaid the debt by the encouragement that it offered, by its mere existence, to European liberalism.

In the course of time, American society lost its idyllic qualities. It lost them primarily because of forces that had been inherent in the American character from the beginning. With their drive toward the domination of nature and toward social and economic success, the Americans could not be content with an agrarian way of life. They preferred both the rewards and the hazards of industrial capitalism, and in doing so they sacrificed most of those features of eighteenth-century life which had appeared so admirable. Those political leaders who wished to keep America a country of small property owners fought a losing battle, not merely because they were defeated by the moneyed interests, but for the more basic reason that their static social ideals were inconsistent with that dynamic quality of the will which characterized American civilization in general. Yet though Americans abandoned the way of life that had developed during the colonial period, they retained many of the attitudes that had been associated with it. Long after the essential features of eighteenth-century society had disappeared, most Americans continued to think in the terms that had been appropriate to the formative early period of their civilization.

☆ ☆ ☆ ☆ ☆ ☆ ☆ ☆ ☆ ☆ ☆ ☆ ☆ ☆

CHAPTER IV

AMERICAN RELIGION

★ ★ ★ ★ ★ ★ ★ ★ ★ ★ ★ ★ ★ ★

To TURN from the politics of eighteenth-century Americans to their religious beliefs seems at first like entering an utterly different world. Men like Franklin and Jefferson believed that if human beings were free from unjust social conditions they could be trusted to behave wisely and virtuously. But according to Jonathan Edwards, who was born only three years earlier than Franklin in the same part of America, all men were by nature utterly sinful and worthy of eternal damnation, and the sole object worthy of pursuit was the salvation of one's soul, not in this life but in the next.

Yet many of the same men who accepted the political ideals of Jefferson also believed in the theology of Edwards, and were able to do so without any sense of inconsistency. The rationalistic deism professed by the more intellectual Americans was not shared by the mass of their fellow citizens. A large proportion of eighteenth-century Americans were adherents of one or another of the evangelical Protestant denominations, and were staunch Calvinists in their general view of life. Calvinism was one of the most vital factors in the shaping of American civilization.

And when one examines the religious development of the Americans, one can discover reflected in it the same psychic tendencies that are so apparent in their political evolution. Projected into theological symbolisms are to be found the same repudiation of external authority, the same confidence in the average man, the same exaltation of the will, and the same belief that evil can be overcome. Franklin and Edwards, in spite of the irreconcilable differences in the beliefs they consciously held and explicitly taught, were representatives of the same basic American character. And it can be argued that that character was reflected more completely and more truly in theology than it was in political and economic theory. In their political ideals, men give expression to what they wish to believe; but in their religion (so long as it remains a vital social force covering every aspect of human life) they show what they really are. A theology is, in fact, a kind of collective poem or work of art that records the secret emotional history of a community. And that drive of the American will, which was the ultimate reason for the failure of the social ideals of eighteenth-century liberalism, was very manifest in the evolution of American religion.

The European mind had been dominated by the sense of a cosmic and social order to which the nature of the individual must be adjusted; and its central religious experience had been a feeling of inner disharmony, of man at war with himself, that resulted in a turning to God for deliverance and salvation. The individual, even when wholly moral and law-abiding in his overt behavior, felt a deep anxiety on account of his own forbidden natural impulses, and became convinced of his own worthlessness and sinfulness. He believed that he deserved punishment and was worthy only of eternal rejection and damnation. But Christianity taught him that if he trusted in God rather than in his own merits he could be released from his anxiety and could achieve salvation in spite of his evil nature. Salvation was the free gift of God to those who had been chosen for redemption; it was acquired by faith, and was not dependent on merit. The penalty for the sins of the redeemed had already been paid through the crucifixion of Jesus Christ. This sense of worthlessness and fear of rejection, which twentieth-century naturalism prefers to describe in the vocabulary of psychiatry, was the very essence of the Christian experience as it was recorded by St. Paul and St. Augustine in the early Christian era, by

Luther in the sixteenth century, and by Kierkegaard and Karl Barth in more recent times; and from it were deduced the theological doctrines of original sin, divine grace, salvation by faith and not by works, the atonement of the cross, and heaven and hell in the hereafter.

These Christian doctrines, in the formulation that had been given them by Calvin, were brought to America by many of the early settlers; and until the nineteenth century they composed the official creed of the American evangelical churches. But in the American environment they were interpreted in a different spirit and made to reflect a different form of experience. The sense of inner conflict and the deep pervasive anxiety that had produced the European conviction of man's basic sinfulness and need for divine deliverance grew less vivid. American Christianity had no vital belief in a cosmic order to which the individual must submit; instead, it saw life in terms of a battle between the human will and the natural world, and had confidence that, with divine aid, the battle would end victoriously.

The beginnings of this religious evolution antedated the settlement of America. For the Calvinist creed, though derived from the European religious tradition, was already particularly well adapted to a race of individualistic pioneers. More than any other form of Christianity, it promoted militancy and self-assurance, and encouraged action in preference to contemplation. It was no accident that so many areas of America were first colonized by members of the Calvinist churches. The Calvinist immigrant was already half an American.

The anxieties and aspirations that are projected in religious beliefs are originally the products of social discipline; and the theology of any community can often be interpreted as a reflection of its experiences in daily living. Calvinism developed chiefly among sections of the European middle class who were already predisposed to an attitude of militant activity. They did more than merely accept those basic institutions which have been common to all European communities: monogamous marriage, the family system, the subordination of women, the disciplining of children, sexual taboos. (Such institutions always involve a considerable repression of natural impulses, and may therefore provoke those feelings of anxiety which appear in theology as a sense of sin.) To these institutions the middle class added others appropriate to their social and economic status. They believed in hard work, thrift, and the avoidance of expensive or time-consuming pleasures. They resented the social superiority of the aristocracy and its addiction to luxury and dissipation; and long before the Reformation they were becoming hostile to the Catholic clergy. They could not approve of a Church that charged high prices for salvation, had little respect for the economic virtues, and regarded the contemplative life as superior to a life devoted to business activity.

To men and women of this kind, the system of thought that was worked out by John Calvin during the Reformation had a special appeal. Calvin's morality, though professedly derived wholly from the Bible, was essentially a bourgeois morality. It regarded hard work at one's regular occupation as a religious duty, and had no place for monasticism or any other form of the contemplative life; it prohibited expensive pleasures and encouraged thrift; it approved of economic success, provided that it was not obtained by unjust methods; and by abolishing the Catholic hierarchy, it made salvation cheap.

Calvinism, moreover, promoted an attitude of extreme militancy and aggressiveness. It divided mankind into two groups, the elect and the damned. Those who had faith in God, who sincerely endeavored to obey the moral rules that God had established, and who were accepted into the Calvinist Church, might feel assured of their own election, and could rely upon God for guidance and protection. The rest of mankind were among the damned. It was the duty of the elect to impose their way of life upon the rest of the human race, if necessary by force, and to see to it that the will of God was obeyed. Calvinism thus led to civil war and revolution, and was the spearhead of the advance of the middle class to political power, in several European countries.

Modern man, imbued with naturalistic modes of thought,

finds it difficult to understand how Calvinism could ever have exercised such influence. Here was a system of beliefs that declared that all men were utterly wicked, that a small minority had been chosen by God for salvation, and that redemption depended not on man's free will but on divine election and predestination. Why were the adherents of such a religion conspicuous not, as one might expect, for a fatalistic acquiescence, but rather for an astonishing energy and force of will? In actuality, the doctrines of complete depravity and of divine election were among the chief reasons for the strength of the Calvinist creed. In common with all other forms of evangelical Christianity, Calvinism declared that man obtained salvation not by good works but by faith, and that the power to achieve a saving faith was the free gift of God to those whom he had elected. When this doctrine is interpreted in terms of the emotional experience it reflected, its power immediately becomes apparent. To the individual who feels any anxiety or emotional insecurity nothing is so paralyzing as the belief that he can win approval, either from his neighbors or from God, only by the quality of his works. But Calvinism taught its adherents that their works were always worthless and that they were right in feeling no confidence in them, but that if they felt a trust in Christ and a willingness to obey him, they could nevertheless be assured of salvation—not because of their works, but in spite of them. Those persons who accepted this doctrine and applied it to themselves had an astonishing sense of liberation, as though a burden had suddenly fallen from their shoulders: they were immediately freed from doubt, insecurity, and anxiety. This instantaneous experience of conversion was, indeed, a kind of rebirth.

Calvinism contained, in embryo or by implication, a number of the qualities that became characteristically American. In certain directions, for example, it encouraged individuals to repudiate external authority and to have confidence in their own judgments and intuitions. The true believer, who had received the gift of saving faith, and who therefore had the Holy Spirit within him, could no longer recognize any merely earthly authority as endowed with superior wisdom. At the same time, however, he must obey the will of God as it had been revealed in the Bible, and must accept the authorized interpretations of that will by the Calvinist Church. Nor was the individual encouraged to theorize and speculate about divine things; the will of God and his purposes in choosing some men for election and the rest for damnation were inscrutable mysteries that man must not presume to investigate. From the beginning, the Calvinist doctrine of saving faith led some persons to maintain that their own spiritual intuitions superseded the written words of the Bible and the decisions of the Church; but such liberalizing tendencies were always repressed with great severity. God could not contradict himself, and the decisions of the Church were more likely to be valid than those of the individual. In general, it was the church members as a group, and not the ministers alone, who decided upon the divine will, though the division of authority was never clearly defined, and conflicts between minister and congregation were not infrequent. Thus the right of the individual to repudiate external authority, though implicit in Calvinism, was in practice narrowly circumscribed.

Calvinism, moreover, viewed life in terms of a battle between good and evil; it encouraged those who were fighting on the side of good to act with great energy and self-assurance; and it offered the hope that evil might eventually be wholly overcome. An omnipotent God was the leader of the forces of good; and he had promised that the earth would someday be the scene of the millennium, during which he would visibly reign over his followers and evil would be obliterated. Many Calvinists studied the prophecies in the Book of Revelation with great care, and believed that the millennium was to be expected in the near future. This Calvinist cosmology was formulated in extremely simple terms, with the convincing and deceptive clarity of a mathematical theorem. Goodness meant faith in God and obedience to his will; every impulse of nature was evil. The Calvinist moral code was not unduly ascetic, but its main characteristic was its emphasis on unremitting self-watchfulness and self-discipline. Any spontaneous emotion, including love for another human being, was likely to be sinful. Starting in early childhood, the good Calvinist was taught to keep constant guard over his own feelings and never to permit himself, even for a moment, to forget his duty to God and the dangers of diabolical temptation. The man who succeeded in this process of emotional inhibition would ascribe little value to intellectual speculation or æsthetic experience, but would excel in the activities of business, politics, war, and pioneering.

Yet at the same time it must not be forgotten that the basic concepts of Calvinism had been derived from the Christian tradition of Europe, even though Calvin had reformulated them with an excessive narrowness, simplicity, and logic, and had adapted them so as to sanctify the acquisitiveness and the social ambitions of the rising bourgeoisie. The core of Calvinism, as of all forms of evangelical Christianity, was man's sense of his own sinfulness and his consequent anxiety and fear of divine anger. The sincere Calvinist believed in human depravity because he felt that he himself was depraved, and he believed in hell because he felt that he himself deserved damnation. There were many unhappy souls in sixteenth- and seventeenth-century Europe who turned to Calvinism not because it sanctified their acquisitiveness and promised them participation in the millennium, but because, more simply and more emphatically than any other branch of Christianity, it declared that the man who trusted in the grace of God and the atonemen made by Jesus on the cross need no longer feel any anxiety on account of his sinfulness.

2

Such was the creed that many different groups of immigrants brought with them to America and that inspired, in particular, the early settlers of Massachusetts and Connecticut in their struggle with the wilderness. Seeing life in terms of a battle between good and evil, these Calvinist colonists identified evil with that American world which they were engaged in subduing, and believed themselves to be crusaders preparing the way for the millennium.

This attitude of militancy is very evident in the early

religious history of New England. The Puritan colonists
regarded themselves, as one of them declared, as the for-
lorn hope of Christ's invincible army, led into battle by
Christ himself. Their task was to create in New England
a kind of installment of the millennium. New England was
"the place where the Lord will create a new Heaven and a
new Earth"; it was to be "a specimen of what shall be
over all the earth in the glorious times which are expected."
And in order to carry out the will of the Lord, the Puritans
must constantly do battle with the devil and his agents.
According to Cotton Mather, they were "a people of God
settled in those which were once the devil's territories. . . .
There was not a greater uproar among the Ephesians when
the gospel was first brought among them than there was
among the powers of the air . . . when first the silver
trumpets of the gospel here made the joyful sounds. . . .
I believe that never were more satanical devices used for
the unsettling of any people under the sun, than what have
been employed for the extirpation of the vine which God
has here planted." [1]

One incidental consequence of such an attitude was that
the aboriginal inhabitants of America were regarded as
the devil's peculiar servants—according to some opinions,
even as his children; and when they resisted the Puritan advance, many New Englanders advocated exterminating
them. One of the most saintly of the New England ministers, Thomas Shepard, described how, during the Pequod
War, "the Providence of God" guided three or four hundred
of the Indians to a place convenient for "the divine slaugh-
ter by the hand of the English." Some were put to the
sword and some were burned to death when their wigwams
were set on fire," until the Lord had utterly consumed
the whole company except four or five girls they took
prisoners" and kept as slaves.[2]

[1] *Edward Johnson:* Wonder-Working Providence of Sions
Savior in New England *(reprinted 1910)*, Book I, Chap. I;
Increase Mather: Icabod *(1729)*, p. 74; *Cotton Mather:* Won-
ders of the Invisible World *(reprinted 1862)*, p. 13.
[2] *Alexander Young:* Chronicles of the First Planters of the
Colony of Massachusetts Bay *(1846)*, pp. 549, 550.

Under such circumstances there was a tendency for the concept of evil to become externalized. Emphasis on man's own evil nature decreased, while there was a correspondingly increased concentration upon the external nature which man must subdue. To some extent, perhaps, these two forms of nature became identified; the American wilderness and the repressed elements in the human personality were both of them abodes of the devil, and both of them must be brought under stern religious control. Thus Puritanism stimulated the drive of the will toward the domination of all forms of nature, both internal and external, and identified this drive of the will with positive good. To tolerate such carnal sins as drunkenness and fornication would provoke the anger of God and would also weaken the community in its struggle to establish material prosperity. In dealing with nature, both internal and external, man must obey God; and as long as he obeyed God he might expect divine assistance. Disobedience and immorality, on the other hand, would be followed by catastrophe, since God would withdraw his support and allow the Puritans to be overcome by their enemies. Throughout the seventeenth century, the main theme of the sermons and official pronouncements of the New England clergy was that obedience to God was the only way to secure worldly prosperity; immorality would be punished by floods, droughts, thunderstorms, earthquakes, shipwrecks, fires, epidemics of deadly diseases, and Indian wars. In the Puritan world nothing was trivial or accidental, and every happening was to be interpreted in terms of the cosmic battle between God and the devil. All material events were signs and symbols of supernatural realities, and should be regarded as rewards for the righteous, as warnings to the wicked, or as omens and tokens of divine purposes.

This view of life had a certain grandeur in spite of its narrowness and the fantastic superstitions which it encouraged; it gave a transcendental significance to every aspect of human behavior. But it inevitably led to self-righteousness and to intolerance. The Puritans were convinced that they knew the will of God and that it was their duty to carry it into effect, if necessary by the use of coercion. One should not exaggerate, however, the severity of the Puritan conscience. They relied upon the Bible as the authoritative word of God, and the Bible does not inculcate excessive asceticism. The New England legal code prescribed penalties for nonattendance at church, sabbath-breaking, idleness, drunkenness, and fornication, and any unrestrained merriment was regarded with disapproval; but a sober and moderate enjoyment of those pleasures which God had provided for the benefit of mankind was encouraged. The Puritans declared that, unlike the Catholics, they did not burden the individual conscience with unnecessary scruples or excessive restrictions.

The psychological evolution of New England may be traced in terms of the weakening of the sense of sin. If virtue would be rewarded with prosperity, then it presumably followed that prosperity was a proof of virtue. As the New Englanders advanced in material security and well-being, they were less inclined to regard themselves as creatures of complete depravity who could be saved only by supernatural grace. The prosperous merchant of eighteenth-century Boston might be still inclined to divide mankind into the saved and the damned, but he had little doubt that he himself was among the saved and that he owed his salvation not to the grace of God but to his own merits. In the American environment, moreover, men had increasingly great opportunities for the expression of aggressive energies and the pursuit of ambition, and (in spite of the Puritan disapproval of certain forms of pleasure) were less restricted by social disciplines than in Europe. And it is when men are inhibited from any overt display of aggression, and their impulses are driven back upon themselves, that they are likely to suffer most acutely from that inner anxiety which theologians know as the sense of sin. In America the individual's chief source of anxiety was the natural environment rather than his own repressed desires; and by battling successfully with the environment he could win security and self-esteem.

The leading ministers of the generation that had colonized New England had themselves known that inner anxiety and sense of divine deliverance on which their theology had been founded. There is a note of genuine personal experience in the autobiographical narrative of Thomas Shepard and in the sermons of John Cotton. There is less of it in the writings of Increase Mather, of the second generation. And although Cotton Mather, of the third generation, laboriously recorded his religious experiences in his diary, and endeavored to reproduce the emotions he regarded as appropriate to a devout Calvinist, it is impossible for the modern reader to take his protestations seriously. He called himself the chief of sinners, but he was much too self-righteous to feel any genuine sense of sin, fear of divine anger, or need for divine grace. Among the ministers of the early eighteenth century, if one can judge from the surviving diaries and autobiographies, the sense of sin almost disappeared.

The result was a steady softening of the Calvinist theology. There was less emphasis on man's depravity and on God's righteous anger, more emphasis on man's ability to save himself and on God's benevolence. Religion began to be identified with reason, respectability, and decorum. But this trend toward religious liberalism was decidedly illiberal in its political and social implications. As the clergy lost their political influence, they began to claim wider powers over their congregations in religious matters and to ally themselves with the wealthy merchants and other conservative elements. As the sense of a direct relationship between the Holy Spirit and the soul of the individual believer became less vivid, the churches became less democratic. If true religion meant respectability and not inner experience, then its chief exemplars were the Boston merchants. Benjamin Colman, for example, who succeeded Cotton Mather as the acknowledged leader of the New England clergy, was both more liberal in his theology and more authoritarian in his views of church government. This growth of a religion of respectability led finally to Unitarianism, which became a recognized and distinct denomination early in the nineteenth century and which was the favored church of the "gentlemen of principle and property" in eastern Massachusetts.

Meanwhile Calvinist churches had been established in

many other parts of America. The Dutch churches in New York had little vitality, and Anglicanism became the predominant creed in that colony. But the French Huguenot communities that settled in several seacoast towns had more religious fervor. Industrious, talented, and strictly disciplined, many of the French families quickly became rich and respectable, and passed through a religious evolution similar to that of the Bostonians. In the eighteenth century came the Scotch-Irish Presbyterians, who turned to agriculture rather than to trade, and became the most vigorous pioneering group along the frontier from Pennsylvania southward. In the courage and the aggressiveness with which they did battle against the Western forests and against the Indians, they strongly resembled the New Englanders of a century earlier. Another Calvinist Church, that of the Baptists, which was more democratic than the Congregationalism of New England, had been propagated in a number of areas by immigrant preachers from Great Britain. During the Revolutionary epoch came the Methodists, who rejected part of the theology of Calvinism, but preached a generally similar view of life. All these organizations had much more vigor than the tepid and formalistic Anglican Church, to which the rich and respectable belonged in New York and in the South, or than the Quakerism of eastern Pennsylvania.

3

The appearance of a distinctively American form of Christianity may be dated from the religious revivals of the 1730's and 1740's, generally known as the Great Awakening. The theology of the Awakening was pure old-fashioned Calvinism, but its social implications were decidedly democratic and individualistic; the tendency to repudiate all external authority, which had always been latent in Calvinism, now became much more explicit. The Awakening swept across farming communities in almost every part of the colonies, especially along the frontier, and only the aristocratic elements were left wholly unaffected by it.

What precipitated the Great Awakening it is impossible to say. Those who took part in it could see it only as the direct handiwork of God and as a probable indication that the long-expected millennium was now close at hand. There were suggestions that America was to be the place where Christ would be born a second time and where sin and evil would be finally destroyed. During the 1730's, religious revivals started independently of each other in several different places, most notably among the Scotch-Irish in Pennsylvania, among the Dutch Reformed churches in New Jersey, and among the Congregationalist churches in western Massachusetts. In the years 1739 and 1740 the English itinerant evangelist, George Whitefield, toured the colonies from New Hampshire to Georgia, preaching and provoking revivals everywhere. The work was then carried forward by the ministers of the different Calvinist churches.

The most effectual revivalist oratory was hell-fire preaching of the crudest and most lurid kind. Congregations were told that every unconverted person would infallibly go to hell and spend eternity in the most horrible torments. Preaching of this kind could easily throw unsophisticated audiences into a state of utter panic, during which men, women, and children wept, screamed, jerked their arms and legs, fainted, and had convulsive fits. Once an individual had been thoroughly infected with this mob hysteria and reduced to a state of abject terror, he usually passed successfully through the crisis of conversion; he resolved to trust in God rather than in his own merits for salvation, and to obey God's will. Henceforth he could regard himself as one of the elect.

Probably there was nothing very profound or complex in the emotional experience of the average convert. The people most susceptible to revivalism were the poorer and less educated farmers and city mechanics, boys and girls (including small children), and Negroes. The available evidence suggests that revivalism brought about a marked improvement in their moral standards. Its most conspicuous and important result, however, was to stimulate the movement toward democracy. Once a plain farmer or mechanic had undergone the experience of conversion, he believed

that he was filled with the Holy Spirit and that—in the eyes
of God—he was superior to those merchants, landowners,
planters, and royal officials who were still among the
damned. And in spite of his lack of education he felt that
his own judgments and intuitions, enlightened by the Spirit,
were wiser than the opinions of the gentlemen of principle
and property. Revivalism was an expression of the American repudiation of authority and assertion of freedom for
the average man.

In the colonies from Pennsylvania southward the revivals
swept across the Scotch-Irish settlements along the frontier.
Presbyterian and Baptist evangelists then began to attack
farming communities that had hitherto been nominally
Anglican or wholly irreligious. Only the planter class remained uninfected, and eventually most of the South outside
the seacoast regions became almost as permeated with
evangelical Protestantism as New England had ever been.
The new evangelical denominations soon began to denounce the privileged position of the Anglican Church
and other aspects of the aristocratic principle. Patrick
Henry first became a popular figure in Virginia, shortly before he won wider fame by his speech against the Stamp
Act, by voicing the resentment of the Presbyterians and
the Baptists against the taxes for the support of the Anglican clergy.

In New England the effects of the Awakening were even
more cataclysmic. Most of the Congregational clergy took
part in it during its earlier stages, but their authoritarian
and conservative attitudes aroused increasing resentment;
and the movement soon passed beyond clerical control.
All over New England many thousands of farmers and
mechanics left the established churches and formed new
"Separatist" congregations of their own, in which every
member, however humble or illiterate, was free to preach
or pray as the Spirit moved him. The writings and exhorta-
tions of the Separatists were filled with denunciations of the
rich and respectable classes and of the privileged and
college-trained clerical hierarchy. The plain citizen, they
declared, if enlightened by the Spirit, needed no professional
guidance. The oligarchy, both in Massachusetts and Con-

necticut, retaliated by declaring the meetings of the Separatists to be illegal, by continuing to tax them for the support of the regular clergy and to send them to prison when
they refused to pay, and by predicting that this spirit of
"enthusiasm" would destroy all moral, social, and political
order. This religious persecution lasted until the War of
Independence, and caused a large number of Separatists to
take refuge in northern New England and New York,
making these areas special centers of religious "enthusiasm."
Both the doctrines of the Separatists and the alarm that
they provoked among the regular clergy and the richer
classes were obvious reflections of the contemporary political conflicts. The revival swept across Massachusetts
during the same period that the struggle between debtor
and creditor interests about inflation was most acute. When
the Revolution came, all the revivalist groups were militant
champions of American rights, while many (though not all)
of the opponents of revivalism were inclined towards
Toryism.

Most of the Separatist congregations eventually joined
forces with the Baptists, though a few remained independent until the nineteenth century. But once the principle of
complete private judgment in religious matters had been
stimulated in this fashion, it could not be checked at any
point. From the time of the Great Awakening there was
a constant splintering of religious congregations into new
sectarian groups, which differed from each other on minor
points of theology or religious practice. As long as New
Englanders retained a vital belief in religion, the demand
of the plain citizen to think for himself continued to produce a proliferation of novel and often eccentric theologies.
At the end of the eighteenth century there was one small
Massachusetts town that contained six different and mutually hostile Baptist congregations.[3] In the year 1805 the
regular Congregationalist minister of Salem gloomily reported that the different sects in that town were "as thick as
the gulls upon our sand-bar, as hungry and as useless." In a

* This was Rehoboth.

lesser degree the same tendency showed itself among the Calvinist churches in Pennsylvania and the South.

It is easy to laugh at the sects, but their significance as reflections of the American spirit should not be overlooked. Most of them claimed to be based on the Bible, and did not deviate far from its traditional interpretations. But there were a few that were bold enough to make a deeper exploration of the possible implications of the Calvinist experience. If God communicated his Spirit directly to the soul of the believer, he might have new revelations going beyond the doctrines of the Bible and of tradition. And if the true believer was genuinely liberated from the burden of his sins, perhaps he might be free to follow his own deepest intuitions without being restricted by any external rules. Such doctrines had been propagated by a few heretical leaders during the European Reformation, and had been preached in early Massachusetts by Mrs. Hutchinson, for which reason she had been banished from the colony in 1638. They began to reappear after the Great Awakening, and were usually accompanied by suggestions that the millennium was close at hand or had already arrived, and that it was now possible for men to live wholly without sin. It was a perilous attitude, since almost any impulse might be attributed to divine inspiration and withdrawn from rational investigation and control; and it could encourage charlatanry and imposture and end in downright lunacy. Most of the self-appointed prophets who appeared in such profusion in New England and the Middle West during the period between the Revolution and the Civil War were conspicuous chiefly for their sexual promiscuity and for their messianic claims. But the complete repudiation of earthly authority and tradition and the belief in the possibility of a sinless existence—both of which were characteristically American attitudes—could also lead to a bold exploration of new forms of human relationship.

The most interesting of the sects were the Shakers and the Perfectionists, though neither of them was destined to achieve such success as Mormonism or Christian Science. The founder of the Shakers was Ann Lee, an immigrant from England who came to America in 1774 in the belief that this was the place appointed for the realization of the millennium. She was an uneducated woman from a working-class background, who appears to have had a genuine piety and spiritual insight. Ann Lee was regarded by her followers as the feminine counterpart of Jesus Christ; God was both male and female, and had therefore to be revealed twice in human form. Since the revelation was now complete, men could live without sin, which meant complete chastity and the abolition of private property and of any use of force and coercion. Ann Lee gathered a number of followers in New York and New England, chiefly among former Separatists and Baptists, and established communities where they lived strictly disciplined monastic lives and devoted themselves to farming and to handicrafts. They became known as Shakers because they were accustomed to dance and shake their bodies during their religious services in order to expel evil influences. When the Holy Spirit was inactive, the dances consisted merely of a rhythmic shuffle, but at times of religious excitement they whirled around like dervishes and fell on the floor in fits. Shakerism continued to increase until the middle of the nineteenth century, by which time there were twenty-seven different Shaker communities, mostly in New England and in the West. In spite of the peculiarity of its religious rituals, Shaker life had an impressive dignity and serenity.

Perfectionism developed at a later period, although it sprang from the same kind of religious background. Its founder, John Humphrey Noyes, a native of Vermont, passed through the experience of conversion in the year 1831, and subsequently decided, after a study of the biblical prophecies, that the millennium was close at hand and that a sinless existence was possible. A life without sin meant a life of love, and the chief obstacles to love were conflicts and jealousies about property and about sex. Noyes, therefore concluded that private property and private marriage should both be abolished; in the kingdom of God all property should be held in common, and every man should be the husband of every woman. "Exclusiveness, jealousy, quarreling have no place at the marriage supper of the Lord. . . . In the Kingdom of Grace marriage does not exist. On the other hand there is no proof in the Bible nor in reason that the distinction of sex will ever be abolished. . . . In the Kingdom of God the intimate union that in the world is limited to the married pair extends through the whole body of communicants. . . . It is incompatible with the perfected freedom, towards which Paul's gospel of 'grace without law' leads, that a person should be allowed to love in all directions, and yet be forbidden to express love except in one direction." [4]

Noyes gathered a group of disciples, and in 1848 they established a perfectionist community at Oneida, New York. Here they maintained their peculiar institutions until 1880, when pressure from the state legislature compelled them to abandon the practice of group marriage. Their thoroughgoing communism involved considerable discipline and regimentation; they did not find it easy to love each other equally, without jealousy or exclusiveness. Probably the colony could not have survived at all if Noyes had not continued to exercise a benevolent dictatorship. Noyes appears, however, to have been a man of complete integrity and quite remarkable psychological insight. Beginning as a religious prophet and mystic, he gradually evolved into a communist sociologist, a student of socialist experiments of all kinds, and a pioneer in the study of methods of contraception and of eugenics. He was one of the boldest thinkers and most interesting characters in nineteenth-century America.

Noyes illustrates in his own person the psychological continuity between the religious utopianism that developed out of Calvinism in the seventeenth and eighteenth centuries and the scientific or materialistic utopianism characteristic of radical movements in the nineteenth and twentieth centuries. The dream of a millennial existence, free from sin and evil, has continued to inspire radicals, whether they follow the teachings of John Calvin or those of Karl Marx. And from the time of the Puritans, who hoped to achieve "a new heaven and a new earth" in

[4] *G. W. Noyes:* John Humphrey Noyes, The Putney Community *(1931)*, *pp. 3, 116, 117.*

Massachusetts, down to the present day, this dream has been particularly associated with the American continent. The belief that America has a peculiar mission to establish a new and higher way of life has, in fact, become a part of the American character, even though few Americans have been prepared to 'interpret it in any very radical fashion. It was not religious mystics or radical agitators but sober political leaders who placed on the Great Seal of the United States the words *"Novus Ordo Seclorum."*

4

Meanwhile the Great Awakening had stimulated a re-interpretation of Calvinist theology; this attracted little attention at the time, but became the dominant influence in American Protestantism throughout the period between the Revolution and the Civil War. This was primarily the work of Jonathan Edwards. As minister of the Congregationalist church at Northampton, in western Massachusetts, Edwards took part in the revivals. Subsequently he spent some years as an Indian missionary at Stockbridge, and was then appointed to the presidency of Princeton, where he died in 1758. His purpose was to formulate a system of divinity that would avoid, on the one hand, the drift toward Unitarianism in eastern Massachusetts and, on the other hand, the disorderliness and eccentricity of the Separatists. On the surface, Edwards's divinity was a mere restatement of the traditional Calvinist dogmas. Actually it was a new system reflecting certain of the basic preconceptions of the American spirit. Edwards made use of European formulas, but in attempting to adapt Calvinism to life as he himself and his neighbors knew it, he unconsciously Americanized it.

The evangelical Christianity of Europe had been founded on man's sense of inner conflict and disharmony and on his consequent conviction of sin and need for divine deliverance. But this did not correspond to Edwards's personal experience. He was not drawn to God by an internal division of this kind. Before his own conversion he had no genuine sense of sin; it was not until afterwards, when he adopted the Calvinist formulas, that he learned to speak of himself as wicked, and then only with an exaggerated emphasis that betrays his lack of genuine conviction. The emotional struggles that preceded his conversion were caused by a reluctance to accept the doctrine of God's absolute sovereignty and to surrender his own will to that of God. He appears to have become convinced of the need for divine salvation not because he felt himself to be filled with sinful desires that he could not control, but because he knew himself to be weak and powerless, and because he saw evil in the external world—in the epidemics of diphtheria that killed infant children, for example, "like the children that were offered up to Moloch . . . who were tormented to death in burning brass." [5] In the Edwardean system, the human will pitted against the environment, not the will at war with itself, was the underlying reality. And man turned to God not so much to be healed of an inner disharmony as to be assured of omnipotence.

This is evident from Edwards's *Personal Narrative*. The crisis that he came to regard as his conversion occurred while he was a student at Yale, and it consisted in a complete surrender of his own will to that of God. It was not preceded by any deep anxiety or conviction of sin, so that it did not conform to orthodox Protestant experience. As late as five years afterwards, Edwards himself was still puzzled because his conversion did not seem to contain "those particular steps wherein the people of New England, and anciently the dissenters of Old England, used to experience it." [6] What religion meant to Edwards was identity with God, so that by merging his own will in that of God— even, as he said, to the extent of being willing to be damned if that would promote God's glory—he could share in God's omnipotence. The sufferings of mankind proved that God was angry with them; but by submitting to God's will the elect individual could participate vicariously in the expression of God's anger and of God's vengeance upon the unregenerate. Power was a quality that Edwards partic-

[5] The Great Christian Doctrine of Original Sin Defended, *Part I, Chap. 2.*

[6] *S. E. Dwight:* Memoir of President Edwards (*1829*), *p. 93.*

ularly liked to ascribe to God. In his *Personal Narrative* he
recorded his special delight in watching it manifested in
thunderstorms.

This lack of any genuine sense of sin is very manifest in
Edwards's famous treatise on *The Freedom of the Will.*
Following the European theologians, Edwards set out to
prove that man could not save himself. But whereas the
Europeans had believed in the necessity of divine grace
because they felt that man's will toward good had been
corrupted and frustrated by his carnal impulses, Edwards
made no distinction between will and impulse. The will,
he declared, always obeyed the strongest motive. The reason why man could not save himself was simply that all
his actions were predetermined, in the last resort by God.
Edwards did not see unregenerate human nature as a
battleground between conflicting drives toward good and
evil; neither did he regard regeneration as a gradual progress toward psychological harmony. Man was a simple
creature, without inner conflicts, who was wholly evil unless
God chose to save him. But when God communicated the
knowledge of himself, then man was irresistibly drawn to
love him and submit to him. It is obvious that Edwards had
no real comprehension of the European doctrine of salvation by grace. *The Freedom of the Will* is an exercise in
logic rather than a record of vital personal experience.

Historically, the most important aspect of Edwards's
theology was his redefinition of the meaning of conversion.
Religion meant the love of God, and was therefore an
emotional experience, and its validity might be judged
by its effects on conduct. It was derived from "a spiritual
and divine light, immediately imparted to the soul by
God." And since the true believer knew God directly, he
could trust his own conscience instead of relying on external authority. "When a holy and amiable action is
suggested to the thoughts of a holy soul, that soul, if in
the lively exercise of its spiritual taste, at once sees a
beauty in it, and so inclines to it, and closes with it." This
was a doctrine with strongly liberal implications, particularly since Edwards abandoned completely the earlier
Puritan belief in a union of church and state and the im-

position of morality by force. True Christian virtue, moreover, meant a love not only for God but also for the
other human beings whom God had made, from which
later theologians deduced that it would manifest itself in
philanthropic and humanitarian activities. This side of
the Edwardean divinity was decidedly progressive and individualistic. It meant the emancipation of American
Protestant ethics from an exclusive reliance upon the moral
rules laid down in the Bible and a recognition of the possibilities of spiritual evolution. "We cannot suppose," said
Edwards, "that the Church of God is already possessed of
all that light . . . which God intends to give it." [7]

Yet while Edwards advocated trust in the conscience of
the individual believer and an ethics of active love, he also
believed in an omnipresent God who was "where every
devil is, and where every damned soul is," [8] and who had
deliberately chosen to consign a majority of his creatures
to eternal torment in hell. Edwards was driven to accept
this belief because otherwise God would not be omnipotent.
And with an extraordinary boldness he set out to rationalize
the whole Calvinist system, instead of recognizing, as Calvin had done, that certain questions were better left in
mystery; he believed that by the exercise of logic and in-
tuition he could tear out the ultimate secrets of the universe.
He believed that God, like an artist, had created the cosmos
for the expression of his own attributes, and had deliberately composed it out of contrasts, light being balanced
against darkness, good against evil, and happiness against
suffering. This meant that God was responsible for hell;
and since the elect in the next life would share in God's
omnipotence, they would join him in enjoying the spectacle
of the damned in torment. The mystical meditations on the
beauty of God and of God's universe that fill Edwards's
writings have an extraordinary charm and intensity of

[7] *Sermon entitled* A Divine and Spiritual Light; A Treatise
Concerning Religious Affections, *Part III, Section IV; Preface
by Edwards to Joseph Bellamy:* True Religion Delineated
(*1750*).

[8] *Sermon entitled* The End of the Wicked Contemplated by
the Righteous.

feeling, but the sermons in which he brought home the reality of hell to his Northampton congregation are like the nightmares of a diseased soul. What is so peculiarly horrible about them is that Edwards always seems to be identifying himself with God, not, like Dante in the *Inferno*, with the sinner. He is never the divided soul, convinced that he himself deserves divine condemnation; he is pure will seeking omnipotence and finding it in fantasies of an inhuman cruelty. For the modern reader it is difficult to understand how a man who preached an ethics of love could believe in a God of cruelty. Yet Edwards himself showed no sign of being disturbed by the apparent discrepancy, nor did his gloomy theology have any shadowing effect on his personality. Throughout his life he showed himself cheerful, patient, hard-working, and most genuinely saintly.

The most significant aspect of the Edwardean divinity is that its inner inconsistencies mirror with remarkable clarity the conflicting tendencies that run through the history of the American spirit. On the one hand it inculcates an American trust in the individual and an American humanitarianism; on the other hand, it gives expression in theological symbols to the drive of the American will towards domination. In the twentieth century, when Edward's theology is no longer regarded as literally true, it is possible to interpret it as a symbolic expression of the deep psychic forces that pervaded the culture that produced it: to consider it, in other words, not as theology but as poetry. His cosmology has, in fact, a kind of morbid and sinister beauty, resembling that to be found in some of the short stories of Poe and in certain surrealist paintings. As a poet, Edwards foreshadowed the two major themes that occupied the great American writers of the following century. On the one hand his doctrine of "a spiritual and divine light immediately imparted to the soul" pointed toward Emerson and Whitman. On the other hand his intoxication with the idea of omnipotence, the cruelty that it implied, and the overweening pride of logic with which he set out to explain the entire universe, represented tendencies that pervaded the writings of Poe and of Melville. If Edwards is judged as an American poet, then only Melville can be said t have surpassed him in depth and intensity of spiritual ex perience. Indeed, in their basic preoccupations the two men had much in common. That drive of the will, both American and Calvinist, which is so conspicuous in Edwards, had its most complete æsthetic embodiment in Melville's Captain Ahab.

But for hundreds of thousands of Americans, during several generations, the theology of Edwards was not poetry, but literal and scientific truth, and the hell he described had a reality surpassing that of material existence. He had little influence in his own lifetime, but his doctrines were propagated and developed further by his friends and disciples until American Calvinism was permeated with them. By the end of the eighteenth century, New England Congregationalism had become almost wholly Edwardean; the Presbyterianism of the middle and Southern states had been deeply affected; and similar attitudes were displayed by the Baptists and the Methodists. After the clergy had been converted to the "new divinity," it was carried to the laity by revivalistic methods. The period from the 1790's to the 1850's was the great period of American evangelism, during which general revivals, at frequent intervals, swept across all of New England except eastern Massachusetts and vast areas of then newly settled areas west of the Appalachians.

The puritanism that resulted from the great revivals was in many ways different from the puritanism of the founders of New England. It was more individualistic and more humanitarian, while at the same time it inculcated a stricter and narrower morality. It accepted religious toleration and the separation of church and state, basing its religion on the private conscience, and it insisted that religion should show itself in practical benevolence rather than in mere obedience to a moral code. Of the many activities that developed out of Edwardean Christianity, unquestionably the most important was the abolitionist movement. Not all the abolitionists were Edwardeans, but the movement derived its strongest impetus from the evangelical churches. Edwards's closest pupil, Samuel Hopkins, was one of the first men to denounce Negro slavery; and his example was followed by Charles G. Finney, the New York evangelist, who founded Oberlin College as an abolitionist center, by the Beecher family, and by other Edwardean revivalists. All the activities of the Edwardeans were marred, however, by their tendency towards fanaticism and self-righteousness. They saw life always in terms of an absolute good in conflict with absolute evil; and they extended their conception of evil to a degree that would have horrified the original Puritans. They were the first opponents of drinking (an idea that originated not with Edwards but with Samuel Hopkins, and of which Lyman Beecher was the first militant exponent), and they denounced smoking, dancing, and most other pleasurable activities. The Edwardean theory that the true believer should show his complete devotion to God by his behavior, and that he should be guided by his conscience rather than by tradition, was essentially progressive; but its concrete results depended upon how it was interpreted. As developed by the later Edwardeans, it was one of the factors that made the American nineteenth century decidedly gloomier and more puritanical than the tolerant and easy-going eighteenth.

Meanwhile the Edwardean theology slowly disintegrated. The conception of a God who had deliberately condemned a majority of his creatures to eternal torment began to seem incredible. The later Edwardeans preferred to emphasize God's benevolence rather than his righteousness, and they transmuted the belief in complete determinism into a belief in complete free will, the doctrines of grace and divine election being lost in the process. A few conservatives remained faithful to the Calvinist dogmas down to the twentieth century, but as early as the Civil War a man like Henry Ward Beecher, in spite of his Edwardean background, was preaching a God of love who wished all mankind to be saved. And with this growth of optimism and of confidence in man's capacity to save himself, the Protestant churches ceased to exert any really vital influence on American cultural development. A majority of the Americans continued to give a nominal adherence to the evangelical denominations, and the churches continued to play an active part in certain political and social movements, particularly in the crusade for the prohibition of liquor. But after the Civil War, Protestantism tended to become, in large measure, a mere reflection of American life rather than a positive and independent force working for the transformation of human nature.

☆ ☆ ☆ ☆ ☆ ☆ ☆ ☆ ☆ ☆ ☆ ☆ ☆ ☆

CHAPTER V

THE REVOLUTION

★ ★ ★ ★ ★ ★ ★ ★ ★ ★ ★ ★ ★ ★ ★

DURING THE COLONIAL PERIOD, which occupies nearly half
the entire course of American history from the founding
of Jamestown down to the present day, American attitudes
and American institutions were slowly taking shape. It was
inevitable that, sooner or later, this process should lead to
an open assertion of American nationality and of American
independence from European control. The immediate cause
of the Revolution was American indignation against specific
acts of oppression on the part of the British government.
But when viewed in more fundamental terms, the war between America and Great Britain was a clash of principles
and ideologies; it was a conflict between European ideas
of class rule and authoritarian government and the drive of
the common man in America for political equality and
economic opportunity. Even if the British government had
done nothing to provoke it, some sort of conflict could
scarcely have been avoided.

The Revolution, as John Adams remarked, was a psychological process before it became a political one.[1] Long before 1763, liberal-minded Americans were coming to believe that their way of life was not only different from that
of Europe, but also superior to it. It was superior in the

[1] *"The Revolution was in the minds and hearts of the people;
a change in their religious sentiments of their duties and obligations." "Who, then was the author, inventor, discoverer of
independence? The only true answer must be the first emigrants."* Works of John Adams *(1856)*, *Vol. X, pp. 282, 359.*

opportunities it offered to the common man and in its higher standards of personal and political morality. Americans who knew anything about the British government were horrified by the habits of class privilege and by the corruption with which it was pervaded; and many others were made conscious of these things by contact with British officials and British military and naval units stationed in the colonies. Franklin expressed a widespread attitude when he suggested that America might be corrupted by too close a union with Great Britain. "When I consider the extreme corruption prevalent among all orders of men in this old rotten state," he wrote from London in 1774, "and the glorious public virtue so predominant in our rising country, I cannot but apprehend more mischief than benefit from a closer union. . . . Here numberless and needless places, enormous salaries, pensions, perquisites, bribes, groundless quarrels, foolish expenditures, false accounts or no accounts, contracts and jobs devour all revenue and produce continual necessity in the midst of natural plenty. I apprehend, therefore, that to unite us intimately will only be to corrupt and poison us also." [2]

Holding such opinions, the Americans protested immediately against British measures that reflected the traditional assumption that colonies should be subordinate to the mother-country. They did not wish to break the British connection. Some of them, particularly Franklin before he had become disillusioned, had dreamed of a perpetual partnership of the English-speaking peoples, in which leadership might eventually pass to the western side of the Atlantic. But the Americans felt that they were entitled to equality with the British and to full self-government. And until the final stages of the controversy they did not recognize that such a claim was contrary to the whole traditional theory of imperialism, and could never be accepted by the British government. Instead of recognizing that they were asserting a revolutionary doctrine, they conducted the argument in legalistic terms, attempting to prove that taxation without representation was contrary to natural law,

[2] *Carl Van Doren:* Benjamin Franklin (*1938*), p. 517.

to the British constitution, and to the colonial charters. They acted with remarkable boldness and political maturity, but they were overanxious to justify their actions in accordance with traditional conceptions of legality. In consequence, they were compelled to exaggerate the misdeeds of the British government and to represent as an intolerable tyranny regulations that appeared to the British to be wholly legitimate and necessary. It was not until 1776, when the English immigrant Tom Paine published *Common Sense,* that the American case was presented in its true colors, as a bold assertion of new principles of government.

And these new principles of government included more than the claim that the inhabitants of a colony should have the same rights as those of the mother country. The American Revolution was a movement toward democracy as well as toward independence, and for this reason it caused internal divisions both in Great Britain and in the colonies. The British people were by no means unanimous; British radicals supported the Americans in the belief that an American victory would advance the cause of freedom everywhere. And the Americans themselves were very deeply divided. Most of the planters and many of the merchants finally accepted independence, but throughout the entire controversy, from 1763 until 1776, the most militant champions of American rights were those Western farmers and urban mechanics who wanted political changes within America. Those Americans, on the other hand, who clung to European principles of government, and who were afraid of the advance of democracy, continued to support British rule. Probably as much as a third of the whole American population was inclined towards Loyalism, and an appreciable number were willing to fight for it. The Loyalists included many of the aristocratic elements in New England, New York, and Pennsylvania, and many of the more recent immigrants in the middle colonies and in the Carolinas.

Before the Revolution, the Western farmers had shown increasing resentment against the domination of the seaboard aristocracies, while in the larger towns—especially in Boston—mechanics, small tradesmen, and journeymen had begun to join political organizations that challenged the control exercised by the mercantile oligarchies. Such men welcomed the Revolution as an opportunity to establish a more democratic form of government and to overthrow economic privilege. Representing the ideal of an agrarian democracy, these American radicals wished the "general happy mediocrity" of American society to be protected and more fully developed. How far the radical leaders were conscious of their objectives it is not easy to determine; but their eagerness in seizing every opportunity to stir up hostility against Great Britain and their unwillingness to accept any compromise settlement suggest that they were motivated by more than a dislike of British taxation. They were opposed to British rule not only because it violated American rights, but also because of the support Great Britain gave to the aristocratic principle in America. This is particularly true of Samuel Adams and his radical associates in Boston. In all his public pronouncements, Adams represented himself as merely defending the liberties of Americans against the attempts of wicked British officials to enslave them. But the pertinacity with which he sought to carry the controversy through to the point of crisis cannot be explained unless we assume that his major objective was to bring about a more democratic form of government in Massachusetts and that he recognized this to be impossible unless Massachusetts became fully self-governing. When independence was finally consummated, it was the spokesmen of agrarian democracy who assumed control in most of the states, and their radical ideals were embodied in the new state constitutions.

Prior to 1763 it had been generally admitted that the colonies were under British sovereignty. This sovereignty had originally been exercised by the king, and had then been assumed by Parliament. Parliament had legislated for the colonies, and its general power to do so, though not clearly defined, had been taken for granted. Except under the later Stuart kings there had been little interference with the colonial legislatures in political matters, but the economic activities of the Americans had been elaborately supervised. Americans were, in general, forbidden to start manufactures that might compete with those of the mother country, and most of their foreign trade had to pass through Great Britain. The general effect of the regulations was to drain money out of the colonies and to cause American merchants and planters to fall into debt to merchants in London. This mercantilist system was an example of one of the general tendencies of all advanced civilizations, both ancient and modern: the tendency of urban business areas to exploit the areas that produce raw materials. On the other hand, the Americans derived from the British connection certain positive benefits in the form of protected markets, bounties for the production of some raw materials, and military and naval protection; and many of the regulations were loosely enforced.

The trade regulations provoked few complaints before 1763, and were not usually listed among the major American grievances after that date. Down to the outbreak of the war, the Americans, while resisting the claim of parliament to tax them, professed themselves willing to accept parliamentary regulation of trade. From the commercial point of view, in fact, many of the American merchants might have preferred to remain inside the British Empire. They opposed many of the British regulations, and felt themselves to be exploited by the British merchants; but in an age of closed mercantilist empires they could expect difficulty in finding new markets to replace those they would lose if they broke the British connection. The major factor in carrying the controversy as far as independence was not commercial interest, but the drive toward democracy. The assumption of some historians that the American Revolution must have been primarily a bourgeois movement instigated by the merchants is an illustration of the tendency to read American history in European terms. The agrarian democracy of eighteenth-century America was brought into existence by the unique conditions of American life, and cannot be paralleled in the history of the leading European nations.

The change in British policy after 1763 was a sequel to the French and Indian War, which had been fought during the previous ten years for the control of the West. From the British point of view, this began as an American war, caused by the expansion of the colonies westward across the Appalachians and their conflict with the French officials and fur traders who were hoping to establish French control over the Mississippi region. The war started in 1753 with an attempt by the government of Virginia to expel the French from the Ohio valley, and the first shots were fired by Virginia militiamen under the command of young George Washington. The struggle gradually developed into the Seven Years' War, in which Great Britain and France fought each other for imperial supremacy in Asia as well as in the western hemisphere, and which ended in the expulsion of France both from most of India and from the North American mainland. Great Britain was left victorious, but with a heavy internal debt and increased responsibilities.

But the war by no means promoted good feeling between the Americans and the British. The Americans, who had taxed themselves heavily to carry on the struggle, were provoked by the many military blunders committed by the British during the earlier period of the war, and resented the arrogant behavior of the British professional officers. They felt that the British had fought the war in America not for their benefit, but for that of the British fur traders, who expected to replace the French in the West. They were beginning to feel that they were capable of attending to their own defenses and to resent their involvement in the power politics of Europe. Why should the road into the Western wilderness run through London and Paris? Why should the ambitions of European kings cause American frontier communities to be massacred by Indians? As Franklin told the British House of Commons in 1766, "the war, as it commenced for the defence of territories of the crown the property of no American, and for the defence of a trade purely British, was really a British war; and yet the people of America made no scruple of contributing their utmost towards carrying it on and bringing it to a happy conclusion." [3] This view of the war eventually led some Americans to form an opinion, which was afterwards

[3] *Ibid.* (*1938*), *p. 348.*

to have a determining influence on the foreign policy of the United States, that the affairs of North America ought to be permanently disentangled from those of Europe.

Left with increased expenses and half a continent to administer as a result of the war with France, British officials set out to make such regulations as seemed most likely to promote the welfare of the empire as a whole. They tightened the enforcement of the trade regulations (which had been notably violated during the war), prohibited migration into the West until the claims of the Indians could be adjusted, posted troops in America to guard against Indian attacks, and began to impose upon the colonies taxes that would meet part of the costs of imperial defense. All these measures were legal if it was assumed that the British Parliament was the supreme imperial authority and that the colonies were to remain subordinate. The English political leaders were lacking in wisdom and insight; none of them—not even Burke or Chatham—had the vision and the far-ranging imperial imagination of the greatest of the Americans; but they were not devoid of good intentions or of the narrower kind of intelligence. But the Americans, as a result both of traditions inherited from British history during the Stuart period and of their own colonial experience, had learned to regard the principle of no taxation without representation as fundamental. This attitude was owing not merely to an understandable dislike of taxes in general—a dislike particularly strong in a country where currency was scarce —but to a farsighted realization that the power to tax could too easily be abused.

Almost everybody in America would suffer as a result of these British measures, and almost everybody wished to protest against them. But the violence of the opposition was wholly unexpected. The mass riots and demonstrations against the Stamp Act, conducted mainly by the urban mechanics under the leadership of such spokesmen of democracy as Samuel Adams, were an indication that new political forces were emerging. These "Sons of Liberty," as they began to call themselves, became the spearhead of the movement toward democracy and full self-government. Their activities are inexplicable unless it is remembered that the internal political conflicts in the colonies were already becoming acute; the actions of the British government should not be regarded as the sole original cause of the convulsion, but rather as the provocation that brought it to the point of crisis. Thenceforth the wealthier classes in America were caught between two fires. Threatened with financial losses by the British measures, the bolder and more enterprising supported the Sons of Liberty; fearful of democracy, the more timid clung to British authority. Except in Virginia, where the planters were deeply in debt to British merchants, and where there were no cities and hence no urban mechanics to conduct riotous demonstrations, most of the aristocratic elements continued to hope for reconciliation rather than for independence.

The Stamp Act was repealed, but the Townshend duties followed, and there were numerous other indications that the successive British governments had no intention of surrendering the principle of British supremacy. The point at issue—whether the colonies were subordinate to the mother country or its equals—was, in fact, irreconcilable. And as invariably happens during a period of prolonged controversy, each side became increasingly exasperated and began to attribute to the other a deliberate malevolence that it did not really possess. The British officials felt that the Americans were a most unreasonable people who would not assume any of their appropriate obligations for the maintenance of the empire that had protected them against the French. Many of the Americans, on the other hand, came to believe that the British government had worked out a long-range plan to deprive them of all their rights of self-government and reduce them to slavery. When two parties reach this degree of mutual suspicion, reconciliation usually becomes impossible.

In 1770 a new British government repealed most of the taxes, retaining only a small duty on tea as an assertion of the principle of British supremacy. Even this tax was not successfully collected, since some of the American merchants were able to evade it by smuggling. This was followed by three years of peace. During this period, the leaders of the Sons of Liberty did their best to keep the controversy alive and to stimulate hostility to Great Britain; and they began to create a new kind of political organization. A network of radical "Committees of Correspondence" was organized, headed mainly by lawyers, merchants, and planters who, for one reason or another, desired political changes, but supported chiefly by the farmers and mechanics. They were guided by political organizers like Samuel Adams in Boston, Isaac Sears, John Lamb, and Alexander McDougall in New York, Charles Thomson in Philadelphia, Samuel Chase in Baltimore, and Christopher Gadsden in Charleston. These organizations were prepared to push the controversy through to the point of crisis on the next occasion when the British government exercised its claim to supremacy.

The final phase of the controversy started in 1773, when the British East India Company was given the right to ship tea direct to America. This meant that the Americans (in spite of the tax) could buy tea more cheaply than ever before, but it also meant that American tea merchants, both those who had paid the duty and those who had engaged in smuggling, would lose their business. Supported by many of the merchants, the radicals represented this measure as a device for bribing the Americans into accepting the principle of parliamentary taxation. The Boston radicals organized the famous Tea Party, after which the British government, thoroughly provoked, retaliated with the Coercive Acts. These showed very clearly that, in the opinion of the British ministers, the colonies had no rights not subject to revocation at the pleasure of the British Parliament. At the same time, by the Quebec Act, the Western territories, where Americans had been hoping to settle ever since the French and Indian War, were annexed to Canada.

In the opinion of the radicals, America now had to choose between resistance and submission. The conservatives continued to hope for reconciliation, and in the Continental Congress, which met at Philadelphia in September 1774 in order to work out a common American policy towards the Coercive Acts, one of their leaders, Joseph

Galloway, put forward a plan for establishing an American legislature that would share authority with the British Parliament. But the radicals neither wanted reconciliation nor regarded it as possible; by a small majority they were able to stop discussion of the plan and to prevent any knowledge of it from reaching the general public. The Congress voted in favor of resisting the Coercive Acts and adopted a stringent economic boycott of Great Britain, the enforcement of which was entrusted to radical committees. These committees, which were now to police the activities of the merchants and prevent them from violating the boycott, began to assume some of the functions of a revolutionary government.

When British troops arrived in Boston to enforce the Coercive Acts, war became inevitable, though the Americans were careful to wait for the British to commit the first overt act. The shooting started in April 1775, when a detachment of British troops marched out to destroy military supplies that were being accumulated at Concord, and was met by American militiamen at Lexington. The subsequent controversy as to which side actually fired the first shot was of significance only as an illustration of the Americans' desire to justify their actions in legalistic terms. But whether they realized it or not the radicals had not really been acting merely in self-defense: they had been working toward a fundamentally new political system, which involved new conceptions of legality and individual rights, and which the British could not accept so long as they clung to traditional ideas of imperialism. The American Revolution, in other words, was a genuine revolution, and not merely a war for independence. This view of the situation was written into the Declaration of Independence of 1776, which justified the American cause not on narrow grounds of legality but on the natural right of all men to freedom, equality, and self-government.

After Lexington and Concord, the remnants of British authority were destroyed; executive power in most of the colonies was assumed by committees of safety; and the Continental Congress assumed responsibility for the conduct of the war. In this fashion a group of lawyers, merchants,

planters, and politicians, most of whom were young men
without executive or military experience, undertook to
determine the destiny of half a continent and to challenge
the trained armies and navies of the world's strongest
power. If they failed, they could presumably expect to be
hanged as traitors.

2

For several years after the outbreak of the war there was
little legal government in America and little regular enforcement of law and order. The Continental Congress
acquired no legal authority to act as a central government
until the ratification of the Articles of Confederation in
1781. A majority of the states were controlled by extra-
legal committees of safety and provincial congresses; subordinate committees assumed control of smaller areas. In
some regions the law courts ceased to function, and there
was a period of what seemed to conservatives to be outright
mob rule. The men in power had not only to raise and
equip an army to fight the British; they had also to meet
the threat of civil war with the Loyalists—a danger that,
as in all such situations, could be met only by terroristic
methods. This phase of American history is essentially
analogous to the Jacobin reign of terror in the French Revolution and to the Civil War in the Russian Revolution. That
the parallel has not been generally recognized is a tribute
to the moderation with which the American radicals used
their power. Although the Loyalists were made to suffer
acutely, and though there was some petty persecution and
paying off of personal grudges, there were very few exe-
cutions, and none without real justification. And in spite of
the obvious need for strong government, the Americans
did not set up a dictatorship. Both the leaders of the
Revolution and the mass of the people viewed political
power with the greatest suspicion, and were not willing to
allow any surrender of the rights of individual freedom.
Living in an agrarian economy of small property owners,
the average American of that epoch had acquired a habit
of acting independently and a hostility to coercion and

regimentation that made any kind of authoritarian regime impossible.

The war was in some measure a class conflict, but the division of opinion among the Americans did not wholly correspond with class lines. A majority of the poorer classes supported independence. The urban mechanics had been the most vigorous opponents of British control ever since the Stamp Act; and after the war started most of the fighting was done by the farmers, particularly by men from the Western frontier communities. On the other hand there were farming areas in New Jersey, Delaware, Maryland, and eastern Pennsylvania, and in the back country of Georgia and the Carolinas, where, as a result of economic interest, local political conflicts, inertia, or recent immigration, the bulk of the population remained Loyalist. Among the wealthier classes, the Southern planters were predominantly in favor of independence; they had little fear of democracy, and resented British economic control. Any doubts they may have felt were removed in the autumn of 1775, when the royal governor of Virginia called for a slave rebellion. In the North the upper class of landowners and merchants was divided. Probably a majority were Loyalist, particularly in New York and Pennsylvania; but a strong minority, including the bolder and more enterprising of the merchants, were for independence. But the most active leaders of the Revolution in the North were men who had previously been excluded from political power because of their lack of wealth and family prestige.

The only crime committed by most of the Loyalists was that they held political opinions different from those adopted by a majority of the Americans; but they were potentially dangerous, and it was necessary to deal with them. At the outset of the war the radical committees visited persons who were suspected of being actively Loyalist and deprived them of their weapons. The more dangerous were arbitrarily arrested and placed in prison, while a few underwent the painful and humiliating experience of being publicly tarred and feathered or ridden on rails, while their houses were ransacked by bands of patriots. The spectacle of some wealthy, dignified, and class-conscious merchant or landowner being treated in this unceremonious fashion by a group of farmers or mechanics directed by a radical committeeman convinced many conservatives that all their fears of democracy were thoroughly justified. A new type of man was achieving power in America; and for lovers of the old regime it meant the end of civilization.[4] In the later stages of the war, when thousands of Loyalists were serving in the British army and others were giving the British information and supplies, the state governments adopted the most stringent anti-Loyalist legislation. Their property was confiscated; and they were completely deprived of all political and legal rights. Probably about eighty thousand Loyalists went into exile during the war. A very much larger number of Americans sympathized with Loyalism but did not commit themselves so openly as to make it necessary for them to become refugees. The ruthless treatment of the Loyalists was a revolutionary procedure that cannot be justified by anything except stringent necessity. Its effect was to weaken that element in America which supported aristocratic principles of government.

The chief achievements of the Revolution, apart from the winning of independence from Great Britain, were to be found in the new state constitutions adopted during the war. The general trend was toward agrarian democracy, though this went much further in some states than in others. In general, the franchise was widely extended, so that most farmers acquired the right to vote; and the Western regions were given fair representation in the legislatures. The transfer of power from the seaboard aristocracies to the small farmers was symbolized by the movement in-

___

[4] *Crèvecœur was one of those who disliked the political changes brought about by the Revolution. Speaking of the radical politicians who were assuming power in rural areas, he declared: "The hypocrisy, slyness, cupidity, inhumanity and abuse of power in these petty country despots are evident and manifest. . . . Ambition, we well know, an exorbitant love of power and thirst of riches, a certain impatience of government, clad under the garb of patriotism and even of constitutional reason, have been the secret but true foundations of this, as well as of many other revolutions."* Sketches of Eighteenth Century America (*printed 1925*), pp. 251, 254.

land of a number of the state capitals.[5] The democratic groups believed in a system of outright and direct majority rule, in which almost all powers should be given to a unicameral legislature subject to reelection at frequent intervals. Their ideas were realized most completely in the new constitution of Pennsylvania, drafted by a convention in which Franklin was the presiding officer, and bitterly opposed not only by Loyalists but also by merchants, such as Robert Morris, who supported independence. After the adoption of these new constitutions, men of a new type were elected to political office even in those states which had remained most conservative. Rural lawyers with small-farmer affiliations, like Patrick Henry in Virginia and George Clinton in New York, sat in the chairs from which the royal governors of Great Britain had been expelled.

Equally important were the economic reforms of the Revolution. The state legislatures came into possession both of the estates of the big Loyalist landowning families and of the public lands that had formerly belonged to the crown. These were broken into small farms and either sold or distributed in the form of bounties to soldiers. Unfortunately, speculators were able to take advantage of this legislation, but the intention was to democratize more fully the ownership of property. The same objective was sought by the abolition in almost all the states of the laws of primogeniture and entail; the purpose was to hasten the rapid subdivision of those big estates which remained and to make it impossible for any landed aristocracy to perpetuate itself in America. Such measures indicated a conscious intention of extending the "general happy mediocrity" of American society. At the same time another European survival—the privileged position of the Anglican Church—was abolished; except in New England, church and state were separated and religious freedom established.

All this was revolution in the complete meaning of the

[5] *State capitals were moved inland during the revolutionary period in Virginia, North Carolina, South Carolina, and Georgia, and soon afterwards in New York and Pennsylvania. Attempts to move the capitals of Massachusetts and Maryland were unsuccessful.*

word. It was an assertion of the new American principles of freedom and equality, and an application of them to the economic system and the distribution of property as well as to political institutions. It was a repudiation of the European principles of class hierarchy and authoritarian government. But meanwhile the War of Independence had to be won. There were several periods between 1775 and 1782 when it seemed possible that the revolutionary cause could not maintain itself, and that the mass of the people, weary of the war and despairing of victory, would swing back to an acceptance of British rule. History is not kind to lost causes, and if this had happened, the fathers of the American republic would presumably have been remembered as a discredited group of radical adventurers, while Loyalist leaders like Hutchinson of Massachusetts, De Lancey of New York, and Galloway of Pennsylvania would have figured as the real heroes of the conflict.

That a democratic people should be able to fight a successful war appears, at first sight, to be paradoxical. By its nature, war necessitates an exercise of authority and coercion that is a negation of democratic ideals. Military discipline is incompatible with a democratic equality and freedom. A democracy that proposes to wage war efficiently must take the risk of temporarily becoming authoritarian. Yet on the other hand those qualities which bring success in war—the qualities of initiative, inventiveness, and moral conviction—develop more fully in a democracy than under a system that is always organized for war. A democracy that temporarily adopts military discipline will always fight a war more successfully (other things being equal) than a society in which military discipline is permanent. And the citizen-soldier, once he has learned the techniques of warfare, will usually defeat the professional as a result of his greater capacity for initiative and his superior morale. The American people excel all others in warfare precisely because they are the least military of all peoples during peacetime.

The military ability of the American was fully demonstrated in the War of Independence. The young men who led the American armies had previously been planters, lawyers, merchants, storekeepers, or farmers, and most of them had had no experience whatever of any kind of warfare; yet these men showed more enterprise and initiative, and in the long run made fewer serious mistakes, than the professional generals of Great Britain. The American private soldier had at first no notion of discipline; he was inclined to disobey orders and to desert in periods of difficulty; and in some of the earlier battles he showed a disconcerting tendency to run away. But he could always shoot better than the British, and with proper training and firm leadership he learned finally how to fight better. The stupidity and the lack of enterprise displayed by the British generals in America have always puzzled historians, who have been driven to suggest that perhaps some of them did not really want to win the war at all. But by eighteenth-century professional standards Generals Howe, Burgoyne, Clinton, and Cornwallis were competent officers who did well in campaigns against other European powers. It is by contrast with the Americans that they appear mediocre or worse. The same difference between the inertia of the professional and the energy and imagination of the citizen-soldier showed itself in the wars of the French Revolution two decades later.

But though the Americans were superior as soldiers, they were unable during the War of Independence to make their superiority effective because of their refusal to submit to any authoritarian government, even as a temporary expedient. Neither the Continental Congress nor the state governments had sufficient power to conscript troops, money, and supplies. The Congress paid its expenses by issuing paper, which depreciated in value and eventually became completely worthless. The inflation and the general disorder enabled clever and unscrupulous business men to make fortunes and to live in the greatest luxury. Government contracts, privateering, and speculation in land and currency created a *nouveau riche* plutocracy who emerged from the war with the pretensions of a new ruling class, more enterprising than the Loyalist aristocracy whom they aspired to succeed, but less cultured and public-spirited. Meanwhile, in a country with nearly two million white inhabitants, it proved to be impossible to keep together an army of sufficent size to win decisive victories. At one time or another, more than one hundred thousand Americans were recruited into the Continental Army, but relatively few of them were willing to serve for more than a few months at a time. At no period were there more than twenty thousand men available for active service at one time, and during a large part of the war the number dropped to about five thousand, whereas the troops at the disposition of the British generals varied between twenty and forty thousand.

Even an army of five thousand could not be adequately fed and clothed. The American soldiers rarely had enough to eat, and could often live at all only by raiding the farms in their neighborhood. The nearest approach to a uniform was the grey linen hunting shirt worn by regiments from the Southern frontier; most soldiers had to wear their own clothes until they were torn to shreds. There were periods when a considerable part of the army was unable to take the field because the men quite literally had nothing to cover themselves with, not even breeches. Men served through winters without blankets and made forced marches on frozen ground without shoes. When the Continental Army shifted its headquarters, it usually left behind a trail of blood from the feet of its soldiers. When one considers the hardships endured by the private soldier under Washington, the lack of any commensurate rewards, and the relative comfort of civilian life, it is astonishing that even five thousand men were willing to continue fighting for the independence of America.

But for Washington's strength of will and powers of command, the army might have evaporated completely, so that the British would have won the war by default. This taciturn, reserved, and diffident Virginia wheat-farmer, whom Congress, on the motion of John Adams, had appointed to command the army, never revealed himself to his contemporaries, and is still no easy man to understand. Unlike most of the political leaders of the Revolution, he was not an intellectual and had little interest in general ideas or theories of government. And he was lack-

ing in the quickness and self-assurance that have characterized so many American men of action. He reached conclusions slowly, and always listened to advice before making a decision. But he had that elemental personal force
and power, the possessor of which always dominates whatever company he enters; and this basic energy, which
might easily have been turned to violent and sinister purposes, was bridled by an equally vigorous moral integrity
and sense of moral principle. Incapable of real personal
intimacy, he did not give the appearance of being a happy
man; and he was more interested in material things than in
human beings. Primarily, he liked to express his will
creatively in some concrete and visible form. He was the
most efficient and the most experimental farmer of his
time, and he dreamed of clearing forests, building canals,
and founding colonies in the West. In this enthusiasm for
material development he was perhaps a better representative
of the American future than any of his contemporaries. He
brought the same constructive energy to his task of holding
together the soldiers whom Congress had put under his
command and transforming them into a genuine army.

Washington's most essential achievement was to keep an
army in the field through the seven years of the war. As
long as he could do this, the Americans were not defeated;
but it is doubtful if they would ever have been victorious if
they had not finally received effective military, naval, and
financial assistance from France. What enabled them to
win their independence was the transformation of the war
into a world-wide conflict between British and French imperialism. Hoping to break up the British Empire and to
regain colonies they had lost in previous wars, the French
aided the Americans from the beginning, and became full
belligerents in 1778. Thenceforth the British had to fight
in Europe and the West Indies as well as in North America.
And though French military and naval assistance to the
Americans was at first disappointing, it proved to be decisive in the final stages of the war.

The British could have won the war if they could have
induced the bulk of the American people to abandon the
hope of independence, and they probably came closest to

it in 1779 and 1780. During the earlier campaigns in 1776 and 1777, General Howe won most of the battles, but the Americans did not lose their self-confidence. In 1776, after the loss of New York and the disastrous retreat across New Jersey, Washington was able to strike back at Trenton and Princeton; and in 1777, Washington's defeats in front of Philadelphia were counterbalanced by the victory of Gates and Arnold over Burgoyne at Saratoga. But in the later phases of the war the main British army, now under the command of Sir Henry Clinton, with headquarters at New York, settled down to a war of attrition, raiding and laying waste American territories. Washington's troops, established farther up the Hudson, could do little to check these activities. At the same time another British army under Cornwallis was winning control over Georgia and the Carolinas, with the assistance of a large number of Loyalists. In these southern states there was a most ferocious civil war between the partisans of British rule and those of independence. Both Loyalists and Patriots formed guerilla bands that plundered, murdered, and devastated the countryside with very little compunction or discrimination. Meanwhile the Congress no longer had either authority or prestige, and was on the verge of total bankruptcy. Sections of the army mutinied because they were not being paid, and the whole of Washington's forces seemed frequently on the verge of dissolution. This was probably the blackest period of the war for the Americans.

The real turning point came in the autumn of 1780, when frontiersmen from the Carolina back country destroyed a Loyalist army at King's Mountain. This was followed by American victories over the British forces in the South, won by the leadership of a Quaker ironmaster from Rhode Island, Nathaniel Greene, and of a farmer and wagoner from the Virginia frontier, Daniel Morgan. Cornwallis was compelled to take refuge on the seacoast at Yorktown, where, in October 1781, he was attacked by Washington and compelled to surrender. This final victory was made possible only by effective co-operation from the French: a French fleet blockaded Yorktown by sea, and nearly half of the land forces under Washington's command were French. After the surrender of Yorktown, the British still held New York and several seaports in the South, but they preferred to make peace with the Americans rather than run the risk of losing India and other parts of their empire to the French by a prolongation of the war. In 1782, a treaty was signed by which Great Britain conceded American independence and accepted American sovereignty over the Western territories as far as the Mississippi.

In spite of their final victory, the Americans found the war a disillusioning experience. They had won their independence, but they could no longer believe so firmly in the principles of individual freedom and equality that they had asserted with such confidence at the beginning of the conflict. The war had been prolonged through seven dreary years chiefly because of the lack of any strong government capable of enforcing discipline and obedience and of conscripting men and supplies. The effect was to cause a reaction back to the European principles of authority and the leadership of an elite. This reaction was most conspicuous among the army officers, who had had the most vivid experience of the evils of weak government. It is not surprising that at the end of the war some of them should have wanted Washington to overthrow Congress by a military *coup d'état*, and that almost all of them should have become advocates of a central government with real coercive power. This change of attitude can be traced in the writings of such a man as Alexander Hamilton, who in 1775 was one of the most ardent exponents of American rights and principles, but who, after seven years' experience as an army officer, wished America to adopt a government modeled as closely as possible on that of Great Britain. It had become plain to many Americans that the loose, undisciplined, and easygoing ways of an agrarian democracy, however much they might promote the individual pursuit of happiness, did not lead to national wealth and power. This widespread change of attitude was one of the most significant consequences of the War of Independence. It was to result, a few years later, in the formation of the federal constitution.

☆ ☆ ☆ ☆ ☆ ☆ ☆ ☆ ☆ ☆ ☆ ☆ ☆ ☆

CHAPTER VI

THE CONSTITUTION

★ ★ ★ ★ ★ ★ ★ ★ ★ ★ ★ ★ ★ ★ ★

WITH THE DESTRUCTION of British rule the rival forces in American society came more directly into conflict with each other. The aristocratic principle had gained new strength as a result of the disillusioning experiences of the War of Independence; and it was now represented not only by those wealthy families who had supported the Revolution and had not been expelled for Loyalism, but also by a new group of speculators and merchants who had grown rich during the war. The conflict between the European ruling-class concept of government and the American doctrine of equality continued for the next half-century. It was not until the Jacksonian era that the evolution toward political democracy was completed.

The most conspicuous results of this conflict were political, but the main issues were at all times economic. Eighteenth-century Americans were not in the habit of divorcing politics from economics; on the contrary, they generally viewed political conflicts in economic terms and regarded political power as a means for securing economic privilege. The economic basis of politics was more apparent to Americans than it was to Europeans, perhaps because it had been demonstrated more clearly in American experience. To a large extent the American aristocratic groups, particularly the big landowners, had initially obtained their economic privileges by the use of political influence. The processes by which they had obtained their property were not hidden in the distant past, as in the case of the feudal aristocracy of Europe.

The Americans were a nation of property owners, and their economy was dynamic and expansionist. The typical American was a man who wished not only to retain the property he had, but also to improve it and enlarge it. As Tocqueville remarked, every poor American hoped to become rich, and every rich American was afraid of becoming poor.[1] All Americans, rich and poor, believed that the state should protect property rights and that it should promote economic opportunity and free enterprise. Locke's doctrine of natural rights was not disputed by any American, whether aristocratic or democratic. But though the Americans were in essential agreement on this basic principle, they differed as to its application. In particular, they differed as to which kind of property most needed protection. This difference was perhaps the main dividing line in American politics.

Locke's explanation of the origin of property rights was as follows: "Every man has a 'property' in his own person; this nobody has any right to but himself. The labor of his body and the work of his hands, we may say, are properly his. Whatsoever then he removes out of the state that nature hath provided and left it in, he hath mixed his labor with it, and joined to it something that is his own, and thereby makes it his property. It being by him removed from the common state nature placed it in, it hath by this labor something annexed to it that excludes the common right of other men . . . at least where there is enough, and as good, left in common for others." [2]

---

[1] *"The desire of acquiring the comforts of the world haunts the imagination of the poor, and the dread of losing them that of the rich. . . . I never met in America any citizen so poor as not to cast a glance of hope and envy on the enjoyments of the rich or whose imagination did not possess itself by anticipation of those good things that fate still obstinately withheld from him."* A. de Tocqueville: Democracy in America, *Vol. II, Second Book, Chap. X.*

[2] *John Locke:* Of Civil Government, *Book II, Chap. 5.*

Such an explanation of how property became private might have been written with the American pioneer in mind. The pioneer went into the wilderness while it was "in the state that nature hath provided and left it in"; he carved out a piece of farmland and "mixed his labor with it"; and thereby he made it his own private property. This was the kind of property right that the American farmer understood and believed in, and which he felt that the state ought to protect.

But mixing their labor with the wilderness was not the only way in which Americans acquired property. If they belonged to the privileged classes, they might also obtain it as a result of political influence or by commercial and financial methods. They could secure grants of Western land from the government, with the right to collect rents from the farmers who were "mixing their labor" with it; they could acquire farm mortgages by lending money to farmers, and could deprive the farmers of their land if the debts were not repaid; and they could obtain from state legislatures charters by which they were authorized to establish certain forms of business enterprise and were sometimes given virtually monopolistic rights—for example, in the construction of a road or a bridge or in the establishment of a bank. Property rights of this kind came under the general heading of contracts. When the richer classes spoke of the protection of property rights as one of the chief functions of government, what they meant was that the government must maintain the sanctity of contracts and must see to it that the obligations of contracts were enforced.

The difference between the property that had originated in the mixing of human labor with the wilderness and the property that had been acquired by means of a contract was never sharply defined. It was, in fact, impossible to draw any clear line of demarcation between these two forms of property. Yet this difference is the clue to much of the political controversy of eighteenth- and nineteenth-century America.

The moneyed classes whose property was derived from contracts were a small minority of the total population;

and they believed that their rights would be endangered by any democratic system of government based on outright majority rule. Their chief political objective, as Madison expressed it in 1787, was therefore "to protect the minority of the opulent against the majority." [3] Distrusting the mass of the people, and believing in the rule of the "gentlemen of principle and property" and of "the wise, the rich and the well-born," they wanted a system of government under which the sanctity of contracts would be legally guaranteed against democratic interference. At the same time they also wanted a government with broad positive powers to regulate economic development, in order that men with political influence could continue to obtain land titles, monopolies, and other forms of economic privilege. The greatest exponents of this point of view were Alexander Hamilton and John Marshall.

This conception of government promised not only to protect the property of the rich, but also to encourage business enterprise and hasten the growth of American wealth and power. It was, in fact, the chief link between the aristocracy of the eighteenth century and the capitalism that succeeded it and developed out of it. But its distrust of the people and its belief in the leadership of an elite were derived from European traditions, and if it was allowed to prevail, it would transform America into another Europe. It would gradually destroy that "general happy mediocrity" which was the most remarkable feature of eighteenth-century American society. There were other Americans who approved neither of aristocracy nor of capitalism, and who regarded this "general happy mediocrity" as America's greatest blessing. Such men began to work out a theory of government appropriate to those classes, comprising the vast majority of the population, who had acquired property not through contracts but by labor—in other words, to the farmers, the mechanics, and those planters who were interested solely in agriculture and not also in land speculation. The resultant philosophy

[3] *Max Farrand:* Records of the Federal Constitution of 1787 *(1937), Vol. I, p. 431.*

of agrarian democracy, which first began to take shape
during the revolutionary period in the writings and political
programs of men like Franklin and Jefferson, which was
systematized a generation later by John Taylor, and which
was carried further by the Jacksonians and in the early
judicial decisions of Roger Taney, was profoundly American, in spite of its indebtedness to European thinkers. It
borrowed some of its concepts from Locke, from the
French physiocrats, and from Adam Smith; [4] but essentially
it was a formulation of American ideals and a reflection of
American experience, and its purpose was to perpetuate
those features of colonial society which had made America
so markedly different from Europe.

In the opinion of the agrarians the reason for the evils
of European society was not merely the lack of political
freedom or the perpetuation of hereditary distinctions; it
was the use of political power by a ruling class in order
to secure economic advantages. "Kings, nobles and priests,"
Jefferson declared, had formed "an abandoned conspiracy
against the happiness of the mass of the people" and had
acquired the privilege of living in idleness at their expense.
"Still further to constrain the brute force of the people,
they deem it necessary to keep them down by hard labor,
poverty and ignorance, and to take from them, as from

[4] *Adam Smith is widely regarded as a spokesman of early
capitalism. Actually his viewpoint was similar to that of the
American agrarians. The main purpose of* The Wealth of Nations *was to oppose government intervention in economic matters on the ground that it resulted in monopolies and special
privileges for the business classes. He advocated competition as
the best method of ensuring that businessmen would genuinely
serve the public interest, and assumed that in a regime of free
competition property would be widely distributed. In Smith's
opinion the interests of the landed and laboring classes were
generally identical with those of the community as a whole;
the special interests of the business classes were contrary to
those of the community (since they usually wished to restrict
production and to keep prices high). Competition was usually
disliked by businessmen, and was a necessary measure of discipline. The American agrarians generally spoke of Smith with
strong approval, while the exponents of business enterprise
(such as Hamilton) criticized him.*

bees, so much of their earnings, as that unremitting labor shall be necessary to obtain a sufficient surplus barely to sustain a scanty and miserable life. And these earnings they apply to maintain the privileged orders in splendor and idleness, to fascinate the eyes of the people, and excite in them a humble adoration and submission, as to an order of superior beings." In such a society "every man must be either pike or gudgeon, hammer or anvil"; and the government was a rule of "wolves over sheep," of "kites over pigeons." [5]

How different was the society that had developed in America, in which the vast majority of the people were independent farmers and were neither exploiters nor the victims of exploitation! Both Franklin and Jefferson followed the French physiocrats in arguing that agriculture was the only honest way of life because it was the only occupation that actually created new wealth; all other methods of making a living were parasitical. "There seem to be but three ways for a nation to acquire wealth," said Franklin. "The first is by war, as the Romans did, in plundering their conquered neighbors. This is robbery. The second by commerce, which is generally cheating. The third by agriculture, the only honest way, wherein one receives a real increase of the seed thrown into the ground, in a kind of continual miracle." The great virtue of American society was that it was composed mainly of producers of this "real increase." This happy condition might not endure indefinitely; the supply of vacant land, even in America, was limited, and when it was exhausted Americans might lose their economic freedom. Franklin predicted that America would lose its unique features when "the lands are all taken up and cultivated, and the excess of people who cannot get land" would be thrown out of employment. "When we get piled upon one another in large cities, as in Europe," declared Jefferson with greater emphasis, "we shall become corrupt as in Europe, and go to eating one another as they do there." But with a vast

[5] *Letter to Wythe, Aug. 13, 1786; Letter to William Johnson, June 12, 1823; Letter to Rutledge, Aug. 6, 1787.*

empty continent before them the Americans need not expect such a fate for centuries.[6]

From this economic analysis the agrarians deduced their
political philosophy. Their primary objectives were to
maintain a genuine equality of economic opportunity and
to make it impossible for men to acquire wealth by any
methods except their own industry and talent. They believed in a democracy of small property owners, and by
democracy they meant outright majority rule; the government should be as close to the people, and as responsive
to the people, as it was possible to make it. Jefferson agreed
that democracy might be dangerous in Europe, where the
mass of the people had suffered for so long from poverty,
ignorance, and exploitation; but among the American
farmers, "enjoying in ease and security the full fruits of
their own industry, enlisted by all their interests on the
side of law and order, habituated to think for themselves,
and to follow their reason as their guide," it was the only
just form of government.[7] While the moneyed interests
wished to limit majority rule in order to protect "the
minority of the opulent," the agrarians saw no such necessity; in America, where the masses of the people were
property owners, and not a degraded proletariat as in
Europe, the majority could be trusted.

Yet while the agrarians believed that government should
represent the will of the majority, they also believed that
its functions should be mainly negative rather than positive.
They regarded any form of power, no matter who exercised
it, as potentially dangerous; this was the strongest of their
convictions, and the one that shows most clearly their
political wisdom. "Mankind," said Jefferson, "soon learn
to make interested uses of every right and power which
they possess. . . . The natural progress of things is for
liberty to yield and government to gain ground." [8] The true
function of government was to maintain order. "A wise

[6] *Carl Van Doren: op. cit., pp. 372, 705; Thomas Jefferson,
Letter to James Madison, Dec. 20, 1787.*

[7] *Letter to William Johnson, June 12, 1823.*

[8] Notes on Virginia, *Query XIII; Letter to Carrington, May
27, 1788.*

and frugal government, which shall restrain men from injuring one another, which shall leave them otherwise free to regulate their own pursuits of industry and improvement, and shall not take from the mouth of labor the bread it has earned. This," he said in his *First Inaugural,* "is the sum of good government." Government should not only be prohibited from interfering with the rights of individuals and from creating a large bureaucratic class who could live at public expense; it should also be prevented from intervening in economic matters, since the effect of any such intervention was always to transfer property and to establish some form of economic privilege. The greatest of all dangers to democratic freedom and equality was the use of political power by an aristocracy, a bureaucracy, a mercantile oligarchy, a pressure group, or any other minority interest in order to increase their wealth or to obtain the privilege of living parasitically on other men's labor.

Holding such opinions, the agrarians did not look with favor on those forms of property which were acquired by contract and not by labor. They believed with Jefferson that "the earth is given as a common stock for men to labor and live on," and that the only natural right of property was "the fundamental right to labor the earth. . . . Stable ownership is the gift of social law, and is given late in the progress of society." And since contractual property rights were created by society and not by nature, it followed that society could alter them. "Whenever there are in any country uncultivated lands and unemployed poor," said Jefferson, "it is clear that the laws of property have been so far extended as to violate natural right." Society could, for example, change the laws of inheritance in order to enforce the subdivision of properties. And since, as Jefferson declared, "the earth belongs in usufruct to the living" and "the dead have neither powers nor rights over it," it followed that debts and other contractual obligations need not, if society so decided, be handed down from one generation to the next. In general, society had the right to break the dead hand of the past in order to prevent the perpetuation of economic inequalities and economic privileges. This did not mean that the state should intervene directly in economic affairs in order to transfer property; but since the general laws regulating the transmission of property were made by the state, they could also be altered by the state in order to preserve "the fundamental right of all men to labor the earth" and to enjoy the fruits of their own labor.[9]

This agrarian philosophy of government was optimistic, idealistic, and humanitarian; it was based on a realistic analysis of society; and it reflected, or appeared to reflect, the wishes and interests of the vast majority of eighteenth-century Americans. Even today the ideal of a property owners' democracy probably has a stronger appeal to most Americans than either of the rival ideologies of big-business capitalism and of socialism. Yet it cannot be maintained that American society has developed in conformity with agrarian principles or that it is still characterized by any "general happy mediocrity." Americans have always liked the economic individualism and independence, the freedom from coercion, regimentation, and exploitation, that the agrarians offered them; but they have never been willing to pay the price that agrarianism would have required.

At the heart of the agrarian philosophy was a confidence in human nature. The agrarians rejected all authoritarian and aristocratic doctrines in the belief that men were good by nature and not merely as a result of social discipline or indoctrination. When men lost their economic independence and became degraded by poverty and exploitation (as in the cities of Europe), their moral intuitions might become perverted and destroyed; but in America men could be trusted to behave virtuously. Man, declared Jefferson, had an innate "sense of right and wrong," which was "as much a part of his nature as the sense of hearing, seeing, feeling." [1] To make men good it was necessary only to make them free. This confidence in human nature is one of the essential foundations of the American democratic faith; for if the moral sense is not innate, then it follows that

[9] *Letter to Rev. James Madison, Oct. 28, 1785; Letter to James Madison, Sept. 6, 1789.*
[1] *Letter to Peter Carr, Aug. 10, 1787.*

men need authoritarian guidance and indoctrination. But in insisting on the innate virtue of individuals, the spokesmen of agrarian democracy did not sufficiently recognize the extent to which individual behavior is shaped and conditioned by prevalent social values and attitudes and by institutions. The preservation of the agrarian ideal required more than individual freedom; it required also the support of appropriate institutions and of a general view of life. And neither the American view of life nor American institutions tended to encourage the kind of behavior that was needed for the preservation of the agrarian economy.

In a country governed in accordance with agrarian ideals, manufacturing could have developed only very slowly, since there would have been no large accumulations of capital and no supplies of cheap labor. But a people like the Americans, with their drive towards the conquest and exploitation of nature, could not be persuaded to reject the promise of wealth and power through rapid industrial development and to content themselves with a relatively static economy. Nor were the Americans, as individuals, ever willing to forego the hope of making money through speculation and through the use of political influence. A nation in which every poor man hoped to become rich and every rich man was afraid of becoming poor could not conduct its affairs with the austerity and self-restraint that agrarianism would have required. Americans were never prepared to reject any way of making a fortune that was not positively illegal, in the eighteenth century as in the twentieth. Indeed, almost every prominent figure in eighteenth-century America, including a number whose political alignments were with the agrarians, engaged in land speculation; and many of them were interested in a bewildering variety of different business enterprises, which often involved political manipulation. With the vast resources of an empty continent to pre-empt and exploit, very few individuals were ever prepared to live by agrarian principles. One must not, in fact, look for much consistency among American political leaders and thinkers. Although two opposite and clearly articulated philosophies of government can clearly be traced in all the political controversies of the post-Revolutionary period, they were never fully embodied in individuals. In practice, men frequently changed sides and advocated different ideas with bewildering rapidity.

It is significant that the most consistent exponents of agrarianism came from Virginia. The Virginia society of this period was more static than that of any other part of the United States; it lacked the restlessness and the dynamism that were generally characteristic of Americans. And while it would be unfair to emphasize the incongruity between the liberal principles of the agrarians and their ownership of slaves, it must be admitted that it was easier for a slaveowning planter than it was for the average small farmer to glorify the agrarian way of life and to denounce quick ways of making money. In Virginia, in fact, agrarian principles eventually crystallized into dogmas of the kind which cause political fanaticism and make peaceful compromise impossible. Jefferson and John Taylor were the intellectual fathers of Calhoun and the Southern secessionists.

Of the two rival philosophies of agrarian democracy and aristocratic capitalism, the former was closer to the conscious ideals of Americans, but their actions were more frequently in conformity with the latter. The final result was therefore somewhat paradoxical. In the political sphere the democratic forces were triumphantly successful. In the nineteenth century, all remnants of class rule were swept away, and the right of the plain people to control the government became an American article of faith. This evolution was virtually completed by the 1830's, and there has been no essential change in the American political system since that date. In the economic sphere, on the other hand, the agrarians lost their battle to preserve the democracy of the small producers. America became capitalistic instead of agrarian, and in doing so it retained economic doctrines that had originally been associated with the aristocratic principle. American capitalism was built on the sanctity of contracts and on the use of political power or influence to secure economic advantages. This practice, which the agrarians had regarded as the most vicious aspect of aristocracy, became, in fact, a normal feature of American political life; originally developed by the moneyed interests, it was eventually adopted also by the farmers and by organized labor.

A political system based on equal rights for all and an economic system characterized by the maintenance of special privileges for a few were essentially incompatible with each other. But they could be combined as long as there was an open frontier and a rapidly expanding economy. Poor Americans hoped to become privileged, and the number of those who succeeded was enough to encourage the rest. Ultimately, however, Americans would have to make a choice. Between Hamilton and Jefferson there could be no permanent reconciliation.

2

The struggle between agrarian and capitalistic principles lasted through the nineteenth century. Yet it can be argued that the decisive engagement occurred at the very outset, and that the agrarians were defeated when they had scarcely begun to fight. For the American Constitution, drafted by the Philadelphia Convention of 1787, was based on aristocratic and capitalistic principles. The importance of this convention in determining the future development of America can scarcely be overestimated. By accepting the Constitution, the people of the United States were virtually deciding that they should not remain a nation of small property owners, but that they should become a capitalistic people, possessed of the greatest wealth and power and of a high standard of living, but divided by the most extreme economic inequalities.

In 1776 new principles of government, reflecting the peculiar conditions of American society, had been asserted and partially put into effect. The political groups then dominant in a number of the states had believed that government should be based on majority rule and should be as close to the people as possible. Distrusting political power, they had felt that the best government was the government that governed least, and had preferred a local government, which the people might more easily control, to any form of centralized authority. And they had wished to subdivide big estates and to make it possible for every man to become a property owner. These principles had reflected the vigorous and self-confident individualism, verging on anarchy, of the American farmers and mechanics. In 1787, on the other hand, fifty-five men, almost all of whom were wealthy merchants, lawyers or landowners, met behind closed doors at Philadelphia in order to draft the charter of a new central government for the thirteen states. Most of them were agreed (according to Edmund Randolph) that "the evils under which the United States labored" were due to "the turbulence and follies of democracy," and that "some check therefore was to be sought for against this tendency of our governments." Believing (as Madison, Rutledge, and Gouverneur Morris explained) that the chief objects of government were "the security of property and public safety," they wished (in Madison's words) "to protect the minority of the opulent against the majority." And they hoped to accomplish these objectives by setting up a central government with broad powers, based (as Madison suggested) on "the policy of refining the popular appointments by successive filtrations," and by depriving the state legislatures of any power to impair the obligations of contracts.[2]

That the Constitution was the product of a distrust of democracy is evident both from the speeches made at the Philadelphia Convention and from the debates of the state conventions that ratified it. Why then did its framers believe that a sufficient majority of the American people would be willing to accept their proposals?

The best argument in favor of the Constitution was the need for defense against foreign encroachments on American rights. The United States was a nation in a world of nations, and the western hemisphere was by no means isolated, either politically or economically. Lacking a strong government, the Americans had almost lost the

[2] *Max Ferrand: op. cit., Vol. I, pp. 50, 51, 147.*

War of Independence; and after peace had been made, their welfare continued to be endangered by the policies of other nations. The British, established in Canada, had failed to withdraw their troops from the Western territories, as provided in the peace treaty. The Spaniards held Louisiana, and were interfering with American trade on the Mississippi and plotting to win control of Kentucky and Tennessee. Meanwhile American merchants were suffering from the exclusionist commercial policies of all the European powers. Strong government is always a potential threat to the freedom of individuals; but as long as the human race is divided into separate nations, whose relations with each other are determined mainly by force, it is always necessary.

Another valid argument was the need to maintain unity among the thirteen states. Different states were coming into conflict about boundaries and about claims to Western lands. On several occasions these conflicts resulted in a use of force and seemed likely to lead to open warfare.

But these were not the arguments that had the greatest weight with the makers of the Constitution. Their strongest motive was the defense of property against "the excess of democracy." According to Madison they were influenced chiefly by "the necessity of providing more effectually for the security of private rights and the steady dispensation of justice. Interferences with these were evils which had, more perhaps than anything else, produced this convention." [3]

The economic disturbances resulting from the War of Independence had sharpened the conflict between debtor and creditor interests; and in a number of the states, debtor interests had succeeded in passing legislation acutely displeasing to creditors. "Stay" laws were enacted, suspending the right of creditors to foreclose on mortgages in default; and during 1785 and 1786 there was a widespread resort to inflation. This tendency was finally brought under control, but creditor groups were profoundly disturbed by it. Even more alarming to the moneyed interests was what happened in Massachusetts. In this state the merchants had

[3] *Ibid., Vol. I, p. 134.*

continued to enjoy legal support in collecting their debts; and in the autumn of 1786 the farmers of the Connecticut Valley region, under the somewhat unwilling leadership of Daniel Shays, attempted to save their farms by resorting to armed rebellion. The rebellion was easily suppressed, but meanwhile the moneyed groups in the state had been thrown into a state of panic. They regarded the rebels, who were merely trying to save their own property from confiscation, as the enemies of all property rights and as the most dangerous revolutionaries.

The extraordinary fears of the aristocratic elements are displayed most vividly in a letter written to George Washington from Boston by General Knox. Knox declared in horror that the creed of the farmers was "that the property of the United States has been protected from the confiscation of Britain by the joint exertions of all, and therefore ought to be the common property of all. . . . This dreadful situation, for which our government has made no adequate provision, has alarmed every man of principle and property in New England. They start as from a dream, and ask what can have been the cause of this delusion? What is to give us security against the violence of lawless men? Our government must be braced, changed, or altered to secure our lives and property. We imagined that the mildness of our government and the wishes of the people were so correspondent that we were not as other nations, requiring brutal force to support the laws. But we find we are men—actual men, possessing all the turbulent passions belonging to that animal, and that we must have a government proper and adequate for him." [4]

The stay laws, the inflation, and the rebellion in Massachusetts caused the aristocratic and business groups in all the states to draw together. Composed partly of those elements in the colonial aristocracies which had survived the Revolution, and partly of merchants who had grown rich during the war, these groups wished chiefly to set up a government that would maintain the sanctity of contracts.

[4] *Quoted by V. L. Parrington:* Main Currents in American Thought, *Vol. I, p. 277.*

Debts must be paid, a sound currency must be maintained, and business enterprise must have political protection and assistance. And as a result of the debtor-class legislation and the inflationary excesses of 1785 and 1786, this point of view now won considerable support among those middle-class citizens, neither creditor nor debtor, who composed the majority of the population. Wanting economic tranquillity, many average Americans were now somewhat disillusioned with democracy, and willing to support a reversion to aristocratic leadership. It was this situation that made possible the calling of the Philadelphia Convention.[5]

The proceedings of this convention should not be interpreted in twentieth-century terms. That its members wished "to protect the minority of the opulent" against the majority did not mean that they wished to set up any authoritarian system of government. In common with all other Americans, they believed in individual freedom, in the maintenance of civil liberty, and in republican principles of government. Nor were they consciously motivated by personal ambition or crude self-interest. What determined their decisions was not their own economic interests, but

[5] *R. H. Lee summarized the situation as follows: "One party is composed of little insurgents, men in debt, who want no law, and who want a share of the property of others; these are called Levellers, Shaysites, etc. The other party is composed of a few, but more dangerous men, with their servile dependents; these avariciously grasp at all power and property; you may discover in all the actions of these men, an evident dislike to free and equal government, and they go systematically to work to change, essentially, the forms of government in this country; these are called aristocrats, m—ites, etc. Between these two parties is the weight of the community: the men of middling property, men not in debt on the one hand, and men, on the other, content with republican governments, and not aiming at immense fortunes, offices and power. . . . These two parties . . . are really insignificant, compared with the solid, free, and independent part of the community." Quoted by V. L. Parrington: op. cit., Vol. I, p. 291. According to Lee the aristocratic party was making use of the alarm caused by the "little insurgents" in order to win the support of the "men of middling property."*

the political attitudes and ideals into which they had been educated. That they were capable of a noble humanitarianism is proved by the abhorrence of slavery expressed several times during their debates, even by the extremely conservative Philadelphia merchant Gouverneur Morris. There were no protests against the declaration of Madison, representing the Southern state of Virginia, that "a mere distinction of color" had become the basis of "the most oppressive dominion ever exercised by man over man." [6] But these men belonged to the eighteenth century, when democracy was still a new, alarming, and untested idea. Differing from the agrarians in their conceptions of freedom and property rights, they regarded it as almost self-evident that the direct rule of the ignorant masses was dangerous, and that the country should be guided by an elite of "gentlemen of principle and property."

Such an attitude is understandable, yet it had little basis in reality. The masses of whom they were afraid were not the oppressed proletariat and peasantry of Europe, but the free and independent property-owning farmers of America. And perhaps the most striking characteristic of these eighteenth-century merchants and planters was that they still thought largely in European terms. The American society of that epoch was unique; but there was as yet no developed theory of government, even among the agrarians, that took account of its unique features. So both for warnings of what to avoid and for models to be imitated, the members of the convention turned to the history of European countries, ancient and contemporary, quoting extensive precedents from the experience of Greece, Rome, Holland, Germany, Poland, and Great Britain. When they shuddered at the dangers of mob rule, they were thinking of ancient city-states and of the mobs of London and Paris, not of the independent proprietors who composed the chief democratic element in America. And when they were horrified by Shays's Rebellion, they were identifying it with European class struggles; they did not sufficiently recognize that the farmers responsible for the rebellion

[6] *Max Farrand: op. cit., Vol. I, p. 135.*

were fighting not for the destruction of all property rights, but for the right to keep property of their own. The agrarian democracy of the American states had a number of weaknesses, which needed remedying; but the fear of the merchants was derived from European, not from American, experience. There was much truth in words written a number of years later by Thomas Jefferson. "It must be agreed," he declared, "that our governments have much less of republicanism than ought to have been expected; in other words, that the people have less regular control over their agents, than their rights and their interests require. And this I ascribe, not to any want of republican dispositions in those who formed these Constitutions, but to a submission of true principles to European authorities, to speculators on government, whose fears of the people have been inspired by the populace of their own great cities, and were unjustly entertained against the independent, the happy, and therefore orderly citizens of the United States." [7]

That the convention was legislating for Europeans and not for Americans was pointed out by one of its members, Charles Pinckney of South Carolina. In a long and carefully prepared speech Pinckney insisted that "we cannot draw any useful lessons from the example of any of the European states or kingdoms," and that "the people of this country are not only very different from the inhabitants of any state we are acquainted with in the modern world; but I assert that their situation is distinct from either the people of Greece and Rome, or of any state we are acquainted with among the ancients." The essential characteristic which made the United States unique was that "there is more equality of rank and fortune in America than in any other country under the sun; and this is likely to continue as long as the unappropriated western lands remain unsettled. . . . Where," asked Pinckney, "are the riches and wealth whose representation and protection is the peculiar province of this present body? Are they in the hands of the few who may be called rich; in the posses-

[7] *Letter to John Taylor, May 28, 1816.*

sion of less than a hundred citizens? Certainly not. They are in the general body of the people, among whom there are no men of wealth, and very few of real poverty." And "this equality is likely to continue, because in a new country, possessing immense tracts of uncultivated lands, where every temptation is offered to emigration and where industry must be rewarded with competency, there will be few poor, and few dependent. . . . We have unwisely considered ourselves," he declared, "as the inhabitants of an old instead of a new country." [8]

This was the wisest speech delivered at the convention, but does not appear to have exercised any influence on its proceedings. Nor did the convention pay much attention to the suggestions of Benjamin Franklin, who was now old and feeble, and whose recommendations, though heard with the respect due to his reputation, were almost invariably ignored. Most of the members remained convinced that the rights of property would be genuinely endangered by majority rule, in America as in Europe; and insofar as what they meant by property was not the ownership of a farm or a plantation but the sanctity of commercial contracts, their distrust of democracy was not without justification.

3

The Constitution drafted at Philadelphia may be viewed from several different angles. It may be considered as a solution to the problem of federalism, as a method for protecting "the minority of the opulent," and as a mechanism of legislation and administration. These different functions have been performed with varying degrees of success.

The members of the convention showed themselves most realistic and most farsighted in their handling of the federal problem. Their task was to create a government strong enough to protect the common interests of Americans, but not so strong that it would obliterate the sover-

[8] *Max Farrand: op. cit., Vol. I, pp. 397–404.*

eignty of the states. This was substantially the problem
that has presented itself, in a much more difficult form,
to the nations of the world in the twentieth century. The
clarity with which the convention understood it is shown
by their realization that the central government must be
more than a mere confederation of states; it must have
direct sovereign power over individuals. As Madison
pointed out, the federal authority could not successfully
coerce a state. "The use of force against a state would look
more like a declaration of war than an infliction of punishment," and would destroy all the purposes of the union.[9]
The government must therefore be able to use force directly
against any individual who broke its laws or failed to perform the duties it prescribed. In this respect the makeis
of the American Constitution showed a clear-sighted intelligence that was lacking in their twentieth-century successors. Madison would have known that the League of
Nations would prove unworkable.

But though the federal government must be sovereign,
it did not follow that it must be the sole repository of
sovereignty. The convention solved its chief dilemma by
the device of dividing sovereign power; some forms of
authority over individuals were given to the new federal
government, while others remained with the states. Political
logicians would have regarded this as impossible; sovereignty was supposed to be indivisible. But the members
of the convention were realistic enough to understand that
what was impossible according to the rules of logic might
be wholly practical in reality.

For a period the convention was deadlocked by the demand of the smaller states for equality with the larger
states. Delaware and New Jersey were alarmed by the
superior size and power of the big states, and convinced
that if their rights were not fully guaranteed they might be
exploited and dominated. This dispute shows very clearly
how far the members of the convention were thinking in
European and not in American terms. Such anxieties would
have been relevant if they had been planning a federation

[9] *Ibid., Vol. I, p. 54.*

for Europe, where men were divided by racial and linguistic differences; but in America, where nothing but geography distinguished a native of Delaware from a Pennsylvanian, there was not the slightest reason for the insistence of the small states on retaining an equality of sovereignty. The dispute was settled permanently by the compromise under which the states were to be represented equally in the Senate, while the membership of the House of Representatives would be based on population.

In attempting to protect the "minority of the opulent" against majority interference, the members of the convention were faced with a more difficult problem. One of their favorite ideas was that somehow wealth and numbers should be balanced against one another; for example, the House of Representatives might represent the people, while the Senate might be based on the aristocratic principle. But they did not dare to adopt property qualifications for admission to the Senate or to give its members tenure for life, and the system of election by the state legislatures was no guarantee of conservatism. The democratic trend in American society was, in fact, so strong that the convention could not reverse it; after British authority had been overthrown and the reforms of the Revolutionary period had been enacted, there was no foundation anywhere in America upon which any kind of permanent aristocracy could be erected. It was suggested by Madison that the formation of a large federal union would, of itself, serve to protect minorities. In the states single economic groups might achieve complete control; but in a large republic, in which there was a great diversity of interests and occupations, the different groups would constantly check each other, so that no compact majority could win power. Madison's analysis, with its suggestion of the value of competition between different pressure groups, proved to be a substantially accurate prediction of how the American federal system would develop; but as the Southern states were to discover, both before and after the Civil War, minority interests were not always secure against exploitation.

In general, the convention tried to limit democracy by

"refining" the popular will through a system of indirect elections for the Senate and the Presidency. At that period it was assumed by all Americans that remote government meant undemocratic government. When representatives were removed from their constituents, either geographically or by indirect election, they were more likely to act independently, and more likely also to respond to pressure from aristocratic and moneyed interests. By its very nature, therefore, the federal government might be expected to be less responsive to popular sentiment than the local governments. In the outcome, however, these attempts to check majority rule proved to be unsuccessful. Indirect elections were no barrier to the growth of democracy. And while the federal government has often been influenced by moneyed interests, it cannot be maintained that it has been less democratic than the state governments. But though the convention failed in its attempt to limit majority control over the legislature, it accomplished its main objective by other methods. Certain guarantees of property rights were written into the constitution; in particular, state governments were forbidden to issue paper money or to impair the obligations of contracts. And the defense of the Constitution was entrusted to a judiciary, which was independent of popular control. Although the Supreme Court was not explicitly given the power to invalidate state and federal laws, there can be little doubt that it was expected to exercise it. The statement about contracts was probably the most important single clause in the whole Constitution.

The Constitution is most open to criticism when it is considered as a mechanism of government. On the one hand, the members of the convention wanted a government with broad powers, which would protect and promote different economic interests. On the other hand they believed that political power was always dangerous. Citing numerous warnings from European history, ancient and modern, different speakers suggested that either the President or the majority of the legislature might assume dictatorial authority, or that they might become the hired agents of some foreign country. For this dilemma they could find no satisfactory solution. Adopting the theory of separation of powers, with which they were familiar both from American experience and from the writings of European theorists, they divided the executive from the legislature, and made rigid rules providing for elections at two- and four-year intervals. Such an arrangement established guarantees against abuses of power by government officials; as long as the Constitution remained in force, neither President nor Congress could arrogate dictatorial authority. Unfortunately it also meant that responsibility was divided, slowness and inefficiency were encouraged, and paralyzing conflicts between different branches of the government were inevitable. In practice it is impossible to make any clear distinction between executive and legislative functions, and efficiency is impossible unless (as under the parliamentary system) the men who make the laws and those who supervise their enforcement are in agreement with each other. But the American Constitution did not make provision for ensuring any such agreement. Even when the President and the majority of the Congress were of the same political opinions, conflicts between them were likely to occur, and responsibility for errors was difficult to fix; and when they were in opposition to each other it became difficult for any action whatever to be taken. And as a result of the election rules and the general lack of flexibility in constitutional procedure, conflicts could not be settled by means of an appeal to the verdict of the people. It was necessary to wait until the time appointed for the next Presidential or Congressional election.

In the course of time the Constitution acquired the qualities of a mythological symbol. Every nation needs some unifying focus of loyalty to which the emotions of its citizens can be attached; and among the Americans, who lacked a hereditary monarchy, a long history, and a common blood and ancestry, the Constitution performed this function. Just as in Great Britain the King could do no wrong, so in the United States the Constitution could do no wrong. According to popular legend as developed during the nineteenth century, the makers of the Constitution had been endowed with an almost supernatural wisdom and foresight and had made provision for almost every possible contingency. But the fact that the Constitution actually worked, and has continued to work for more than a century and a half, does not prove that it had any extraordinary merits. The primary reason for the success of the American form of government was not the wisdom of the Philadelphia convention but the character and traditions of the American people. Eighteenth-century Americans could have made almost any constitution work.

Any form of government is essentially a complex of habits; and since men change their habits slowly and only with reluctance and alarm, new institutions cannot be adopted if they involve too sharp a break with previous custom. The most perfect constitution will fail if it is suddenly imposed upon a people unaccustomed to self-government. But as a result of many generations of experience, not only in the colonies but also in the England of the Stuarts and the medieval kings, the American had become habituated to the election of representatives, the acceptance of their decisions, the settlement of disputes by legal procedure, and the judicial protection of individual rights. They were willing to accept compromises, and they were not torn apart by irreconcilable political ideologies. The Constitution was, in certain respects, an extremely clumsy mechanism of government; it was successful because of the political maturity of the nation that adopted it.

In the course of time, moreover, the Americans worked out new political mechanisms, which were not incorporated into the Constitution or foreseen by the men who made it, but which were essential to its success. The chief of these was the party system, which originated in the 1790's but which assumed a new and permanent form, uniquely American, half a century later. By means of the party system, the different sectional and class interests acquired organization and coherence, and the executive and the legislature were brought into closer contact with each other. After the establishment of political democracy in the 1830's, it was this system, and the habits and conventions associated with it, which actually controlled the political evolution of America. The Constitution established the framework within which parties operated; but insofar as the spirit was more important than the letter, the party system was more important than the Constitution.

After the convention had finished its work, the Constitution was submitted for ratification to specially elected conventions in the different states. The aristocratic and moneyed groups were almost unanimously in favor of it; the agrarian elements were preponderantly against it. Agrarian spokesmen complained that too much authority was being concentrated in the new federal government, and that civil liberty and democratic control were not sufficiently assured. R. H. Lee of Virginia, for example, criticized the "strong tendency to aristocracy now discernible in every part of the plan," and declared that "every man of reflection must see that the change now proposed, is a transfer of power from the many to the few." [1] But the agrarian opposition was disorganized and lacking in outstanding leaders, and had no alternative program of its own. After elections in which only about one third of the electorate appears to have voted, every state was persuaded to ratify. In a number of the states the majorities in favor of the Constitution were narrow, and in several of them the popular vote (though not the final vote of the state conventions) was opposed to ratification. It is probable that the Constitution would not have been ratified at all if it had not been generally assumed that Washington would be the first President. In order to remove the fears of the opposition, it was agreed that the Constitution should be amended by the addition of a Bill of Rights guaranteeing the essential liberties of individuals against federal interference. These limitations upon the power of the state have generally been regarded as the most praiseworthy feature of the American form of government. It should be remembered that they were the work not of the moneyed interests (who wanted a strong government, provided that they could control it) but of the agrarian and democratic elements who stood for the principle of majority rule.

But once the verdict of the people had been fairly given and the Constitution had been ratified, all groups loyally

[1] *Quoted by V. L. Parrington: op. cit., Vol. I, p. 290.*

accepted it and set out to make it work successfully. This complete abandoning of opposition was followed by a curious reversal of the original position of the two parties. The supporters of ratification, known as Federalists, continued to believe in a strong federal government that would give positive aid to business expansion, and began to extend federal power beyond the written words of the Constitution. The agrarian elements (including a few persons who had supported the Constitution, but consisting preponderantly of those who had opposed it) now claimed that the Constitution itself was an ideal form of government, provided that it was interpreted narrowly and literally. Assuming the name of Republicans, they accused the Federalists of violating it and of trying to remodel it along European lines. Thus the original opponents of the Constitution were transformed into its most enthusiastic champions.

Yet there can be little doubt that it was the Federalists who were more faithful to the spirit of the Philadelphia Convention, if not always to the letter. And after the elections of 1800, when they lost control of the executive and the legislature, they continued to control the judiciary, from which their spokesman, John Marshall, handed down decisions protecting the property rights of moneyed interests. These were denounced by the Republicans as unconstitutional, but were actually in full accord with the initial purposes of the Constitution. In the long run, Marshall's verdicts maintaining the sanctity of contracts had a greater influence on the development of American society than all the electoral victories of the agrarians. They created a legal structure within which capitalism could develop, free from interference by agrarian legislatures.

Obviously men must have a reasonable assurance that contracts will generally be fulfilled; otherwise all economic activity will be seriously impeded. On the other hand, when contracts are clearly contrary to justice or to the public interest, they should be subject to revision. To consider all contracts, of whatever nature, as sacred means that future generations will be perpetually in subjection to the dead hand of privilege and vested interest established in the past. But it was this doctrine—that all contracts, however acquired and of whatever nature, were sacred—which was preached by the Federalists and upheld by John Marshall, and which became the chief link between the aristocracy of the eighteenth century and the capitalism of the nineteenth.

Marshall's classic assertion of the sanctity of contracts was made in the Dartmouth College case. Dartmouth College was a corporation that had acquired a charter in the year 1769. When the state of New Hampshire tried to alter the charter in order to transform the college into a state university, the trustees of the college appealed to the law courts. Marshall declared, in a verdict given in the year 1819, that a corporation charter should be regarded as a contract, and hence that Dartmouth College was immune from political interference. In this particular case (though not in the implications to be drawn from it) Marshall's decision was probably in accord with the public interest. The full meaning of the doctrine, as interpreted by conservative judges, can be seen more vividly in two more extreme examples: *Fletcher versus Peck,* and the Charles River Bridge case.

Fletcher versus Peck resulted from the famous Yazoo lands fraud. A corrupt Georgia legislature sold thirty-five million acres of public land to companies interested in speculation at a price of less than one and one-half cents an acre. The people of Georgia were infuriated by the fraud, and the next legislature rescinded the sale. The matter eventually reached the Supreme Court, which decided that the original sale was legally a contract and therefore protected by the Constitution. Actually the companies did not regain possession of the land, but (in spite of violent protests by the extreme agrarians) were paid compensation by the federal government.

The Charles River Bridge case was not decided by the Supreme Court until 1837, by which time Marshall was dead and the agrarian Roger Taney was Chief Justice. In 1786 the State of Massachusetts had granted a charter to a corporation for the purpose of building a bridge across the Charles River and collecting tolls from all persons who used it. Forty years later the corporation was still collecting tolls, and its profits had amounted to thirty times its original investment, while the value of its stock had risen by two thousand per cent. The Massachusetts legislature then voted that a second bridge should be built, upon which no tolls should be charged at the end of six years. The owners of the first bridge claimed that this was a violation of their contract (even though they had never been explicitly given monopolistic rights). Taney, in accordance with his agrarian convictions, supported the legislature, declaring that the public interest was more important than the alleged property rights of the bridge corporation. To the admirers of John Marshall such a ruling was horrifying. They felt that the doctrine of the sanctity of contracts had been repudiated, that all property rights had become unsafe, and that the American government no longer gave protection to the "minority of the opulent" and had been perverted into a system of outright majority rule. Marshall's friend Justice Story declared that "a case of grosser injustice, or more oppressive legislation, never existed," while Chancellor Kent, the most famous legal scholar in the country, asserted that the decision "undermines the foundations of morality, confidence and truth. . . . What destruction of rights under a contract can be more complete?" he asked. "We can scarcely avoid being reduced nearly to a state of despair of the Commonwealth." [2]

[2] *Quoted by A. M. Schlesinger, Jr.: The Age of Jackson (1945), p. 327.*

☆ ☆ ☆ ☆ ☆ ☆ ☆ ☆ ☆ ☆ ☆ ☆ ☆

CHAPTER VII

CAPITALISM
AND AGRARIANISM

★ ★ ★ ★ ★ ★ ★ ★ ★ ★ ★ ★ ★ ★

THE MOST IMPORTANT PROBLEMS confronting the new federal government were in the sphere of foreign policy. Most of the western hemisphere was controlled by European empires, which would limit the expansion and threaten the security of the United States, and which were hostile to the republican principles that she represented. It was in dealing with this situation that the Americans showed their political maturity most clearly. Washington and his immediate successors laid down the foundations of an American foreign policy with a remarkable good judgment, far-sightedness, and certainty of touch. By taking advantage of European conflicts they achieved their main purposes so successfully that for several generations thereafter Americans were able to forget about international power politics.

The most vital American interest was security against any possible attack. The expulsion or neutralization of the European imperialisms in the North American continent was therefore the principal American objective. If this was accomplished, then the Americans could settle the empty Western territories and develop a peaceful way of life in complete safety, instead of maintaining large armed forces, which would be an economic burden and would inevitably stimulate militaristic, authoritarian, and antirepublican attitudes. In the eighteenth century the two oceans could be regarded as a sufficient protection against threats from outside the western hemisphere.

The second American interest was access to foreign markets, and this had no hemispheric limits. American merchants traded with Europe and with the Far East. American governments opposed commercial barriers, wished to see the destruction of closed mercantilist empires, and advocated an open-door policy, seeking trading rights on equal terms with all other nations rather than monopolistic privileges. And during periods of European warfare, when neutral commerce was restricted by blockades, they asserted the doctrine of the freedom of the seas.

In addition to these vital material needs, Americans had an interest in the extension of free institutions. The conflict between republicanism and autocracy, in the eighteenth century as in the twentieth, necessarily affected international relations. And while aristocratic Americans were inclined to support aristocratic forces elsewhere, the democratic elements, who believed that the United States represented new and beneficent principles of government, wished to see these privileges extended to the whole human race. Such an attitude caused them not only to support republican movements in other countries but also to advocate the territorial enlargement of the United States herself. This could easily degenerate into a self-righteous imperialism, as occurred later in the nineteenth century when the slogan of "Manifest Destiny" became popular; yet it was not without justification. As long as American practices were in conformity with American principles and did not involve racial discrimination or economic exploitation, the extension of the United States did mean the extension of freedom. In consequence the most democratic of Americans, from Jefferson down to Whitman, were often the most expansionist. When men have genuine faith in a political creed they always wish to universalize it, although (if their creed is a liberal one) they do not always regard territorial annexation as a justifiable method of doing so.

When Washington became President the immediate necessity was to ensure the survival of American institutions rather than to extend them. Washington had little of a crusading spirit, although even he believed that the success of the American experiment was of vital concern to humanity. His main preoccupation was to assert an independent American policy, free from colonial attitudes and based on genuine American interests. Americans should therefore refuse to be drawn into European contentions that did not concern them. How far such a doctrine (as it was stated in the *Farewell Address*) should be construed as isolationist depends upon how American interests are interpreted. The most lasting significance of the *Farewell Address* lies in its warning to Americans to think in American terms and to abandon "permanent inveterate antipathies against particular nations and passionate attachments for others." In a nation of immigrants divided into different racial groups who have maintained traditional antipathies and attachments for different European nations, this advice has often been violated (particularly by politicians seeking the votes of hyphenated Americans) and has constantly needed reaffirmation.

The French Revolution began a few weeks after Washington's inauguration, opening a period of general European warfare that lasted until 1815. Lacking a strong navy, the United States was unable to maintain her doctrine of freedom of the seas, and her attempts to do so caused an undeclared naval war with France in 1798 and a series of controversies with the British that culminated in the War of 1812. On the other hand, the Americans could win from the warring powers concessions that were of much more vital importance to their future security. Washington stopped British and Spanish encroachments on the American territories in the West; Jefferson purchased Louisiana, extending the boundaries of the United States as far as the Rockies; Madison began the acquisition of Florida; and Monroe finished the annexation of Florida and induced the Russians to relinquish their claims to the Oregon Territory. This remarkable growth made the United States virtually immune from possible attack, although the Americans had hoped to complete the process by the acquisition of Cuba and of Canada. But as long as Cuba remained Spanish and was not transferred to some more vigorous power, there could be no danger from that direction. And after the War of 1812 (which the United States had fought not only to protect her commerce but also in the hope of expelling the British from North America) Great Britain agreed to boundary settlements along the Canadian border, thereby ensuring American security on the north.

Meanwhile the remainder of the American continent had revolted against European control. The peoples of Mexico and South America, stimulated by the example of the United States, began to fight for their independence in 1810 and had gained it everywhere by 1825. Although the United States viewed their struggles sympathetically, she actually did little to help them, and they turned chiefly to British merchants for supplies and to British seapower for protection. But in 1823, when there were rumors of intervention by European monarchies, the American government made an extraordinarily bold and farsighted statement of its attitude. In the Monroe Doctrine were reflected all three of the basic preoccupations of American foreign policy: the desire for territorial security against European imperialism, the desire for open markets and the destruction of closed mercantilist empires, and the desire for the extension of republican institutions. It had little influence at the time it was issued; the Latin Americans owned their independence primarily to themselves and secondly to the British navy. But it was of immense importance in its foreshadowing of a future program of Pan-Americanism.

After 1823 Americans were no longer required to think seriously about foreign affairs until the twentieth century. The United States was safe from any possible aggression. The general world trend towards freer trade and the dissolution of colonial empires gave Americans access to markets. Liberal institutions were gaining ground everywhere. This long period of security was brought about chiefly by the course of events in Europe, but it was due also to the good judgment of early American diplomacy. And in the twentieth century, when the rise of Germany and Japan altered the balance of world forces, the diplomacy of the United States continued to be guided by the same preoccupations as in the period of Washington and Jefferson, although on a larger geographical scale. American security now required the destruction of aggressive imperialisms not only in North America, but also in western Europe and in eastern Asia.

2

For the first twelve years after the adoption of the Constitution American internal development was controlled mainly by the Federalists. Composed of the merchants and other moneyed elements, of the more theocratic of the clergy, and of those Southern planters who regarded land-owning as a business rather than as a way of life, they believed in the leadership of "the wise, the rich and the well-born." Their ability, their patriotism, and their devotion to republican principles were unquestionable; but what they meant by republicanism was the protection of the minority of the opulent and not the rule of the majority. Thinking in European rather than in American terms, they had a wholly irrational fear of the mass of their fellow citizens.

The desire to reshape America in accordance with European attitudes was, in fact, the keynote of the Federalist period. It was shown not only in its politics and in the pretentiousness of its social life, but also in its art. The favorite Federalist painter was the Europeanized Gilbert Stuart, who presented men and women as conventionalized examples of aristocracy, not with that honest and unflattering portrayal of individuality that had distinguished the early work of Copley. In architecture the period was marked by the beginning of the Greek revival, which dominated American building for the next two generations. The Greek revival was not an especially aristocratic movement; it represented an attempt to find a style that would be appropriate to a republic; one of its chief early exponents was Thomas Jefferson. But marking a sharp break with the tradition that had been developing during the colonial period (as shown, for example, in Independence Hall, Philadelphia), it reflected a lack of confidence in the possibilities of an indigenous culture. And although the imitations of Greek temples that it produced often had considerable dignity and grace, they were not wholly suited either to their functions, to their environment, or to their material.

Washington and Adams were both of them sympathetic to the Federalist attitude, although both of them governed as Presidents of all the people. But the leader of the Federalists was Alexander Hamilton. Of all the great men who have contributed to the development of the United States, Hamilton was the least American. Born in the West Indies, he had come to New York at the age of eighteen to seek his fortune; and after serving as an officer through the War of Independence, had married into one of the surviving aristocratic families of the Hudson Valley, and become a lawyer in New York City. He was vain, arrogant, and ambitious; but he had a superb courage, frankness, and self-assurance; and he was undeviatingly honest and sincerely devoted to the public interest as he saw it. Jefferson's conviction that Hamilton was plotting to destroy the liberties of Americans by establishing a monarchy was as unjustified as Hamilton's belief that Jefferson was "a contemptible hypocrite" [1] whose policies must lead to general anarchy and ultimately to dictatorship. Within somewhat narrow limits Hamilton's intelligence worked with an extraordinary clarity and inventive power; but he had no breadth of sympathy and little imagination. In particular, he lacked the capacity to understand the country to whose service he had devoted himself. His vision was restricted by the beliefs of eighteenth-century Europe. He assumed that the masses must always be governed by an elite, working through a strong and paternalistic state, and that the only alternative was a mob rule, which meant anarchy or tyranny or both. The whole purpose of his political career was to establish in America those institutions that had maintained strength and stability in European countries, particularly in Great Britain. The special qualities of America—particularly of the new

[1] *Letter to J. A. Bayard, Jan. 16, 1801*

America of Western farmers and frontiersmen, with their independence of spirit and their confidence in themselves —were beyond his comprehension. He despised the slipshod and undisciplined agrarian way of life, in which a man was free to work or be idle as he pleased. Taxes, he declared, were positively beneficial, since they compelled men to be industrious. The career of such a man, in such a country, could only end unhappily, since he was struggling to dominate forces which he never understood. Before he was killed by Aaron Burr, Hamilton was convinced that his career had been a failure. "This American world," he said, "was not made for me." [2]

Although Hamilton's political ideas went down quickly to defeat, his economic program had a lasting influence on American development. Believing in government by and for the rich, he favored close collaboration between the federal government and the moneyed classes. And wanting the United States to become a strong and wealthy nation, he hoped for a rapid development of manufacturing and believed that this could be promoted by appropriate federal policies. He was therefore an advocate of government intervention in economic affairs and of certain forms of national planning, and a critic of the laissez-faire theories of Adam Smith. He was a rigid believer in private enterprise; but he argued that it should be guided and assisted by the government. This became the permanent attitude of American business. In later generations business leaders sometimes declared that they disliked government intervention and spoke the language of *laissez faire*. But in reality they were opposed only to those kinds of intervention that were intended to police business practices or to give direct protection to other elements in the community, such as agriculture and labor. Like Hamilton, they believed in private enterprise and in the sanctity of contracts; and like Hamilton, they believed also that it was the function of the federal government to give them positive assistance.

The financial program that Hamilton put forward while he was Secretary of the Treasury in Washington's adminis-

[2] *Letter to Gouverneur Morris, Feb. 27, 1802.*

tration meant, in general, the use of political power to give economic privileges to the moneyed classes. By funding the government debt at its face value (in order, as he explained, to maintain the sanctity of contracts) he enriched a small group of speculators, who had bought up a large part of the debt at a small fraction of its nominal value. By chartering a bank and giving it authority to issue notes (while the government restricted itself to the coinage of gold and silver, issuing no paper money), he transferred to private citizens virtual control over the nation's currency and the power to make profits from it. And in his *Report on Manufactures* (which had little influence on legislation until the next generation) he advocated protective tariffs and the payment of bounties and subsidies for the encouragement and enrichment of manufacturers. He and his associates also looked with favor on the acquisition of Western lands by moneyed groups for speculative purposes, and on the granting of privileges to business corporations chartered by state governments. All this was admittedly legislation for the benefit of the rich; but while the agrarians denounced it as undemocratic, Hamilton was quite honest and consistent in believing that by consolidating the power of the upper classes and providing them with capital for investment he was making America into an orderly, disciplined, hard-working, and wealthy nation.

The Republican Party originated in 1791, when a group of Southern opponents of Hamilton, headed by Jefferson, began to form alliances with anti-Federalist groups in the North. For the next decade there was bitter conflict between the two parties. The Federalists were aided by the greater prestige of their leaders and by the continued influence of aristocratic and theocratic principles of government among a considerable body of the people. But the democratic spirit was now recovering from the disillusionment following the War of Independence. Farmers and urban mechanics began to form democratic clubs similar to the Sons of Liberty a quarter of a century earlier.

What finally ruined the Federalists was fear—fear of mob rule at home, and fear of the French Revolution abroad. The political influence of irrational emotions of this kind is often underestimated. Historians are too inclined to assume that human behavior can always be explained in rational terms, and—in the case of the Federalists —they have sometimes argued that their policies were based on deliberate calculation. Yet one cannot read the speeches and private letters of the leading Federalists without concluding that their panic was genuine, and that it drove them to courses that could end only in their political destruction.

The Federalist majority in Congress did not share Washington's coolness of judgment about the war in Europe. As a result of their political convictions, they had a permanent attachment to Great Britain and an antipathy to Revolutionary France; and they became convinced that the French were plotting to attack the United States from outside, and were at the same time trying to undermine her institutions by propaganda from within. During the Adams administration they made preparations for war; and believing that radical propaganda was a genuine menace to American society, they passed the Alien and Sedition Acts of 1798, which in violation of the Bill of Rights (and contrary to the wishes both of Hamilton and of President Adams) drastically limited freedom of speech and press. The Sedition Act was then enforced with excessive severity by a Federalized judiciary. But as became evident a year later, the French government had no serious designs against America. Disgusted by the war policies of the Federalists, American public opinion swung over to the Republicans.

In the election of 1800 the aristocratic principle made its last open stand in American political history. Federalist orators and clergymen suggested that civilization was in danger and that the election of Jefferson to the Presidency would mean a mob rule similar to what was supposed to have occurred in France under the Jacobins. It was alleged that there was an international conspiracy for the overthrow of culture and tradition, that the Republicans would establish a dictatorship and a reign of terror, and that they would abolish religion, marriage, and the family. The outcome was a decisive victory for Jefferson. It may be stated, to the credit of the American people, that whenever a political party in America has abandoned rational argument and succumbed to panic, it has committed a suicidal error. Unfortunately this is one of those lessons that men never learn from the past, and that have to be repeated in almost every generation.

3

In Jefferson's opinion the election of 1800 was the equivalent of a revolution. It meant the overthrow of men who had been attempting to build in America a class society copied from Europe and a reaffirmation of those principles of government that had been asserted in 1776. The agrarian democracy of the mass of the people had achieved political power, and the government of the United States had become Americanized.

The spokesmen of agrarian democracy had hitherto expressed themselves more boldly in practice than in theory. American political theory had been borrowed from Europe, and European writers had no conception of the unique kind of society that had developed in America. The concrete legislation of the Revolutionary epoch had been more significant than the appeals to natural rights with which it had been justified. Men had spoken of freedom in vague and general terms, but what they had chiefly meant was the right of every individual to economic independence. During the struggle with Hamiltonianism, however, the agrarians had begun to work out their political principles in more specific detail. It is possible that if agrarianism had acquired a body of political doctrine a generation earlier, before instead of after the drafting of the Constitution, the subsequent history of the United States might have been decidedly different.

Jefferson was the most gifted of the agrarians; but he never expounded his beliefs in any systematic form. For a detailed statement of agrarian principles one must turn to another Virginia planter, John Taylor of Caroline. Taylor is now remembered only by historians. His writings are rambling, repetitious, badly organized, and sometimes ungrammatical. After the triumph of industrialism, moreover, American history was rewritten in conformity with the

capitalist viewpoint, and it became inconvenient to recall
a thinker whose protests against the dominance of the
moneyed classes had been so outspoken and so unambigu-
ous. But the reader who has enough perseverance to cope
with Taylor's forbidding style can discover in his writings a
singularly penetrating interpretation of American society.
Unlike many of his more famous contemporaries, Taylor
understood what America meant; he deduced his principles
from American experience and not from irrelevant European speculations. In his own day his attitude was in no
way novel; he put on paper the doctrines in which all the
agrarians believed. But in the twentieth century, when the
true meaning of the American agrarian tradition has been
largely forgotten, he seems not only profound but also
remarkably original.

Taylor was primarily an enemy of aristocracy, and he
interpreted aristocracy wholly in economic terms. He defined it as "an accumulation of wealth by law without industry." The basic principle of a just society was that the
individual should be able to acquire property only by the
exercise of his own industry and talent. Property that was
"fairly gained by talents and industry" was based on
natural right, and no government could justly interfere
with it. In an aristocratic society, on the other hand, a
ruling class used its political power to acquire property
that had been created by the labor of other people. Any
law that had the effect of transferring wealth from those
who actually produced it by their own labor was inherently
unjust. Such interferences with the natural rights of property were as tyrannical as restrictions on political freedom.[3]

In the past the aristocratic principle had been represented
by clericalism and feudalism. These had now been replaced
by a new kind of aristocracy, a capitalist aristocracy of "patronage and paper," which operated by more subtle and
indirect methods. Instead of exploiting the mass of the
people directly and openly, like their feudal predecessors,
the aristocracy of patronage and paper created a compli-

[3] *John Taylor:* Inquiry into the Principles and Policy of the
Government of the United States (*1814*), *pp. 113, 275.*

cated legal and financial system by which they were able to acquire wealth that they had not actually earned. The wealth that was created by the labor of the mass of the people was transferred to the moneyed class by such devices as the payment of high rates of interest on the national debt, the issuance of paper money by the banks, the tariff (which enabled manufacturers to charge higher prices), the granting of monopolistic privileges in corporation charters, and speculation in stocks and real estate.

On the one side were the "agricultural and mechanical classes," who could earn property only by honest labor; on the other side were bankers, factory owners, government creditors, and other moneyed groups, whose claims to property were derived from their political influence and from legalistic construction and were not based on natural right and justice. Taylor insisted that these two kinds of property must be carefully distinguished, and pointed out that the aristocracy of patronage and paper was in the habit of confusing the public mind by trying to identify them and by representing agrarianism as an attack on all forms of property. "The grossest abuses artfully ally themselves with real and honest property," he said, "and endeavor to excite its apprehension, when attempts are made to correct them, by exclaiming against the invasion of property and against levelism." The wealth the businessman gained by speculation or through political influence was essentially different from the property the farmer acquired by mixing his labor with the wilderness; yet by claiming that both were forms of the natural right of property the businessman would mislead the farmer and secure his political support. Taylor also denounced the Federalist doctrine of the sanctity of contracts. He recognized that this doctrine, when applied to contracts that had been fraudulently obtained or that had the effect of enriching moneyed groups at public expense, would perpetuate inequalities, privileges, and vested interests. "Whenever the public good and a contract with an individual come in conflict," he pointed out, with obvious reference to such cases as *Fletcher versus Peck,* "public faith is made to decide that the contract shall prevail." Such a doctrine "becomes the protector of political fraud; it compels a nation to be an accomplice in its own ruin; it takes from it the right of self-preservation; and it becomes the modern subterfuge of the modern aristocracy." [4]

The use of political power to transfer property was regarded by Taylor as the basis of the class societies of Europe. "A sovereignty over private property," he said, "is the European principle of government, to which I ascribe most of the European oppressions." The purpose of the American Revolution had been to destroy this principle and thereby to create a regime of economic freedom and justice. The mass of the American people, according to Taylor, had wanted a society based on the natural right of property; each individual would have been free to acquire property by his own industry and talent; and the government would have been prohibited from making laws transferring property from those who had actually earned it. This was the American ideal, and its realization would have made America a unique example of freedom and equality. But unfortunately the Americans had failed to remain true to their own principles. The Federalist Party, tricking the American people by representing themselves as the defenders of property rights, had reintroduced the European system of government and had thus "revolutionized the revolution." [5]

The government, under Hamilton's guidance, had claimed a sovereignty over the natural right of property and "a power for creating pecuniary inequalities." It had enriched speculators at the expense of the mass of the people by its public debt policy. It had given to bankers "an irresponsible, uncontrolled, unpunishable, unelected power over the national purse," instead of recognizing that "currency and credit are social rights" that should be controlled by the elected agents of the people alone. It had assumed the power to enrich manufacturers by the tariff, to grant privileges to corporations by charters that, even

[4] *John Taylor:* Tyranny Unmasked (*1822*), *p. 308;* Inquiry, *pp. 70, 112.*

[5] *John Taylor:* Construction Construed and Constitutions Vindicated (*1820*), *p. 268;* Inquiry, *p. 253.*

when "given corruptly by government, are said, like the oracles, to be sacred," to bestow pensions and other grants on favored individuals, and to create a large bureaucracy supported by taxation. Unless the agricultural and mechanical classes could abolish these "property-transferring" laws, keep the powers of the federal government within narrow limits, and regain the economic freedom for which they had fought in the Revolution, then the whole country would eventually fall under the control of "a vast pecuniary aristocracy." And "if our system of government produces these bitter fruits naturally, it is substantially European; and the world, after having contemplated with intense interest and eager solicitude the experiment of the United States, will be surprised to find, that no experiment at all has been made, and that it still remains to be discovered, whether a political system preferable to the British be within the scope of human capacity." [6]

Although Taylor regarded farming as the ideal way of life, his doctrines were not intrinsically hostile to commerce and manufacturing. Believing in a regime of genuine *laissez faire*, he favored the free exchange of goods between one country and another. And while he deplored the new industrial system that was beginning to develop in New England, declaring that "the profits earned by factory laborers go to an owner," he attributed its evils to the political power of the factory owners. If the farmers were prosperous, instead of being plundered by the moneyed classes, and if the Western lands were kept open for settlers, then employers could get labor only by paying high wages. Thus the farmers and the urban workers had a common interest in preventing the establishment of economic privilege and in keeping America primarily a country of free individual small producers. [7]

The enforcement of these agrarian principles was perhaps the only method by which the Americans could have kept their economic freedom. But even if the American

---

[6] Inquiry, *p. 364, 375,* Tyranny Unmasked, *p. 207,* Construction Construed, *pp. 2, 11, 186.*

[7] *John Taylor:* Tyranny Unmasked, *p. 207.*

people had been willing to display the necessary austerity and self-restraint, it was probably too late to undo the work of the Federalists. Nor were Jefferson and the other Republican leaders the men to attempt it. The result was that within twenty years both the federal and the state governments, although still under the control of the same political party, were outdoing Hamilton himself in the enactment of "property-transferring" laws and the bestowal of economic privileges on bankers, manufacturers, and speculators. The alleged revolution of 1800 proved in the long run to be no revolution at all.

Jefferson was the most widely talented American of his generation; but he was too intellectual to be an effective man of action and too complex to become the embodiment of a program. Resembling Franklin both in the variety of his interests and in the coolness of his emotional temperament, he was a naturalist, an inventor, an agriculturalist, an architect, a musician, a philosopher, and a connoisseur of wine and cookery as well as a politician; and he could use words more effectively than any other figure in American history. But although he could voice democratic aspirations and hatred of class rule with a stirring and unrhetorical eloquence, he was not a fighter; and his actions were usually milder and more devious than his phrases. He lacked, moreover, the common touch and had the personal tastes and habits of an aristocrat. He believed in government for the people; but how far he also believed in government by the people seemed occasionally to be ambiguous. Much of the complexity of Jefferson's character was suggested in the house he built and designed for himself at Monticello. With its excessive elaboration, its echoes of European models, and its somewhat chilly magnificence, it lacked both the charm and the comfort of the more simple and less self-conscious buildings of earlier periods, such as Washington's Mount Vernon. Unlike Washington, Jefferson never quite succeeded in being himself.

There were similar ambiguities in the Republican Party that Jefferson organized and led. As the agrarians were never tired of pointing out, individuals possessed of political power are likely to develop different interests from their

constituents; and this was as true of the Republicans themselves as of any other group of politicians. In particular,
many of the Northerners in the party were decidedly more
interested in patronage than in principle. The New York
Republicans, for example, were led by George Clinton, who
had risen to power during the Revolution as the representative of agrarian democracy but who was now chiefly interested in keeping control of the state and in distributing
offices among his numerous friends and relatives, and by
Aaron Burr, a gifted, likable, and profligate adventurer of
a type very rare in the United States but frequent in some
European countries, particularly in the eighteenth century.
Thus the Republicans combined a genuine idealism with a
practical politics that was sometimes tricky and dishonest.

Actually the Jeffersonian period was singularly barren in
positive achievements. Having adopted the position of strict
construction, the Republicans were precluded by their own
theory from recognizing that the Constitution should be
amended if agrarian interests were to be safeguarded. They
did nothing to develop more effectively democratic mechanisms of government. Although they reduced taxes, they did
not dare to make any general revision of Hamilton's funding and banking system. And although they attacked the
Supreme Court, causing it so much alarm that it retreated
from the extremely partisan attitude it had displayed
hitherto (in its enforcement of the Sedition Act, for example), they failed to make any fundamental change in its
principles and personnel. Jefferson's timid policies eventually caused Taylor and other consistent agrarians to go into
opposition, while former Federalists who were disgusted
with the suicidal behavior of their own party—such as
John Quincy Adams—found it possible to turn Republican
without any real change of principle.

The final abandonment of agrarian principles was caused
by the conflict with Great Britain. This was another example of that fatal dilemma which, as long as force remains
the only arbiter in international affairs, must always im-
pede every attempt to create a genuinely free society. During Jefferson's second term he attempted to retaliate for
British and French attacks on American commerce by

ordering all American ships to remain in port. In view of
the popular indignation in the United States it is probable
that he could not have remained passive; but the enforcement of this embargo necessitated an increase in federal
power and an interference with individual liberty much
more drastic than anything ever attempted by Hamilton. In
Taylor's opinion it would have been better to let American
merchants look out for themselves. After the election of
Madison to the Presidency the country slowly drifted into
the War of 1812, for which British seizures of American
ships and British impressment of American seamen were
the chief provocation. And like the previous struggle with
Great Britain a generation earlier, the war was a disillusioning experience. The government displayed the greatest inefficiency, and only Andrew Jackson's victory at New
Orleans saved the Americans from a sense of general
humiliation. The most important result was a growth of
nationalistic sentiment; the United States must be built
into a strong and rich country, guided by a paternalistic
government. This conviction swept away what remained
of agrarian principles among the Republicans in Congress.

What actually happened after the war was that Hamiltonian economics began to be democratized. The new
factory system, which had originated in England in the
eighteenth century, was introduced into the Northern part
of the United States; and there was a rapid growth of
industry. At the same time a vast movement of people
westward into the Mississippi Valley was under way, enabling shrewd individuals to make big profits from land
speculation. The federal government assisted these processes
by adopting a protective tariff and by subsidizing corporations engaged in building roads and other internal improvements; while the state governments chartered vast numbers
of banks and allowed them to issue notes almost indis-
criminately, thereby causing inflationary conditions that
stimulated still further the passion for speculation. Many
Americans were no richer than before; and the craftsmen
and mechanics were decidedly less prosperous, since they
were losing their economic independence and undergoing a
gradual transformation into wage earners, and their early

attempts to form trade unions were declared illegal by the
judiciary. But it was becoming easier for those who were
cleverer or more fortunate than their neighbors to make
money; and plenty of Americans who belonged to neither
of these categories never stopped dreaming of it. The
benefits of Hamiltonian economics were no longer restricted
to an elite of the wise, the rich, and the well-born. Under
such conditions the austere principles of the agrarians no
longer had much popular appeal. The typical spokesman
of the new era was Henry Clay, who called himself a disciple of Jefferson but whose "American System" was a
democratic version of Hamiltonianism. With great personal
charm, stirring eloquence, and a complete lack of any
genuine sense of principle, Clay popularized the vision of
an America made rich and strong by federal subsidies
and distributions of privilege. As early as 1822 John Taylor
felt that the battle for economic independence was already lost. In a long diatribe against the protective tariff
he declared that, as a result of the property-transferring
program of the federal government, the whole country was
being "turned into one great factory," and its citizens were
"under a necessity of yielding up the profits of their labors
to a combination of legal capitalists." [8]

4

In the long run Taylor's predictions proved to be substantially correct. But the struggle was by no means ended.
On the contrary, the election of Andrew Jackson to the
Presidency in 1828 was followed by a return to agrarian
principles. Jackson and his followers fought for these principles with a much greater courage and consistency than
had been displayed by Jefferson; and as long as Jackson
himself remained in office his personal popularity with the
mass of the people made it possible to carry through a
program that offended every privileged group in the
country.

Jackson's election was due initially to political rather

[8] *Ibid., p. 207.*

than to economic factors. He reached the Presidency as the representative of the plain people. After generations of controversy public opinion had now accepted the doctrine of equal political rights for all, and the final victory of democracy came about so quietly that it has sometimes been overlooked. For like most political reforms it did not wholly fulfill either the hopes of its supporters or the even more extravagant fears of its opponents.

The new Western states that came into the Union after 1800 adopted universal manhood suffrage from the beginning. Starting with Maryland in 1810, the older states gradually followed suit, abolishing the property qualifications that had been established during the Revolution. During the 1820's there was a vast increase in the number of voters, caused not only by the extension of the franchise but also by the growth of popular interest in politics. The members of the electoral college began to be chosen by direct popular vote in each state and no longer by the state legislatures, as hitherto. And the choice of candidates for office, instead of being made by the members of Congress and of the state legislatures assembled in the party caucuses, was now assumed by popular conventions in which the rank and file of the party supporters were more adequately represented. More important than these technical changes was the growth of a new spirit. The plain people had come to believe that the mysteries of government should no longer be left to the richer and better-educated classes, and that any man from any social background might aspire to political leadership. They wanted an increase in the number of elective positions, rotation in office for public officials, and a new kind of man in control of the government.

Astute politicians who understood what was happening set out to manipulate and direct this popular sentiment; and in their search for a national leader they turned to Andrew Jackson. In the presidential elections of 1824 and 1828 there were few specific issues. The Federalist Party was now dead; all the candidates were Republicans, and all advocated similar programs. But the underlying question was whether the average citizens of America were qualified not only to vote but also to hold office. Jackson was defeated by John Quincy Adams in 1824, chiefly because popular election of the electoral college had not yet spread to a sufficient number of states. But he was triumphantly elected in 1828 as the embodiment of the new doctrine of political equality.

The surviving believers in the aristocratic principle no longer dared to denounce the principle of popular government, except in private; but they made amends by vilifying its exponents, with such success that even today it is not always easy to appraise them fairly. American history has never wholly lost a certain Federalist bias. Until recently it was customary to attribute all Jackson's policies to personal quarrels and antipathies and to political ambition, not to any coherent principles. Yet in accepting him as the symbol of their aspirations the plain people of America were following a sound instinct.

With little education and no intellectual interests, Jackson had in superlative degree those moral qualities of courage, tenacity, self-confidence, and personal loyalty that Americans have always most admired. His whole life was one long battle, on an epic scale, against obstacles that might have driven weaker men to suicide. Born on the borders of North and South Carolina of immigrant Scotch-Irish parents, he had fought and nearly died in the War of Independence while a boy of only thirteen. Before his fifteenth birthday all his immediate relatives were dead, and he was left, without resources, to make his own way in the world. Working as schoolteacher, saddler's apprentice, and lawyer's clerk, he was able to scrape together enough money to become a qualified lawyer, and then migrated to the frontier country of Tennessee. In this wild and lawless environment where a man could not survive unless he was quick with a gun, he soon rose to prominence. Tennessee's first Congressman and afterwards a Senator and a judge, he engaged in duels, could defend himself in rough-and-tumble fighting, and played for a few years the role of an ambitious landowner, trader, and land speculator. Meanwhile he had married a wife to whom he was most devotedly faithful for the rest of his life but who—through

a legal misunderstanding—was still technically the wife of
another man at the time Jackson married her. Henceforth
this unlucky complication was publicized by Jackson's opponents, with scandalous embellishments, whenever he ran
for office. Soon after the turn of the century he relinquished
his ambitions and settled down to the life of a cotton
planter, partly in order to spare his wife's feelings, partly
because his speculations had turned out unfortunately as
the result of the failure of a business firm and he was
heavily in debt. From this time on he was rarely solvent,
although he operated his plantation efficiently and industri-
ously, and was saved from total ruin only by breeding a
race horse that earned twenty thousand dollars in prize
money. In 1812 he emerged from his retirement, first to
lead the Tennessee militia against the Indians and, afterwards to defend New Orleans against a British invasion.
He had no training for military command; but unlike
most other militia officers, he could make himself obeyed
and could inspire his men with his own indefatigable determination and capacity for endurance. In the Battle of
New Orleans he won a crushingly decisive victory over
some of the most experienced troops in the British army.
Physically, he never recovered from his exertions during
these campaigns. His digestion was permanently ruined;
he had chronic headaches; he suffered from dropsy; and
he developed tuberculosis, which ate away one lung. But
he was now the most popular man in America. And his
amazing courage and strength of will enabled him not
merely to stay alive, but to serve for eight years as President and to reach the ripe old age of seventy-eight.

Taking office in his sixty-second year, at a time when
he was suffering not only from his physical maladies but
also from the recent death of his wife, he was not expected to be a vigorous President. Nor had his previous
statements indicated that he would follow any particular
line of policy. Yet although Jackson had never formulated
his political convictions in intellectual terms, he felt and
acted as an agrarian. His own experiences had taught him
the perils of speculation; and it had taught him also that in
a society dominated by the moneyed interests it was diffi-

cult for honest men engaged in productive labor to pay
their way. As he declared in his farewell address, he believed that the government should be administered for
the benefit of "the planter, the farmer, the mechanic and
the laborer" who "form the great body of the people of
the United States." These classes "all know that their success depends upon their own industry and economy, and
that they must not expect to become suddenly rich by
the fruits of their toil." Yet "they are in constant danger
of losing their fair influence in the Government" as a
result of "the power which the moneyed interest derives
from a paper currency, which they are able to control,
[and] from the multitude of corporations with exclusive
privileges which they have succeeded in obtaining in the
different states." [9] The main purpose of Jacksonianism, and
of the Democratic Party which took shape under Jackson's leadership, was to put an end to the exclusive privileges of the moneyed interest. The Jacksonian radicals believed in the maintenance of effective competition, and
argued that the growth of monopoly was due to grants of
special privilege by the government and not to genuinely
economic processes.

Jackson's most effective support came not from the agricultural sections but from the cities of the Northeast. Here
the growth of the factory system and the increase of manufacturing, banking, and internal-improvement corporations, often endowed by state charters with monopolistic
privileges, were causing wide resentment. In this section
the American ideal of a property owners' democracy was
already disappearing. A few intellectuals began to play with
the idea of a socialist Utopia; but the mass of the people
were not willing to abandon the hope of economic independence. They wanted more effective realization of the
ideal of equal rights for all, by means of such reforms as
free universal education, abolition of imprisonment for
debt, and prohibition of special privileges for corporations.
In such cities as New York there was an extraordinary

[9] *J. D. Richardson:* Messages and Papers of the Presidents,
Vol. IV, p. 1524.

proliferation of radical programs and political movements. In 1835, when conservatives tried to break up a radical meeting by turning off the lights and the radicals were able to proceed by striking matches, then known as "locofocos," a new word was added to American political terminology. Henceforth the radical of the Jacksonian era was known as a Locofoco. Locofocoism represented the struggle of the unprivileged to maintain the "general happy mediocrity" of agrarianism in a society increasingly dominated by moneyed and speculative interests. The principal spokesman of Locofocoism was the New York journalist, William Leggett. A disciple of Adam Smith and of John Taylor, Leggett ascribed the growth of inequality to interferences with the natural right of property by federal and state authorities, and declared that democracy could be maintained by narrowly limiting the powers of the government, by maintaining a regime of strict *laissez faire,* and by keeping the Western lands open for settlers and preventing them from becoming the property of wealthy speculators.

Jackson was aided by such fellow agrarians as Senator Benton of Missouri and Roger Taney of Maryland, and by a small group of personal advisors, mostly newspapermen, who became known as the "kitchen cabinet"; but his closest associate and chosen successor was Martin Van Buren of New York. Van Buren's political dexterity, his lack of frankness and preference for devious and diplomatic methods, and the sophisticated elegance of his personal tastes and way of living convinced most of his contemporaries that he must be thoroughly insincere. Americans have never found it easy to understand complex characters of this kind. Yet it was not merely by his gift for diplomacy that Van Buren won Jackson's affection. Judged not by his words but by his record, he was a consistently democratic statesman from his early attempts to abolish imprisonment for debt down to his last political action when he headed the antislavery Free Soil ticket in the election of 1848.

Viewed in broad terms, the economic program of the Jacksonians (which was never fully put into effect) was an attempt to maintain the ideal of a property owners' democracy, in general accord with the doctrines of John Taylor. Its guiding principle was that political power must not be used for the creation of economic privilege. On the one hand, the government must no longer give assistance to favored business corporations; on the other hand, the power to form a corporation, instead of being treated as a privilege with monopolistic implications (as in the case of the Charles River Bridge), should become a right equally available for all. Beginning with the Maysville veto of 1830, Jackson put a stop to the voting of federal money to internal improvement corporations; while his followers in the Northern states worked for the enactment of "free banking" and general incorporation laws, by which the formation of a bank or any other corporation would no longer require a special grant from the legislature. These laws would make it impossible for state governments to give favored business groups immunity from effective competition.

The major political battles of the Jacksonian era were fought about banking and the currency. Unlike their predecessors of the Revolutionary epoch, the Jacksonians believed that the producing classes, even when in debt, were not genuinely benefited by inflation, which raised prices and encouraged speculation; and they believed that control over the currency should belong to the government rather than to private banking interests. They wished to restrict the currency to gold and silver, to deprive the bankers of their power to issue notes that circulated as money, and to abolish the privileges that had been granted by federal charter to the Bank of the United States. The chief support for this program came from the urban workers, who were hard hit by rising prices, rather than from the Western farmers; but it had the full support of Jackson himself, who had fought against inflation in the state of Tennessee before he became President at a time when most of the farmers were clamoring for more bank paper. Jackson was an agrarian by conviction, not for political expediency.

During Jackson's second term he fought a long and bitter struggle with the Bank of the United States and with its president, Nicholas Biddle. From the capitalistic viewpoint the bank was a soundly managed institution that had discouraged inflation; but its policies benefited the business rather than the producing classes, while its power over the national economy and its corrupt connections with politicians and newspapers made it a threat to democratic government. Jackson succeeded in destroying the bank; but the government money that it had held was at first transferred to the state banks, which were less soundly managed and more inclined to resort to inflation, and this resulted in an increase in the circulation of paper. Jackson then attempted to drive bank paper out of circulation by issuing the Specie Circular of 1836, which declared that henceforth the government would receive only gold and silver, not bank notes, in payment for public land. During Van Buren's administration the divorce between the federal government and private banking was completed by the establishment of the Independent Treasury.

These measures were a heroic attempt to check the rising tide of capitalism and force the country back to an agrarian way of life. There could be little business expansion and few speculative profits without an expanding paper currency. But capitalism had already advanced too far to be overthrown, and the Specie Circular was followed by a sudden price deflation and a business depression. Jackson had been able to force through his program solely because of his personal popularity. By normal standards such measures as the Maysville veto and the Specie Circular would have meant his political suicide; he was fighting for economic democracy, but he was also frustrating the hope of speculative profits and the propensity for seeking government favors, with which a large part of the American people had already become infected. But while all the moneyed interests denounced him as a tyrant and an economic ignoramus, nothing could impair his hold over the mass of the electorate. But Van Buren, who succeeded Jackson in 1837, did not inherit Jackson's popularity; and when he resolutely adhered to agrarian principles through the depression and refused to give business any assistance, the ordinary voter began to turn against him.

Meanwhile the American party system was assuming a new form. While Jackson's supporters called themselves Democrats, his opponents organized themselves into the Whig Party. The Whigs, inheriting the Hamiltonian tradition, were for the most part the representatives of special privilege; they consisted of Northern moneyed interests, of some of the richer Southern planters, and of middle-class citizens who were not yet privileged but hoped to become so. Such Whig leaders as Daniel Webster preserved much of the old Federalist belief in a ruling class. But to the more clear-sighted Whig politicians it had now become obvious that no party that openly supported aristocratic principles could hope to win an election. New situations required new techniques; and candidates for public office must henceforth preach democracy even when they did not intend to practice it. The economics of Jacksonianism must be defeated by the adoption of its politics. This change of attitude was of great importance in the evolution of the American form of government.

The most astute of the Whig leaders was Thurlow Weed of New York. Since Weed always moved behind the scenes and never cared to hold any office himself, he has been almost forgotten by posterity; yet he was one of the key figures in American political history. The first fully developed specimen of the political boss, he taught the moneyed interests to use the techniques of democracy. By profession a newspaper editor, first at Rochester and afterwards at Albany, he devoted his life primarily to the arts of party management. Although he believed in Hamiltonian policies, his first concern was always the winning of elections; and when a policy failed to appeal to the voters, he preferred to repudiate it. He built a powerful political machine in New York, based on a skillful use of patronage and distribution of favors, which captured the state from the Jacksonians in 1838. And in 1840 he was largely responsible for the strategy that enabled the Whigs to win the Presidential election.

For this election the Whig politicians refused to nominate

any of the outstanding party leaders. Instead they picked a relatively obscure individual, General Harrison by name, who was in no way qualified for the Presidency but who could be presented to the voters as a Whig variant of Andrew Jackson. Harrison had won a battle over Indians twenty-nine years earlier, and was—as far as anybody knew—a man of simple and unassuming habits. The strategy of the Whigs was to ignore every important issue, and to argue that Harrison was more democratic and closer to the plain people than was Van Buren. They organized uproarious mass rallies and demonstrations at which thousands of persons sang songs praising the homely virtues attributed to General Harrison and ridiculing Van Buren's aristocratic tastes. These methods swept Harrison into the Presidency by an overwhelming majority.

The election was of little immediate importance. Harrison died a month after taking office; and his successor, John Tyler of Virginia, whom the Whigs had nominated for the Vice-Presidency in order to attract Southern votes, reverted to agrarian principles. Although Weed and his fellow technicians of the Whig Party repeated their 1840 victory in 1848, when they organized the nomination and election of General Zachary Taylor, the agrarian control over the federal government was not finally broken until 1861. Through the forties and fifties the moneyed interests gained some political advantages, but they won no decisive victory.

Yet in retrospect the campaign of 1840 appears as a landmark in American political history. In the first place, Weed and his associates had discovered that the best way to win an election was to nominate an obscure figure who could be recommended on the ground not of his talents, but of his identification with the plain people. Henceforth this technique was frequently employed by both parties, the result being a marked decline in the standards of the Presidency; after 1840, men of great ability became Presidents only by accident. And in the second place, the 1840 election meant that both parties had fully accepted democracy and were competing with each other for the votes of the plain people. In the future there were no obvious class differences between them, nor were there any clearly defined differences of principle. In the competition for votes the original lines of distinction became blurred, and each party acquired an almost unlimited flexibility. There were radical Whigs, like Horace Greeley, and Whigs who admired Thomas Jefferson, like Abraham Lincoln. Stephen Douglas, who was the real heir of Henry Clay in the advocacy of government aid for business, called himself a Democrat, and so did a number of the most aristocratic Southern planters. It was at this period that the American party system acquired that independence of economic and class divisions that all Europeans and many Americans have always found so anomalous and bewildering.

5

The economic results of Jacksonianism were transitory. The ultimate defeat of agrarianism was inevitable because not enough nineteenth-century Americans were genuinely willing to live by agrarian principles. The purpose of those principles was to maintain a society of freedom and democracy; but although the Americans believed in freedom and democracy as ideals, the austerity and self-discipline that agrarianism required were wholly contrary to the character of a pioneering people. In a country where the drive toward material success was so widespread and where every poor man hoped to become rich, it was impossible to maintain an economic program designed to prevent the making of speculative profits and the use of political influence to secure economic advantages. Men who were agrarians by conviction and not for expediency were rare, and those groups who denounced most loudly the special privileges of other people frequently abandoned agrarian principles when they saw an opportunity to win privileges for themselves. Congress would usually vote for Hamiltonian measures, such as a tariff or an internal-improvement bill, if a sufficiently large proportion of the electorate were included in the distribution of favors. In consequence the use of political power to secure economic advantages gradually revived during the forties and fifties, and became an established American practice after 1861.

The political developments of the Jacksonian era, on the other hand, had a lasting influence. Since 1840, in fact, there has been no fundamental change in American political mechanics. And as a result of the victory of democratic principles, and of the acceptance of that victory by the politicians of both parties, the American political system acquired certain unique characteristics, which have persisted down to the present day.

The chief feature of the American system has been the separation of the political parties from the economic and class interests that they represent. This is a phenomenon that cannot be clearly paralleled in any other country in the world. Among the European and Latin American peoples, parties have normally been the direct political embodiments of social classes. In England, for example, political conflicts since the first Reform Bill have been based first on the opposition between the landowning and the manufacturing interests and afterwards on the opposition between capital and labor, and most of the political spokesmen of these groups have been themselves economically identified with them. The average conservative politician of today is himself a company director; the average labor politician is a trade-union leader. In America there was a similar affiliation between politics and economics during the conflict between Federalism and Republicanism; Hamilton founded an industrial corporation, and Jefferson was a tobacco planter. But after the transformation of the Whig Party, under the guidance of men like Thurlow Weed, the parties began to develop into independent entities that no longer reflected class differences. It is true that some economic groups retained permanent party allegiances; after the Civil War, for example, the cotton planters were always Democratic while heavy industry was always Republican. But the parties themselves grew into organizations of professional politicians who lived by patronage and whose primary concern was not to serve some particular economic interest but to be elected into office.

Political theory, even in America, has always been dominated by European conceptions; and doctrinaires of all schools have always been baffled by the American party system. Insofar as it fails to conform to European standards, it has been regarded as a puzzling and reprehensible aberration. Parties, it is declared, ought to represent hostile principles and economic interests, and politicians ought to be motivated by higher considerations than a desire to support themselves by officeholding. Yet the American system was the product of a natural evolution; it came into existence because of the growth of democracy, and it acquired its special characteristics because they were appropriate to the needs and desires of the American people. In reality the American party system is an admirable mechanism of self-government. The greatest defects of the American form of government, if it is considered as an instrument of democracy, are to be found not in the party system but in the Constitution, with its division of responsibiltiy and its complicated machinery of checks and balances.

For more than a hundred years Americans have been in the habit of denouncing their politicians as greedy, unprincipled, and dishonest. Insofar as this practice serves to maintain a proper spirit of humility among the elected representatives of the sovereign people and prevents them from usurping dictatorial authority, it is not to be deplored. Yet many of the attacks on the American politician are due to a misunderstanding of his true function. The Constitution makers, distrusting democracy, tried to establish the rule of an elite; but America became democratic in spite of the Constitution. And in a democracy the ultimate decisions depend on the movements of public opinion. The duty of the politician in a democracy is not to guide and direct popular sentiment or to legislate in accordance with some program of his own but to interpret the will of his constituents and to carry it into effect. As the instrument of the electorate he must be a specialist in understanding popular sentiment, in weighing the relative strength of divergent opinions, and in working out compromises that will satisfy as many different groups as possible, always with the knowledge that the penalty for failure may be defeat at the next election. Such a task requires a flexibility and a bargaining capacity which are incompatible with rigid principles and convictions; but nobody who genuinely believes that men in the mass are capable of self-government can regard it as ignoble. It is undeniable that the American politician frequently develops certain occupational weaknesses: that he responds too readily to pressure from organized minorities and that he is too often inclined to appeal for votes by demagogic slogans and appeals to mass prejudice. But judged by his fidelity to his constituents, he has not performed so badly as his detractors have insisted. When errors have been made it is usually the electorate that is responsible, although the politician, as the whipping boy of the sovereign people, must usually take the blame.

Two rival parties are essential to good democratic government. Government under a one-party system is always inefficient and always undemocratic. But when both parties are competing for the votes of the same body of citizens, it is unnecessary that they represent hostile principles of government or rival economic interests. One of the great merits of the American system is the flexibility with which each party can change its principles in accordance with changes in the sentiments of the electorate. In this manner government always represents the wishes of the majority; political conflicts never become irreconcilable; and since a minority party can always hope to win a majority if it interprets the popular will more accurately than its rivals, the rule of the people is maintained by constant and effective competition. And to the extent that the party system loses this necessary flexibility, it ceases to ensure effective government. The politician who sticks to the same set of dogmas in defiance of his constituents and the voter who always votes for the same party ticket without regard for the qualifications of the party nominees are violating the spirit of American democracy. This kind of rigidity is encouraged by the tendency to interpret the American form of government in European terms instead of recognizing it as a unique creation serving the needs of a democratic people.

The special features of the American system are exemplified most fully in the office of the Presidency. This is a unique position which should not be identified with that of a European prime minister, who is chiefly the leader of a party. Perhaps the closest historic parallel to the American Presidency is to be found in popular monarchy as it was exemplified by the English Tudors or by Henry of Navarre. Since the election of 1840 there have been few great Presidents; but the qualities required in a democratic President are so unusual that it is doubtful whether any alternative method of selection would have produced better results. The President is primarily the representative of all the people; he needs above everything to be skilled in interpreting popular sentiment and experienced in the ways of politics and to have an infinite flexibility. A man of the greatest ability who lacks the political sense or whose principles are too rigid will certainly be an unsuccessful President. To be great a President needs also to have imagination and courage; but how far any particular individual will develop these qualities can rarely be predicted in advance. The greatest of the Presidents was an obscure Illinois politician who had had no previous executive experience and had never previously shown any unusual ability. But being himself one of the plain people, Lincoln understood what they wanted; and when he became President he set out single-mindedly to make himself their servant. When he believed that the people were willing to support action, he showed imagination in translating their wishes into a specific program and courage in fighting for it; but he never regarded himself as wiser than his constituents. Denounced as a dictator by some and as dilatory, compromising, and unprincipled by others, he was guided at all times by his mystical self-identification with the average citizens of America and his belief that as President of all the people he was not an independent agent but merely the instrument of the general will. Without this kind of humility no President can achieve greatness.

Critics of the American form of government, both conservative and radical, are usually motivated by a desire to put into effect some particular program which they believe to be beneficial to the mass of the people but which may be contrary to their wishes. They denounce the typical politician, who regards himself as the delegate of his constituents, and call him timid and dishonest; but they are really betraying a lack of confidence in democracy. For under the American form of government it is usually the people and not the politicians who are responsible for major errors. When the government is so responsive to mass sentiment, there can be no substitute for popular vigilance and enlightenment. The worst feature of American politics has been the power of organized minorities, particularly when supported by money, to secure legislation contrary to the public interest. But what enables a minority to get what it wants is the apathy of the average voter and his habit of voting blindly for the nominees of the party to which he chooses to belong. A Congressman cannot always be expected to resist the pressure of a minority group capable of deciding an election if he cannot count on the support of the majority of the voters irrespective of party labels.

The American government has now been democratic for more than a hundred years; yet democracy must still be considered as an experiment. Have the mass of the people sufficient wisdom to govern themselves without the guidance of an elite? In a society without an established church, without an aristocracy, and without any privileged caste of scholars or administrators, will the average citizen display the necessary political intelligence and the necessary moral capacity for self-sacrifice, and will he understand and remain loyal to those fundamental social principles upon which civilization is based? For a hundred years the critics of democracy, both conservative and radical, have been shuddering at the dangers of popular rule; and it is still too early to say confidently that they are wrong. For the most part the American people have decided correctly on major issues, and they have rarely erred in appraising the relative qualifications of the presidential candidates presented for their choice; and although they have also committed gross errors, they have usually tried afterwards to rectify them. But so long as they had an open frontier, an expanding economy, and no international problems, they did not require any remarkable wisdom in order to conduct their affairs successfully. The crucial, and still undecided, test of the American democratic principle did not begin until the twentieth century.

☆ ☆ ☆ ☆ ☆ ☆ ☆ ☆ ☆ ☆ ☆ ☆ ☆ ☆

CHAPTER VIII

THE CONQUEST
OF THE WEST

★ ★ ★ ★ ★ ★ ★ ★ ★ ★ ★ ★ ★ ★

MEANWHILE the migration into the West, which was the main substance of American history for nearly three centuries, had continued with a growing momentum. At the time of the Revolution the frontier line ran down the Appalachians, and only a few hunters and fur trappers had penetrated into the rich forest country on the farther side of the mountain ranges. The Americans had spent a century and a half in settling the coastal plain along the Atlantic. But after independence had been won, the conquest of the West began. During the next two generations the Americans moved into the basin of the Mississippi from the Great Lakes down to the Gulf of Mexico. By 1840 they had occupied an area of nearly seven hundred thousand square miles west of the mountains. Its population already amounted to nearly six and a half million.

From its source in Lake Itasca in Minnesota the Mississippi flows for twenty-five hundred miles before it reaches the Gulf, gathering tributaries from a region as large as half of Europe. Before the coming of the Americans much of this vast territory was unbroken forest, although in the West where the land began to slope upwards toward the Rockies there was open grassland. The French had been the first white people to explore the country, and a few French settlements had been founded during the eighteenth century. But mainly it had remained unconquered wilderness, inhabited only by a few tribes of nomadic Indians. With its rich soil, its varied mineral resources, and its broad waterways, it presented the Americans with opportunities unequaled in the whole of recorded history.

During the period of the Revolution a few pioneer families established themselves in the forests of Kentucky, fighting prolonged and bloody wars with the Indians. The great migration began after the War of Independence. During the 1780's men and women were driving pack horses and Conestoga wagons across the mountain ranges of Pennsylvania and through the Cumberland Gap in Virginia until they reached one of the tributaries of the Mississippi, where they built themselves boats and floated downstream into the Western wilderness. Others moved up into the Appalachian plateau itself—an isolated region where they quickly lost contact with the American life around them, so that social development became immobilized at the point at which it had first been settled; in the twentieth century its inhabitants were still living and thinking like the frontiersmen of a hundred years before. In this fashion Kentucky and Tennessee were settled. Ohio became safe for colonization after the Indians had been defeated in 1794, and the frontier line was then pushed steadily westward across Indiana and Illinois, provoking a second Indian war in 1811 and a third in 1832. In this region two streams of migration met and mingled, one from Massachusetts and Connecticut and the other from Virginia. To the south of Tennessee, in the regions along the Gulf, the Indians were crushed by Andrew Jackson during the War of 1812. This hot and fertile country was settled by farmers from Georgia and the Carolinas, some of whom brought with them Negro slaves and established plantations for the growing of cotton. By the 1830's the Mississippi had become a busy artery of commerce; every year thousands of flatboats loaded with Western flour and Southern cotton were floated downstream to the seaport of New Orleans, whence the boatmen returned up the river by steamship. The pioneer line had long since crossed the river into the prairies of Iowa and Missouri and the hill country of Arkansas.

Throughout this epic of expansion the ax and the rifle of the pioneer, by which the white man imposed his will upon the wilderness, were the symbols of civilization. A vast process of destruction was needed in order that the country might become habitable. The frontiersmen, with their extraordinary skill of hand and eye and their almost claustrophobic hatred of the ways of settled society, made their way through the forest in order to kill animals for food and fur. Some of them, like Daniel Boone of Kentucky, earned a permanent place in the memory of Americans. The first settlers, who were usually men of a shiftless and barbaric breed, burned away trees in order to make clearings where they could grow corn. Less restless and more purposeful citizens following in their footsteps expanded the clearings into farms and built houses instead of log cabins. As the population grew, the forest steadily receded; its wild life was massacred; and the Indians succumbed to the white man's liquor and diseases, or were ruthlessly pushed westward across the prairie. Riverside settlements, where men congregated for trade, grew into towns with churches and courthouses and central squares modeled on those of Massachusetts or Virginia. And with the advent of the aggressive merchant, lawyer and speculator and—in the South—of the slaveowning cotton planter, the pristine equality of the frontier began to disappear, and a more complex social organization gradually took shape.

The flow of migration was always largest after a period of business depression in the East. Yet it was something more positive than sheer economic need that drove the Americans into the West. Economic opportunities for the average man were diminishing in the Atlantic states; but there was little acute poverty, nor did the migrants belong, in general, to the wage-earning class. Young men and women turned to the West because it promised an escape from social discipline, because by growing up with a new country they could find wider opportunities and more easily achieve wealth and leadership, or simply in order to prove their strength and give significance to their lives. With the opening of the West the restlessness that had brought the first Americans across the Atlantic became a stronger and more widespread national characteristic. Pioneer families often moved every few years, becoming habitually rootless and nomadic as they followed the frontier line from Kentucky into Indiana and thence across the prairies of Illinois and Iowa. And it was by no means only the poorer and more ignorant of the Americans who responded to the magnetic attraction of the frontier. Travelers in Western forests would sometimes meet with literate and cultivated New England or Virginia families who were living in log cabins, raising their own food, and rearing children without benefit of civilization.

Although the federal government exercised a general supervision over the settlement of the West, the migration was a spontaneous movement of individuals; and they did not forfeit any of their political rights by leaving the seaboard regions. This was colonization on the ancient Greek model rather than on that of the European empires in that the colonists were not held in subordination by the states from which they had come. It had been decided during the period of the Confederation that the West should be gradually organized into new self-governing states which would be admitted into the Union on an equality with the original thirteen. The federal government controlled the sale of public land, requiring settlers to pay for legal titles of ownership (although there were always large numbers of squatters, who felt that access to unoccupied land was their natural right and saw no reason why they should pay for it). It regulated the government of a territory as long as it was too thinly inhabited to qualify for statehood. And it assumed responsibility for dealing with the Indians. But in spite of the fears of Eastern conservatives, who felt that the Westerners had become ignorant barbarians and could not be trusted with political power, it never attempted to hold the West in political subjection.

During the first settlement of a new area there was indeed a descent into barbarism, but this rarely lasted for more than a few years. The movement into the West was not merely a migration of individuals; it was also a migration of institutions. Almost all the pioneers were natives of

America, since there was little immigration from Europe between 1776 and 1840; and they brought with them the political habits that prevailed in the seaboard states. As soon as possible they would set up those institutions of self-government with which they were familiar, and would begin building schools and founding newspapers. The transplanting of the essential elements of American civilization into the Mississippi Valley region was often astonishingly rapid.

Yet the Mississippi Valley never became identical with the East. The Westerners were changed by their crossing of the Appalachians in somewhat the same fashion that their ancestors had been changed by the Atlantic passage. Spiritually, as well as geographically, they had come further from Europe. They had a stronger belief in political democracy and in equality of opportunity. They were also more individualistic and more self-assertive. They had less respect for established principles and traditions and for polished manners and cultural interests that served no obvious purpose, and were more inclined to judge everything in pragmatic terms. Vehemently nationalistic and owing allegiance to the Union as a whole rather than to any particular section, they loved to proclaim the greatness and the uniqueness of the United States. And although their patriotic boasting often seemed blatant and offensive, they had sound reasons for it. For the special virtues of the American way of life were more fully realized in the Mississippi Valley, particularly in the small towns of the Middle Western region where Negro slavery never penetrated, than in any other part of the country. Living among an abundance of natural resources and organizing their society on a basis of genuine democracy, the people of this region developed a neighborly kindliness, generosity, and sense of human equality that were peculiarly American. Middle Western society was organized for the benefit of the average man; and those with unusual talents and sensitivities sometimes found it oppressive. But the majority of its inhabitants had good reason for believing that the United States represented an attempt to create a new and higher mode of civilization.

During the period of the migrations, however, the most obvious characteristics of Mississippi Valley society were its exuberant animal vitality and its pride in its own growth. The plain citizens who crossed the Appalachians were engaged in one of the biggest enterprises in human history; they were conquering an empire and settling it with a rapidity that dazzled the imagination. The transformation, within two generations, of millions of acres of forest into farms, plantations, and cities was so unprecedented that it produced a kind of permanent spiritual intoxication. It is not surprising that the Westerner should have become uninhibited, loquacious, fond of magniloquent oratory, and accustomed to thinking in terms of the immense.

The Westerners loved to tell stories, and their wonder at their own achievements led them to create a new folklore in which the physical prowess of the frontiersman was celebrated and humorously exaggerated until it became mythical. The hero of the Western tall tale, like Mike Fink the Mississippi boatman, or David Crockett of Tennessee, was "half-horse, half-alligator, and a little touched with the snapping-turtle"; and he could perform the most extraordinary feats of strength and skill, often with an element of callousness or even of wanton cruelty in them. As his legend expanded he was gradually elevated into the role of a demigod and attributed with supernatural powers. Mike Fink could "out-run, out-jump, out-shoot, out-brag, out-drink, an' out-fight, rough-an'-tumble, no holts barred, any man on both sides the river from Pittsburg to New Orleans an' back ag'in to St. Louiee." [1] In later stories of Fink, Crockett, and other Western heroes, they could swallow thunderbolts and ride on streaks of lightning. This Western humor of overstatement, beginning in oral storytelling and developing into journalism, became an American tradition. Out of it developed a prose style, with colloquial rhythms and vocabulary and a fidelity to American emotions and concrete American experience, that deviated sharply from English models and that was

[1] *B. A. Botkin:* A Treasury of American Folklore (*1944*), p. 57.

afterward (as in the speeches of Abraham Lincoln and
the novels of Mark Twain) refined into literature.

During the middle decades of the nineteenth century the
Mississippi was indeed an amazing spectacle. The steam-
boats that ran for two thousand miles from New Orleans
to St. Louis and up into the prairie country of Iowa and
Illinois carried a great variety of human types; and what
was common to all of them was their exuberant self-confidence and their freedom from external restraints. Their
manners were crude, and their appetites were frequently
gross; they included an abnormally large proportion of
gamblers, swindlers, and charlatans; but they rarely lost
their gusto for living or their sense of humor. Ambitious
business entrepreneurs and land speculators, loud-voiced
political orators, itinerant troupes of actors and vaudeville
performers, Methodist and Baptist evangelists threatening
sinners with the pains of hell, preachers of strange new
religions, medicine vendors promising miraculous cures,
fraudulent real-estate promoters, professional pickpockets
and confidence men, along with travelers from Europe taking notes on the strange ways of American democracy—all
these passed up and down the great river, mingling with the
farmers of the prairies, the planters and their Negroes
from the cotton states, and the French-speaking merchants
of New Orleans. Western life often horrified European observers by its lack of discipline and social refinement; but
it had an epic quality although it never found its Homer.

Yet this Western exuberance, reckless and extravagant
as it so often appeared, was never wholly unchecked; and
as society became more settled the restraints upon it grew
stronger. From the beginning the principal restraining influence appears to have been that of the women. One of
the most conspicuous characteristics of American life noted
by all foreign observers was that women were becoming
more independent and more influential than in any other
country in the world. Sharing equally in all the labors and
dangers of pioneering, in addition to breeding the enormous
families that had become customary in all parts of America,
and frequently living in communities where their value
was enhanced by scarcity, they no longer had the pro-

tected, sheltered, and subordinate status of their European cousins. They were able to develop their own potentialities for initiative and leadership. And it is the consensus of opinion that they used their power to impose discipline, standards of refinement, and a strict morality, and to curb the more lawless and unruly proclivities of the male. Europeans frequently praised them highly. Tocqueville marveled at their competence and their self-assurance, and declared that the prosperity and strength of American civilization were due primarily to the superiority of its women.[2] The American male, on the other hand, while submitting to the standards of order that the women imposed and accepting them as right and necessary, was inclined at the same time to resent these restrictions upon his masculine freedom. He could sympathize with Mark Twain's Huckleberry Finn when he decided "to light out for the territory ahead of the rest, because Aunt Sally she's going to adopt me and sivilize me, and I can't stand it. I been there before." A novelist of a later generation, in revolt against a civilization dominated by Aunt Sally's, declared that they "had broken the moral back of a race and made a nursery out of a continent." [3]

To the influence of women was added that of the Protestant churches. The original irreligion of the frontier did not endure. Evangelists soon went to work in the Mississippi Valley and made it the most religious part of America. The inhabitants of the Valley responded quickly to the more emotional forms of religious appeal, of the type that had originated with the Great Awakening and been systematized by Jonathan Edwards, and the power of the churches was established through a series of violent and hysterical revivals. Western religion was similar to that of the New England Puritans and the Southern Scotch-Irish, but there was less interest in doctrine and in the higher forms of spiritual experience and more emphasis on practical results. It was essentially an instrument for imposing

---

[2] A. de Tocqueville, Democracy in America, *Vol. II, Third Book, Chapter XII.*
[3] *F. Scott Fitzgerald:* Tender is the Night, *Part II, Chap. 23.*

social order and discipline. The churches in this region were, for example, always in the fore-front of the movement for prohibiting the consumption of alcohol.

As civilization developed, moreover, a more complex social structure took shape, and the West became less free and less egalitarian. As everywhere in America, the sentiment of equality was the product of frontier conditions and of an abundance of natural resources; it was never fully safeguarded by institutions. And while frontier life was neighborly and co-operative, it was also individualistic. The man of strong will and driving ambition could attain power and transmit social prestige to his children; the weak, the improvident, and the unlucky suffered defeat. Men's fortunes depended primarily on their natural qualities, not on inheritance; and as long as the country was not fully settled and the frontier remained open, opportunities were abundant. But there was always a trend toward the growth of social distinctions, based mainly on monetary standards; and this grew stronger after the Civil War when the simple agrarian life of the early West began to give place to industrialism. A kind of natural aristocracy soon came into existence, composed mainly of those who deserved to take the lead by virtue of superior energy and practical intelligence, although it also included shrewd men of business who made fortunes, sometimes fraudulently, by moneylending, land speculation, or preemption of natural resources. At the bottom of the social scale in many Valley communities were squatter families, frequently suffering from malaria or some deficiency disease, who continued to live like animals in tiny cabins and to cultivate plots of ground to which they had no legal title. Class lines always remained fairly fluid and never destroyed that basic sense of the dignity of every individual that was the spiritual foundation of American democracy; but as time went on, social distinctions became more noticeable. An individual's ancestry, his occupation, his church, his social affiliations, his political opinions, and the location of his home all became indexes for defining his status in the community.

With the growth of social and economic complexity the

political attitudes of the Mississippi Valley gradually turned away from their original agrarianism and became more Hamiltonian. In the 1830's the West was permeated with the doctrines of Jacksonian democracy. As an agricultural and a debtor section it wished to protect the property rights of the farmer and to restrict those property rights derived from contractual obligations. Western states passed laws making the farmer's homestead immune from seizure on account of debt claims; they endeavored to protect the actual occupants of the land, even when they were squatters, in preference to wealthy land speculators, and to change the public-land system in order to safeguard squatters' rights; and after unfortunate experiences with paper money they limited the right to establish banks or prohibited banks altogether. Yet the West never accepted the doctrines of Virginia agrarianism completely; its attitude was always pragmatic and not based on consistent principle. Needing access to markets, it wanted a strong federal government that would subsidize the building of roads, canals, and other internal improvements, and was never concerned about the dangers inherent in such a use of political power to bestow economic privilege. As the section grew more prosperous and the influence of wealthy business men became stronger, it became more willing to support other Hamiltonian measures. In the 1850's the slavery issue changed the political allegiance of the upper Mississippi Valley, which became henceforth a stronghold of the Republican Party. It continued to believe in democracy and in the ideal of a society of property owners; but its typical spokesmen (like Abraham Lincoln) saw no incompatibility between such an ideal and a program of government protection for the obligations of contracts and government aid for business expansion.

2

To the west of the valley of the Mississippi the land sloped upward into the region of the Great Plains, beyond which lay the Rocky Mountains. Almost all this country suffered from a scarcity of water, and as late as the 1830's

much of it was known as the Great American Desert and
regarded as unfit for white settlement. Men believed that
in Iowa and Missouri the frontier had come close to its
appropriate limits, and that the Far West should be left in
perpetuity for the buffalo and the Indian. Yet during the
next decade the insatiable restlessness and land hunger of
the American brought about new conquests, and the pioneer caravans headed for the Pacific coast.

The mountains of the West were first explored by fur
trappers working for commercial companies with headquarters in Missouri. During the 1820's and 1830's men
like Jim Bridger, Jedediah Smith, Kit Carson, and John
Colter were wandering to and fro across the deserts and
over the Rockies, opening trails and often spending months
in complete solitude. These "mountain men" served as
guides for the military expeditions, sent out by the federal
government and headed by men like John C. Fremont,
that mapped the country and reported on its economic
resources. Meanwhile traders opened a caravan route across
the plains from Missouri to Santa Fe, New Mexico. The
explorations ended the belief that the West was uninhabitable. Much of it was not yet United States territory.
The Southwest officially belonged to Mexico, and the far
Northwest was under joint American and British control.
But the nationalistic Americans of the Mississippi Valley
began to speak of the "manifest destiny" of the United
States to control the entire continent and to dream of
expansion to the western ocean.

It was in the 1840's that the drive of the pioneers reached
its zenith. Several years of economic depression were followed by an even more insistent revival of the urge to
migrate. For Americans Utopia has always lain a little
beyond the horizon, and men who had not found it in
the Mississippi Valley, and whose optimism was still unconquered, turned again toward the setting sun. But now
they were no longer content merely to move on into the
next belt of unoccupied territory. Instead of settling the
Great Plains, they set out to cross the two thousand miles
of mountain and desert to the coast of the Pacific.

Every spring through the 1840's the pioneer caravans

gathered at Independence, Missouri, for the march into the West. Like all the American migrations, this was a movement of plain citizens, many of them mature men and women accompanied by children; and since the equipment and supplies for the journey cost up to a thousand dollars, they were by no means of the poorest class. They usually traveled in covered wagons—singularly graceful vehicles, shaped like ships on wheels, roofed with white canvas for protection against the weather, and drawn by oxen. At Independence they organized themselves into parties and elected leaders. And through the summer and autumn they were driving their ox teams up into the Great Plains, over the passes of the Rockies, across the alkali deserts of Wyoming and Utah, and through the Pacific ranges. For six months and two thousand miles they were dependent entirely on their own resources.

Some parties met with utter disaster, like the Donner party in 1846 that failed to complete the crossing before the winter snows made the California mountains impassable. Caught by winter on the wrong side of the ranges, the majority of the party acquitted themselves as nobly as had the Plymouth Pilgrims in their similar plight two hundred and twenty-six years earlier; a few, on the other hand, lost every vestige of humanity and sank into cannabalism. Almost every party reached the Pacific hungry and ragged, leaving behind them across the prairies and the deserts a long trail of graves and ox-bones and abandoned wagons and possessions. Yet in spite of every catastrophe the Americans continued coming to the Pacific every year in larger numbers.

Most of the emigrants wanted to settle in the fertile coastal regions of California and Oregon. But there was one group that was looking for seclusion—the Church of the Latter-day Saints, popularly known as the Mormons. Mormonism was in many ways a characteristic expression of Mississippi Valley psychology during the pioneering period. With astonishing self-assurance Joseph Smith had found a profession for himself as an inspired prophet and had proceeded to invent a new religion in the same way that other plain citizens were starting new industrial enterprises or settling new territories. Extroverted, agile, and spiritually shallow, he was totally lacking in any genuine emotional insight and integrity; he was neither a mystic like Ann Lee nor a serious thinker like John Humphrey Noyes. But he had an infectious gaiety and zest for living. His religion was pieced together out of fragments of Puritan theology, which he reshaped to suit the optimistic and practical spirit of the time, made more colorful by the addition of a theatrical ritualism, and spiced—at least for the inner circle of male apostles—with sexual license. It was a creed for plain people, containing nothing beyond their comprehension and promising them, if they had industry and courage, Utopia in this world as well as heaven in the next. And it was remarkably well adapted to the ideas and aspirations of the unsophisticated Western Americans of the period. To the men of the Mississippi Valley it was by no means incredible that an ordinary contemporary American should be receiving new revelations from God, like the prophets of the Bible. Thousands of them were willing to suffer poverty, hunger, persecution, and possible death rather than abandon the faith that Smith had given them. But wherever the Mormons settled, whether in Ohio or in Missouri or in Illinois, they came into conflict with their Christian neighbors. In 1844 Smith was lynched, and his followers decided to go to a new country. Brigham Young became their new leader, and in 1847 he led them across the mountains to the shores of the Great Salt Lake in Utah. Here, in territory that earlier explorers had pronounced to be an uninhabitable desert in which no crop would ever grow, they began to build their Utopia. Disciplined by a sense of religious vocation and guided by a skillful and self-assured leader, the Mormons gradually won prosperity. Hard labor and artificial irrigation caused the desert to blossom astonishingly.

The migration into the Western territories made it inevitablé that they should become United States property, whether by negotiation or by war. It was easy to establish American sovereignty over Oregon by peaceful agreement with Great Britain. But the republic of Mexico, as the heir of the Spanish Empire, was the legal owner of California and of much of the Rocky Mountain region, although she had no effective control over them. Lacking the aggressiveness and acquisitiveness of the Americans and torn apart by internal social conflicts, the Mexicans had not colonized their northern territories and were unlikely ever to do so, but they were not willing to abandon their sovereignty over them. Americans had already moved into Texas, which also belonged to Mexico, and in 1836, disgusted by Mexican misgovernment, had successfully rebelled and declared themselves an independent republic. In 1845 Texas, at its own request, was admitted into the United States, after which Mexico broke off diplomatic relations in protest against what she regarded as an act of aggression. This was followed by a series of disputes and, in the following year, by war. President Polk found what he regarded as sufficient legal reasons for going to war, but his real motive was a desire to annex California. A native of Tennessee, he was a spokesman of Mississippi Valley nationalism and expansionism. American armies invaded Mexico and fought their way into its capital city, and in 1848 they dictated terms of peace. Mexico lost more than half of her total territory—a deprivation which she has never forgotten— and the United States acquired title to California and the other regions of the Southwest.

It is impossible to approve of the seizure of California. Yet it must be recognized as inevitable that the more vigorous and aggressive of the two races should take possession of it, and it is improbable that the Mexicans would ever have surrendered it voluntarily. The Americans cannot be called imperialistic since they had no desire to conquer and enslave a foreign race. They were merely assuming, in accordance with long-established frontier attitudes, that they had a right to occupy an empty and fertile territory, with or without legal title.

With the annexation of California the drive into the West, which had started at Jamestown and Plymouth more than two hundred years earlier, had reached its limits. Some Americans were already looking still farther into the west and were dreaming of an American hegemony over the Pacific Ocean. New England merchants had traded with

China since the 1790's. Regular diplomatic relations were established during the 1840's, and a decade later Perry forced the Japanese to take cognizance of the Western world. Through the middle years of the nineteenth century, whalers, traders, and missionaries were visiting the Pacific islands and preparing the way for American domination over the entire ocean. The two expansionist movements from Europe, which had carried some groups eastwards around Africa to India and the East Indies and others westwards into the continent of America, were now beginning to meet each other. But this American conquest of the Pacific, whenever it should occur, would be different in character from the conquest of the continent. It would be accomplished by military, diplomatic, and commercial methods, and not by the spontaneous migrations of individuals.

Meanwhile there were still vast empty spaces in America to be occupied, and the process of expansion was not completed for another half-century. Hitherto men had come West in search of land for agriculture. But in 1848 the pioneers found a new motive. Gold was discovered in California. The result was a sudden mad rush of adventurers from all over the country, which increased the population of the state by more than three hundred thousand in ten years. Covered wagons rolled over the trails across the Rockies by tens of thousands, while other gold seekers took ship around Cape Horn or came by way of Panama. Very few of them emerged any richer than when they started; the profits from the gold rush went chiefly to the storekeepers and the owners of saloons and gambling houses in San Francisco and in the mining camps. As so often in America, adventurers and dreamers opened up the country; but it was the cautious and hard-headed businessmen who eventually became the masters of it. Yet once the hope of sudden wealth had been stimulated, it was not easily abandoned. For several decades after the first rush to California optimistic prospectors were wandering over the Western mountains in quest of gold and silver, and there was a whole series of similar movements when precious metals were discovered successively in Colorado, in Nevada, in Arizona, in Idaho, and in Dakota.

The miners were too migratory to establish a settled society. When gold or silver was discovered, a mining town would grow within a few months, fully equipped with stores, theaters, saloons, and brothels; and a few years later when the mines were becoming less productive most of the population would move elsewhere. With its extravagant hopes and unrestrained individualism and its lack of any established habits of law and order, the mining town during a boom period represented the most extreme expression of one aspect of American development. But the miners were the first men to open up large areas of the mountain country. And some of the mines, after being taken over by business corporations capable of installing proper equipment, became permanent sources of profit.

A similar individualism and exuberance characterized the life of the cattlemen, who were the first to take possession of another region of the West. The Great Plains, on the eastern side of the Rockies, provided excellent grazing, and during the 1860's the raising of cattle became a profitable occupation. The two decades following the Civil War were the period of the open range when vast herds of cattle could move freely over an immense area stretching across the breadth of the United States. The Chisholm Trail, along which hundreds of thousands of cattle were driven in a year, ran from Texas into Montana. The cowboys who accompanied them acquired their costume, and their way of life from the *vaqueros* of northern Mexico; and like the Gauchos of Argentina of an earlier generation, they left behind them the memory of a peculiar gallantry and virility, and of a talent for melody and folk ballads, which made them one of the most romantic elements in the American tradition. But the cattlemen's frontier lasted for a mere twenty years. In the 1880's the herds were decimated by severe winters; and the Great Plains began to be transformed into private ranches and farm properties guarded from encroaching animals by barbed wire.

Meanwhile the railroad had come to the West. The first

transcontinental line was completed in 1869, and four others were in operation before the end of the century. And with the railroads came hundreds of thousands of farmers who settled wherever the land seemed fertile, in addition to ploughing up, in the Great Plains and elsewhere, large areas that should have been left to grass. Immigrants from Europe were now pouring into the United States, and much of the farm land both in the Middle West and in the areas west of the Mississippi was occupied by Germans and Scandinavians. As always, the establishment of civilization was accompanied by a vast process of destruction. After several decades of bitter and bloody warfare the surviving Indians of the West were gathered into reservations and compelled to submit to white control. And the immense herds of buffaloes, originally numbering millions, were slaughtered so wantonly and so persistently that the animal soon became almost extinct.

Thus the free and adventurous life of the early West continued only for a few decades. Before the end of the nineteenth century almost every part of the country had been settled, and the frontier line had ceased to exist. Law and order and all the institutions of a settled society had been established over the whole area of the United States. And although Western life retained much of the sense of spaciousness and of unlimited opportunity it had acquired during the process of settlement, the economic pattern imposed upon it was not that of eighteenth-century agrarianism but that of the new big business society that had developed in the Northeast.

The completion of the conquest of the continent marked the end of an epoch in American history. There was still vacant land in the West; and there was still a tendency for the population to move westwards. But agriculture was no longer a profitable or attractive occupation. The glamor and the big rewards were now to be found elsewhere. The men of strong will and driving ambition were now imposing their mastery not merely upon the wilderness but also upon other human beings; and the ambitious and the discontented were drawn not to the frontier but to the cities. Henceforth the children of the pioneers must face new tasks of a different nature and a much greater complexity.

CHAPTER IX

THE AGRARIAN MIND

★ ★ ★ ★ ★ ★ ★ ★ ★ ★ ★ ★ ★ ★ ★

DURING THE TWENTY-FIVE YEARS preceding the Civil War all the tendencies implicit in American civilization came to a kind of culmination. Political democracy had triumphed; and in spite of the advance of capitalism, a "general equality of condition" was still (as Tocqueville declared in 1835) the "primary fact" about the Americans. Men in America, he declared, were "on a greater equality in point of fortune and intellect, or, in other words, more equal in their strength, than in any other country in the world, or in any age of which history has preserved the remembrance." [1] The pioneering energy that conquered the West was at its zenith. The growing sectional conflict had not yet reached the point of crisis. Everywhere there was an extraordinary sense of exhilaration; in the American world the wildest ambitions and the most impossible ideals seemed capable of fulfillment. The country abounded in Utopian experiments, in new religions, and new social philosophies promising the millennium. Some of the manifestations of America's self-confidence were crude and unlovely; as foreign visitors discovered, there was too much nationalistic boasting and too much insistence on the backwardness of Europe. But faith in the American experiment could also stimulate men of finer grain. This was a period of vital and profoundly American literature.

The civilization of the United States has never been

---

[1] *A. de Tocqueville:* Democracy in America, *Vol. I, Introduction and Chapter III.*

very friendly to purely æsthetic activity. Emphasizing quantity rather than quality, and measuring achievement too often in commercial terms, it has attributed little value to those subtle intellectual creations beyond the grasp of the average man. Moreover, the spirit of the country has always encouraged a versatility and an adaptability which are incompatible with the highest professional attainments. Tocqueville pointed out that "if the American be less perfect in each craft than the European, at least there is scarcely any trade with which he is utterly unacquainted. His capacity is more general, and the circle of his intelligence is enlarged." [2] In spite of these impediments great writers have appeared in America, although they have failed to find the encouragement and the critical understanding needed for the full development of their powers, so that none of them has ever grown into that happy and productive maturity that has been possible for the greatest of the Europeans.

Yet although the American writers of the 1840's and 1850's found themselves in an unsympathetic environment, they were themselves a part of that environment; unlike some of their successors, they did not attempt to repudiate it. They shared the general confidence in the unlimited potentialities of democracy. They used American imagery, adopted American themes, and thought in American terms. More deeply, they explored and interpreted the hidden psychic tendencies pervading the society that had produced them. Their ability to objectify these tendencies in symbolic terms is what makes them perennially significant.

The greatest art is always symbolic in that its imagery is a reflection of profound emotions that cannot be wholly comprehended by means of intellectual formulas. Symbolism is very different from allegory, which is a deliberate and conscious manipulation of images in order to illustrate some intellectual doctrine or idea. The symbolic artist explores, and gives expression to, deep psychic forces within himself, embodying them in images that are their objective correlatives. And insofar as he is a representative product

[2] *Ibid., Vol. I, Chap. XVII.*

of a particular society and is sensitive to its psychic tendencies and attitudes, his work will enlarge our understanding of that society. The writer who devotes himself wholly to the symbolic expression of his emotions and ignores society may, in fact, give us a much more significant revelation of social forces, on a much deeper psychic level, than is provided by those realistic writers who deliberately set out to describe and interpret the society of their time. The important American writers of the pre-Civil War period, particularly Melville, wrote symbolically, and not realistically, without conscious awareness of the social implications of their work. But since they were deeply American, in the quality of their emotional experience as well as in their conscious beliefs, their work had a profound social significance. They gave expression to attitudes that were true not only of themselves but of all Americans.

By liberating men from social restraints and encouraging them to seek the fulfillment of their desires and ideals through the conquest of the wilderness, the civilization of America had produced contradictory tendencies. The hope that had gradually taken shape in America was that of a society characterized by a universal freedom and equality in which all men could live without frustration and without fear. But this hope could not be realized unless it permeated men's minds and guided their actions with the compulsive power of a religion. Americans must not only talk democracy; they must feel and act as democrats. But meanwhile individual Americans had acquired an energy and confidence of the will that too often resulted in an unrestrained drive towards domination and exploitation, in spiritual as well as in material things. And in proportion as they acquired power and privilege, they were inclined to repudiate American ideals and to turn back to the European doctrines of order, authority, and class hierarchy. If the democratic hope was to be realized, then the Americans, as individuals, must feel a spontaneous loyalty toward it and must be willing to act freely in harmony with it. But how was this loyalty to be developed? Did men become more willing to recognize the rights of others and more devoted to ideal values in proportion as they achieved moral freedom and a fuller self-realization, or was it always necessary to maintain some kind of external moral authority? Were men, in other words, good by nature or only as a result of social discipline? This was the fundamental dilemma of American civilization and the central theme of its literature.

What was lacking in America was any deeply felt sense of a social order to which the individual regarded himself as subordinate and through which he could achieve self-realization. Europeans had always believed in some kind of ideal harmony, implicit in society and realized in the cosmos, which gave meaning and significance to the lives of individuals and upon which moral values and standards depended. This notion of an organic social order has assumed very different manifestations, reactionary, liberal, and revolutionary; but it has always been an element in the European mind. It appears in the conservative belief in social hierarchy, in the liberal doctrine of natural law, and in the Marxist philosophy of a dialectical progress towards a kingdom of freedom. But the Americans had no such sense. The struggle between man and his environment, rather than the interrelationship of man and the social order, was the primary American situation. And as long as the necessity of struggle was the paramount factor, men were inclined to think in terms of personal failure or success; and the individual, lacking the sense of belonging to an order larger than himself, was likely to feel isolated and alone.

The European novel during the nineteenth century was largely concerned with sociological analysis. Society was portrayed on a broad canvas, and individual characters were presented as specimens of social classes and types. The central theme was usually the struggle of a young man to establish himself in the social organism, often through a process of successful climbing culminating in a good marriage. Novelists displayed varying attitudes toward the values of bourgeois society, but they rarely suggested that it was possible for individuals to repudiate them. The heroes of American fiction, on the other hand, have mostly been divorced from all social ties and obligations except those of loyalty to personal friends and comrades. Of obscure origin and background, they have represented the ideal of a natural virtue and integrity which owed nothing to external discipline and indoctrination and would, in fact, be endangered by social pressure. American novelists have been relatively uninterested in describing and analyzing social types, and have generally regarded organized society as corrupt or oppressive, so that the hero can preserve his virtue only by rebellion or escape. Man can achieve integrity not through membership in the community but by asserting himself against it. And since marriage normally means the acceptance of social responsibilities, it has often been presented in American fiction not as a consummation but as a trap, any happy sexual fulfilment being usually extra-marital. Early American writers, in fact, displayed remarkably little interest in normal love. Except in the novels of Hawthorne, sexual emotion is either non-existent (as in Emerson and Thoreau) or presented in decidedly morbid forms (as in Poe and Melville, and probably in Whitman).

This view of life, which was derived from the whole pioneering and frontier experience, may be regarded as a kind of American myth, and can be traced in both the popular and the serious literature of America. On a relatively superficial level, it was first fully expressed in the Leatherstocking novels of Fenimore Cooper. Cooper's frontiersman, with his isolated life, his innate sense of justice, his loyalty to his Indian comrades, and his claustrophobic compulsion to escape from an expanding civilization, established a pattern that has largely permeated the American literature of popular entertainment. A long series of heroes have exhibited a primeval independence by protecting their friends and doing battle for a justice that was not supported by social institutions. The theme has been exemplified in the dime novels about frontier life that were written in the later nineteenth century, in Owen Wister's *Virginian* and other cowboy novels, and in the "tough" detective stories of Dashiell Hammett and Raymond Chandler. More serious writers, on the other hand, while accepting the same dichotomy between natural virtue and social corruption, have been unable to regard it optimistically. If the individual can preserve his integrity only by rebellion or flight, he is doomed in the end to be defeated. This is the reason for the pessimism of Melville, of Mark Twain, and of a long series of twentieth-century novelists.

Sooner or later, if the American world was to fulfill its promise, Americans must regain the sense of a social order, but in terms appropriate to the democratic ideal and not borrowed from Europe; and they must develop a deeper emotional allegiance to democratic values and standards of behavior. The necessity did not become urgent until the conquest of the continent had been completed, although John Taylor and the Virginia agrarians had attempted it prematurely on the relatively superficial level of political and economic theory at the beginning of the nineteenth century. On a deeper spiritual level the same problem was faced by the American writers of the forties and fifties. And being concerned not with the analysis of a society, but with the most elemental problems of man's place in the universe, some of them went more deeply into the human situation than any of their European contemporaries except the Russians, in spite of their lack of breadth and variety. As D. H. Lawrence said, they reached a verge.

2

The writing of imaginative literature began to be regarded as a serious profession, for the first time in the history of the United States, by certain natives of New York early in the nineteenth century. But the best of the New Yorkers were not more than tellers of stories, although Washington Irving told them gracefully and Fenimore Cooper with a broad sweep and a masculine verve and vigor. The more important American literature originated a generation later, and all of it (except the work of Poe) was directly or indirectly a product of New England. In spite of the emotional inhibitions and rigid self-control it encouraged, the Puritan tradition could stimulate the imagination, although creativity could not have free play as long as the Calvinist dogmas were accepted as literally true. Puritanism had established among the New Englanders a respect for intellectual labor and a concern for spiritual problems such as were absent elsewhere in America. It had also given them the habit of regarding material things as signs and tokens filled with religious meanings; and it had inculcated a complex of attitudes that were not merely in harmony with the American spirit but were, in a sense, the quintessence of it, and by means of which the varied impulses and aspirations of the American world could be brought to a focus. When the New England mind turned to literature, therefore, its products were likely to be serious, symbolistic, and deeply American.

The so-called flowering of New England was restricted to the area in eastern Massachusetts that had adopted Unitarianism. But although Unitarianism had destroyed the authority of Calvinist dogma, it was itself an arid and illiberal creed. The poetic and radical idealism of its greatest leaders, William Ellery Channing and Theodore Parker, was by no means shared by their contemporaries. More typical of the Unitarian spirit were such men as Andrews Norton, who clung to the authority of the Bible, regarded any kind of spiritual emotion with suspicion, and considered obedience to a moral code to be the essence of religion. Unitarianism was the religion of the rich and respectable; it offered little encouragement to men of inquiring temperament.

The initial impetus toward bolder ways of thinking came from outside. During the 1810's and 1820's New Englanders with intellectual inclinations began to visit Europe and to discover the European writers of the romanticist period. Some of them studied the German philosophers and their English interpretors, such as Coleridge and Carlyle; and from these sources they derived ideas that encouraged them to revolt against the pale negations of the Unitarian creed. They learned in particular that man could apprehend religious and moral truths directly and intuitively and did not need to be guided by any external authority. This doctrine became the main principle of the transcendentalist movement, which began during the 1830's and of which Emerson was the leading spokesman.

But although the immediate stimulus that led to transcendentalism was European, that philosophy itself was essentially a revival of certain elements in the Puritan tradition that had been suppressed by Unitarianism. The early Puritans had believed that man could know truth by direct revelation, although they had also believed that this revelation was the gift of God and that it was confined to the elect. Jonathan Edwards had spoken of "a divine and supernatural light immediately imparted to the soul." And Puritan heretics, such as Mrs. Hutchinson in the 1630's and the radical sects after the Great Awakening, had declared that when men were enlightened by God, they need not obey authority. The transcendentalists inherited this Puritan attitude, and added to it a confidence in human nature and a denial of original sin which they derived from the democratic and optimistic spirit of nineteenth-century America. Emersonianism was Calvinism modified by the democratic belief in man's natural goodness.

Emerson left the Unitarian pulpit in 1832 and settled for the remainder of his life at Concord as a kind of lay preacher to the universe. Since childhood he had lived a consecrated life; and he devoted himself to the tasks of intellectual exploration and leadership with the wholehearted seriousness and integrity with which his clerical ancestors had served their Calvinist God. He was a shrewd observer and an acute critic; he was capable of profound psychological insights; and he had a talent for phrasemaking that has rarely been equaled in English literature. But the discipline of his New England upbringing and the purity of his own nature prevented him from exploring the more ambiguous and sinister aspects of the human psyche and from facing all the possible implications of a doctrine of moral freedom. In consequence he did not sufficiently come to grips with the real problems of American life. His writings were important largely in that they reflected and crystallized the main intellectual tendencies of the American civilization of his time. Presenting in concentrated form the spiritual results of two centuries of developmer.t, they demonstrated both what had been accomplished and what was lacking. It was this that made them such a valuable point of departure for men of a younger generation. Emerson was a stimulating influence chiefly because he left his disciples dissatisfied.

The main burden of all Emerson's writings was confidence in the spiritual potentialities of human nature. "In all my lectures," he declared, "I have taught one doctrine, namely the infinitude of the private man." This was Calvinism without the belief in divine election; and it was also a mystical reinterpretation of the American faith in freedom and equality. Emerson believed that every individual had the truth within himself; and that in proportion as men learned a genuine self-reliance, then any restrictions upon their freedom would become unnecessary. "As the traveller who has lost his way throws his reins on his horse's neck and trusts to the instinct of the animal to find his road, so must we do with the divine animal who carries us through the world." He applauded the "gradual casting-off of material aids, and the growing trust in the private self-supplied powers of the individual," and looked forward to a society of free men in which order would be "maintained without artificial restraints as well as the solar system." "The appearance of character," he declared, "makes the state unnecessary. . . . He, who has the law-giver, may with safety not only neglect, but even contravene every written commandment." [3]

Such doctrines were a justification of the gradual dissolution of the European concepts of order, authority, and social hierarchy that had occurred in America. Emerson was urging his fellow citizens to assert the spiritual, as well as the political, independence of America, and to accept the full implications of the American faith. He was a liberating influence in that he stimulated men to abandon dogmas that had lost their meaning, and gave them courage to rely on themselves. "I unsettle all things," was his own boast. "No facts are to me sacred, none are profane; I

[3] Journals (1909–14). Vol. V. p. 380. Essays (reprinted in Riverside Library, 1929), Vol. II, pp. 31, 206, 210. Complete Works (1888–1893), Vol. I, p. 336.

simply experiment, an endless seeker with no Past at my back." [4]

But if all men relied on their own "self-supplied" powers without the guidance of dogmas or institutions, was there any guarantee that they would co-operate with each other in a democratic way of life? Would Emerson's self-reliant American display a necessary moral restraint, or would he be predatory and acquisitive? Emerson could denounce the commercialism and the materialistic ambitions of his contemporaries with a Hebraic severity. But although the difference between the self-reliance that was moral and spiritual and that which was predatory and acquisitive was clear enough in his own mind, he did not succeed in making it sufficiently clear in his philosophy; and with his deep-rooted American confidence in the individual and suspicion of authority, he was not willing to recognize that the individual cannot realize all his moral and spiritual potentialities unless he is aided by appropriate social institutions. He had a tendency to evade these problems by retreating into a mystical religiosity that had little relation to the real world. He displayed at times a naïve optimism as characteristic of the America of his time as was his democratic idealism.

God, he declared, was everywhere, and evil was an illusion that had no reality. To be truly self-reliant was to be "inspired by the Divine Soul which also inspires all men"; and the Divine Soul would not contradict itself. And since the universe was an expression of God, and God was moral, it followed that all things worked together for good. "An eternal beneficent necessity," he said, "is always bringing things right. . . . The league between virtue and nature engages all things to assume a hostile front to vice. The beautiful laws and substances of the world persecute and whip the traitor. He finds that all things are arranged for truth and benefit." For Emerson, as for his Puritan ancestors, this meant not only that virtue would be rewarded with success but also that success was a proof of virtue. "Success," he said, "consists in close ap-

[4] Essays, *Vol. I, p. 297.*

pliance to the laws of the world and since these laws are intellectual and moral, an intellectual and moral obedience. . . . Money . . . is, in its effects and laws, as beautiful as roses. Property keeps the accounts of the world and is always moral. The property will be found where the labor, the wisdom and the virtue have been in nations, in classes, and (the whole lifetime considered, with the compensations) in the individual also." [5]

In the agrarian America in which Emerson grew up such ideas had some plausibility. But self-reliant individuals were already building a new kind of America in which money was no longer as beautiful as roses. Emerson lived to see the corruption and the unrestrained acquisitiveness that followed the Civil War; and the spectacle profoundly disturbed him, although he was unable to recognize that the attitudes exemplified in his writings had helped to bring it about. "I see movements, I hear aspirations," he said in 1867, "but I see not how the great God prepares to satisfy the heart in the new order of things. No church, no state emerges; and when we have extricated ourselves from all the embarrassments of the social problem, the oracle does not yet emit any light on the mode of individual life. A thousand negatives it utters, clear and strong, on all sides; but the sacred affirmative it hides in the deepest abyss. . . . The gracious motions of the soul—piety, adoration—I do not find." Now that the old religions were dead, "we are alarmed in our solitude; we would gladly recall the life that so offended us. . . . Frightful is the solitude of the soul which is without God." In these words there was a note of despair, and Emerson's remedies did little to dispel it. "Heroic resolutions," he said were needed. "A new crop of geniuses" might be born who with "happy heart and a bias for theism" would "bring asceticism and duty and magnanimity into vogue again." God's communications with mankind were as yet intermittent, but later there might be "a broad and steady altar-flame." [6]

Emerson's most notable disciples were Thoreau and

[5] *Ibid., Vol. I, p. 111; Vol. II, p. 221.* Complete Works, *Vol. VI. p, 100; Vol. X, p. 189.*
[6] *Ibid., Vol. X, pp. 208, 218, 220, 221.*

Whitman. Each of them, in different ways, devoted his life to the problem Emerson had left unsolved: the problem of finding a harmony between individual self-reliance and the ideal of democracy. And each of them assumed, in accordance with their American faith, that such a harmony could be found if men were willing to carry their spiritual explorations to a sufficient depth.

Thoreau found an answer for himself, but his solution was too radical and required too heroic an austerity to become a model for others. Similar to Emerson in his general view of life, but spiritually of tougher grain with a more uncompromising conscience, he was determined to prove his self-reliance by living it. Completely unacquisitive, he believed that the most genuinely satisfying experiences were to be found in contemplation and in direct contact with the realities of nature; and he set out to discover a mode of existence that could give him what he most valued and that he could justify to his own conscience. He solved his problem by the drastic procedure of reducing his economic needs to an irreducible minimum and fulfilling them by the labor of his hands. Despising the new industrial society and regarding all government as intrinsically evil, he was a one-man secessionist from the American state. And this secession was genuine, as he proved when he helped fugitive slaves to escape and went to jail rather than pay a tax during the war with Mexico. In a sense he was the perfect agrarian, the most complete embodiment of the ideal American of the Virginians, cherishing his own moral and economic independence and refusing to exploit others. But although he found the best way of life for himself, as is demonstrated by the sustained note of mystical ecstasy that pervades his books and journals, he was not likely to be imitated by other Americans.

Whitman approached the problem from the other end, not by searching for an ideal way of life for the American individual and using it as a standard for the judgment of society, but by re-creating in his imagination the ideal American society and then reshaping himself into a model specimen of an American citizen. His early interests were chiefly political. As a young journalist he shared the radical enthusiasms of Jacksonianism and of the New York Locofocos, and acquired the agrarian belief in a property-owners' democracy. He declared in *Democratic Vistas* that "the true gravitation-hold of liberalism in the United States will be a more universal ownership of property," and that the stability of the country depended on "the safety and endurance of the aggregate of its middling property own-ers." But he felt that America required more than a demo-cratic politics and economics. Unless democracy "goes deeper, gets at least as firm and as warm a hold in men's hearts, emotions and beliefs as, in their days, feudalism or ecclesiasticism, and inaugurates its own perennial sources, welling from the centre forever, its strength will be defec-tive, its growth doubtful, and its main charm wanting." Americans must become democratic in spirit as well as in the external organization of their society. The influence of New England transcendentalism inspired him to set about creating an appropriate form of literature for democracy. "I was simmering and simmering," he declared; "it was Emerson brought me to boil." [7]

With his defective taste, his crudities of language, and his love for windy and pretentious rhetoric, Whitman was not a great poet, or even a poet at all, except in snatches. He was only a first rough sketch of an American writer—certainly not a finished portrait. Yet the critical opinion that places him at the center of American literary history is not unjustified. By attempting to make himself an embodiment, almost a mythical symbol, of the democratic way of life, he did succeed in uncovering some of the fundamental problems confronting American society. The fact that Whitman himself, as a private person, was not really so virile and carefree as his public role required him to be, does not invalidate his conclusions.

Whitman declared in *Democratic Vistas* that the material achievements of the Americans had not been matched by any corresponding spiritual growth. "I say that our New World democracy, however great a success in uplifting

[7] Complete Poetry and Selected Prose, *edited by E. Holloway (1938), pp. 663, 679. V. L. Parrington:* Main Currents in American Thought, *Vol. III, p. 78.*

the masses out of their sloughs, in materialistic development, products, and in a certain highly-deceptive superficial
popular intellectuality, is, so far, an almost complete failure
in its social aspects, and in really grand religious, moral,
literary and esthetic results. In vain do we march with unprecedented strides to empire so colossal, outvying the
antique, beyond Alexander's, beyond the proudest sway of
Rome. . . . It is as if we were somehow being endow'd
with a vast and more and more thoroughly-appointed body,
and then left with little or no soul." And this lack of a native American "religious and moral character beneath the
political and productive and intellectual bases of the
States," and the consequent reliance upon European standards and beliefs, would have the most sinister consequences.
The Americans could not remain a great people unless they
lived by the moral values of their democracy and had a
vital faith in them. "The United States are destined either
to surmount the gorgeous history of feudalism, or else
prove the most tremendous failure of time." Democracy
must acquire the emotional power of a religion. According
to Whitman, it should be the function of American art to
give it this power by creating symbolical and mythological
embodiments of it that would capture the imagination.[8]

For Whitman, democracy included both equality and
freedom; it meant "the leveler, the unyielding principle of
the average," and at the same time it mean "individuality,
the pride and centripetal isolation of a human being by
himself." These two principles, "confronting and ever
modifying the other, often clashing, paradoxical, yet neither
of highest avail without the other," could be harmonized
only by means of love—not merely "amative love" but
also the "loving comradeship" for which Whitman used
the word "adhesiveness." Only through the growth of "adhesiveness" could American democracy be spiritualized
and its materialism and vulgarity overcome. To glorify
"the manly love of comrades" was the central purpose
both of Whitman's poetry and of his personal life.[9]

But although Whitman himself succeeded in living by

[8] Complete Poetry and Selected Prose, *pp. 659, 661, 666.*
[9] *Ibid., pp. 686. 710.*

these democratic values, he was able to do so only because
he was by no means a typical American. This is the most
important conclusion that emerges from his life and writings. He had none of that aggressive and acquisitive energy
Americans brought first to the conquest of the continent
and afterwards to the building of an industrial society. Nor
did he have that corresponding inner energy of the Calvinist conscience that led to the suppression of sensuous impulses and the drying up of the springs of emotion. He
was a man of relaxed will. He did not wish to dominate
nature, either in the external world or within himself, but
to contemplate it and enjoy it. The deeper meaning of
Whitman's poetry is not only that democracy requires the
sense of human solidarity, but also that this sense is possible only through a relaxation of moral tension. But this
was a lesson Americans were not likely to appreciate. For
as the more imaginative writers of the period clearly re-
veal, the strongest trait of the American character was
the drive of its will; and insofar as the will was competitive
and acquisitive, either in material or in spiritual things, it
would destroy "the manly love of comrades."

3

While Emerson, Thoreau, and Whitman were concerned
with what America ought to be, Poe, Hawthorne, and Melville indicated what America actually was. These three
writers, so different from each other in all their personal
qualities, were alike in their basic preoccupations. Each of
them saw life in terms of a battle between the will of man
and his environment; for each of them there was nothing
higher than the individual will, so that man, instead of
subordinating himself to some ideal order or harmony, was
tempted to strive for omnipotence; and each of them expressed his view of life, not in the superficial terms of
realistic description, but by means of symbols which had
a deep emotional meaning. All three, in other words, were
profoundly American; and by setting their works beside
those of European writers, it is possible to formulate certain conclusions about the American temperament and

view of life. European writers, with their deep sense of
social order and discipline, have usually presented men
and women as torn between conflicting loyalties or between impulse and moral obligation. But the American
conflict is between the will and nature. The characters in
American fiction (like the sinner as envisaged in the Edwardean theology) have usually been relatively simple
creatures with little inner complexity who have embodied
some aspect of human will or appetite. There are no Ham-
lets in American literature.

Poe is the least important of the three writers since all
of his work had the morbid and febrile qualities of his
unbalanced temperament. He was the victim of neurotic
compulsions in his writing as well as in his personal life.
He is significant chiefly because his neuroticism assumed
a characteristically American form. This becomes plain
when he is contrasted with some European writer with
comparable talents and similar emotional insecurity: for
example, Coleridge. The European writer takes his bearings
from the social order, and he may either rebel against it
(like Coleridge in his youth) or idealize it and submit to
it (like Coleridge in his old age). But Poe found himself
in a void and could seek to make himself secure only by
means of a fantastic exaggeration of the drive to power.
He became pure will seeking omnipotence. In this respect
he is comparable to Jonathan Edwards. In the poet, as in
the theologian, the craving for omnipotence resulted both
in a presumptuous attempt to explain the entire universe
by logic (as in *Eureka*) and in fantasies of inhuman
cruelty.

Both Poe's limitations and his achievements were due
to his striving for omnipotence. As he explained in his
critical writings, he regarded the writing of poetry as an
intellectual exercise the purpose of which was to evoke in
its readers "a pleasurable elevation or excitement of the
soul." [1] He attempted to ennoble this theory by indulging
in some pseudomystical speculation about Beauty; but what
it really meant was that a poet should experiment with
emotional effects in order to concoct verbal drugs or stimu-

[1] *"The Poetic Principle,"* Works *(1895), Vol. VI, p. 13.*

lants that would display his power over his audience. Poe's own poems were in conformity with this æsthetic theory; they were literary cocktails, valuable solely for their capacity to produce a "pleasurable" but transitory "elevation or excitement." But in a number of his short stories he gave expression to his will to power more sincerely and directly, and with more interesting results. He had two favorite themes, each of which had a symbolic significance. His most powerful stories dealt either with sadistic fantasies of torture and murder (as in *Hop-Frog* and *The Cask of Amontillado*), or with the fantasy that if the will of man were sufficiently strong, it could conquer even death itself (as in *Ligeia* and *The Case of M. Valdemar*). He also delighted in exhibitions of extraordinary intellectual power, and this fascination with the idea of omniscience led him to invent the detective story. The most significant sentence in all Poe's writings is the quotation from Joseph Glanvil he used as an epigraph for *Ligeia*: "And the will therein lieth, which dieth not. Who knoweth the mysteries of the will, with its vigor? For God is but a great will pervading all things by nature of its intentness. Man doth not yield himself to the angels, nor unto death utterly, save only through the weakness of his feeble will."

Hawthorne, on the other hand, was a man of low emotional pressure who adopted throughout his life the role of an observer. Remaining always aloof from the world around him, he was able to record what he felt with a remarkable balance and detachment. Since he had no strong need within himself to dominate his environment, he could portray fairly and dispassionately the consequences of such a need in others. But since he lacked the compulsive drive of the writer who is himself the victim of conflict and must find a way of salvation, his work lacked force and energy. Carefully and delicately constructed, it was deficient in color and drama and almost passionless.

Hawthorne differed from most other American writers in attributing blame to the individual who became isolated. Isolation was the punishment of pride and egoism, which for Hawthorne were the roots of all evil. Many of his short stories dealt with different manifestations of these basic sins and with the consequent loneliness of the sinner. But while Hawthorne condemned the individual rebel, he was also convinced of the corruption of society. Virtue was to be found not in conformity to social forms and institutions, but in the practice of love and humility; and as long as the human heart remained unregenerated, all projects for social reform were futile. For Hawthorne, as for most other American novelists, the main positive value was comradeship. This attitude was stated in the short stories, often with an excessive reliance on allegorical imagery, and explored more deeply in the four novels. All of these present a favorite symbol, of the meaning of which Hawthorne was probably not fully aware, but which provides the clue to his general view of life.

Hawthorne was descended from one of the judges in early Massachusetts who had convicted the Salem witches. This episode in his family history made a deep impression on him, which was reinforced by prolonged reading of the works of Cotton Mather and other colonial chroniclers. The image of the judge condemning the witch appears, either explicitly or by implication, in each of his novels. To a large degree, in fact, all of them are organized around it so that they present different renderings of the same central theme. And because of the symbolic meaning of this theme Hawthorne's novels are a significant commentary on the American character, more particularly in its Puritan manifestations.

The Puritan sought to dominate nature, both within himself and in the external world; and these two forms of nature had a tendency to become identified. This identity could be symbolized in the figure of the witch. The witch represented the prohibited elements in man's own evil nature, particularly the sexual elements; she also represented the evil forces in the American wilderness, which, as the Puritans believed, had formerly been the devil's own territory. Thus the judge condemning the witch could stand for the whole drive of the American will toward the conquest of nature and the elimination of evil. What is most remarkable about Hawthorne's treatment of this theme is the scrupulous detachment with which he presents both sides of the conflict and refuses to identify himself with either. If the four novels are considered together, then it appears that the judge has been guilty of a selfish lust for power that will eventually cause his destruction ("God hath given him blood to drink" is the curse upon the judge in *The House of the Seven Gables*). At the same time, the witch is the victim of sinister forces that are equally destructive. Nor does Hawthorne show any real conviction that this conflict can be resolved in terms of some higher unity and harmony. His conscious attempts to find a resolution are feeble and unconvincing. At bottom he felt that the struggle between the will and nature was ultimate.

The first and greatest of the novels, *The Scarlet Letter,* presents the essential ingredients of the theme, though the judge and the witch do not appear directly. But the selfish and domineering intolerance of the judge are embodied in Roger Chillingworth, while Hester Prynne, with her unrepentant sexuality and her rebellious independence of mind and spirit, plays the role of the witch. Along with the unhappy Dimmesdale, who is trapped between them, these characters are presented in a series of tableaux which are somewhat lacking in action but which illustrate different aspects of Hawthorn's subject. But the special beauty of *The Scarlet Letter* is derived not from any psychological analysis, but from its emotional overtones. On the one side is the little Puritan settlement at Boston, with its righteous, domineering, intolerant, and acquisitive citizens; on the other side is the vast unconquered forest, in which Hester is condemned to live after her sin, and which is the home of the devil and the meeting place of witches and the source of all that is wild, chaotic, and uncontrolled. Such a setting inspired Hawthorne to do his best work because he was writing, not merely about Hester Prynne, but about the whole American experience.

In the other three novels Hawthorne did not succeed in extracting as much emotional resonance and reverberation from his theme. *The House of the Seven Gables* deals explicitly with the judge and the witch, the image being extended into the nineteenth century by the device of identifying witchcraft partly with mesmerism and partly with a general spirit of rebellion. But the issues of the conflict are presented with little force, and the transformation of the witch from a woman into a man (in the person of Holgrave) deprives the symbol of most of its power. The marriage between the descendant of the judge and the descendant of his victim is perhaps intended as an allegory of ultimate reconciliation; but since these two commonplace and good-natured characters have not inherited the violent and sinister qualities of their ancestors, their marriage has no genuine symbolic value. *The Blithedale Romance,* on the other hand, has more emotional force although less clarity. The self-righteous and domineering Hollingsworth is the magistrate; while Zenobia and her husband, the mesmerist, represent witchcraft. In Zenobia, who has more sexual allure than Hester Prynne, Hawthorne for the first time succeeds in giving the witch image its full meaning. But although Zenobia is duly condemned and driven to her death by Hollingsworth, the implications of the story are clouded by too many meaningless complications. Finally, in *The Marble Faun,* the weakest and most confused of the four novels, there is no figure who clearly stands for the magistrate, and the witch (Miriam), after being wrapped in a sinister atmosphere of diabolism that Hawthorne does not succeed in making convincing, is left to find her own way to perdition.

Melville's central theme was essentially the same as Hawthorne's, although it was expressed through very different symbolisms and with a violence and passion that gave his novels an incomparably greater vitality. While Hawthorne surveyed the American scene by candlelight, Melville started a conflagration in which he was himself almost consumed; but it was the same landscape the two men were illuminating. Melville had none of Hawthorne's cool objectivity; he was himself a victim as well as a recorder, and he had to work his way through to some kind of personal salvation. His unique distinction is that he succeeded in finding it. He is the one American writer of whom it may be said that he mastered the American experience and then went beyond it.

Melville wrote three books of major importance: *Moby Dick, Pierre,* and *Billy Budd. Moby Dick* and *Pierre,* appearing in 1851 and 1852 respectively, both dealt with the problem of the American will. *Billy Budd,* written in 1891 and not published until 1924, may be described as a resolution of the problem. The rest of Melville's works were less ambitious, although all of them had unusual qualities, and at least one of his shorter stories, *Benito Cereno,* was a masterpiece.

Moby Dick is not only the greatest book written by an American; it is also the greatest American book. In choosing to write a story about a monomaniacal sea captain chasing a whale, Melville hit upon a symbol that brought all his emotional resources and attitudes into play and that—since his approach to life was profoundly American—became a revelation of the whole American character. He said himself that he did not fully understand the meaning of what he was writing. On the surface he was telling a story about a whale, and *Moby Dick* can be read and enjoyed on this level. But it also has symbolic meanings sufficiently indicated in the course of the narrative. For Captain Ahab and the crew of the *Pequod* the white whale was "the gliding great demon of the seas of life"; and their determination to kill the whale was a determination that evil could be conquered and destroyed. And for Melville's Ahab, as for all Calvinists, evil was both external and internal. The sea was the universe, and Moby Dick stood for the untamed forces of nature with which man must do battle. But the sea was also "the visible image of that deep, blue, bottomless soul, pervading mankind and nature," and Moby Dick was the "incarnation of all those malicious agencies which some deep men feel eating in them." He was "that intangible malignity which has been from the beginning; to whose dominion even the modern Christians ascribe one-half of the world. . . . All that most maddens and torments; all that stirs up the lees of things; all truth with malice in it; all that cracks the sinews and cakes the brain; all the subtle demonisms of life and thought; all evil, to crazy Ahab, were visibly personified, and made practically assailable in Moby Dick." [2]

In Melville's Ahab the drive of the American will is carried to its furthermost limits. For him, as for Poe, there is nothing higher than the will, yet the will must go down to ultimate defeat. Man cannot conquer nature, nor can he destroy evil, either without or within. "Though in many of its aspects the visible world seems formed in love, the invisible spheres were formed in fright." But Melville, unlike Hawthorne, tends to identify himself with the rebellious individual, recognizing his pride and self-will, but at the same time admiring them. "The intrepid effort of the soul to keep the open independence of her sea" is better than to hug "the treacherous, slavish shore," even though man does not know where he is going and must finally be submerged. The *Pequod,* and Melville with it, is "not so much bound to any haven ahead as rushing from all havens astern." Ahab is crazy, and the inevitable ending of his impossible quest is that the *Pequod* is destroyed by Moby Dick, and "the great shroud of the sea rolled on as it rolled five thousand years ago." But Ahab is in no way comparable to a hero of European tragedy who (like Œdipus or Macbeth) is destroyed by sinning against some higher law or against the cosmic order. In the gloomy and anarchical universe of *Moby Dick* no such order exists. [3]

Pierre can best be read as a commentary on *Moby Dick.* As a novel it is a total failure; its style is stilted and unnatural; its characterizations are implausible; and its plot is fantastic. But it has the same theme as *Moby Dick*—the attempt of man to conquer evil, and his inevitable failure— and it suggests reasons for that failure that could not be presented in a novel about whaling. Pierre is a young idealist who is determined to make no compromises with his environment. At the beginning of the novel he possesses all the advantages of wealth and social position, and is

[2] Moby Dick, *Chap. 35, 41 (Modern Library edition, pp. 157, 183, 186).*

[3] *Ibid., Chap. 23, 42, 96, 135, pp. 105, 194, 421, 565.*

about to be married. But when he discovers that he has an illegitimate sister who has been brought up in obscurity, he determines that the wrong done to her must be rectified. He takes her under his protection; and in order to prevent scandal, he pretends that he has married her. This act of idealism is followed by a series of catastrophes; and finally Pierre goes down to total defeat, destroying not only himself but also both the two women he loves. His defeat is due, not only to the power of evil in his environment, but also to ambiguous tendencies within himself that he scarcely understands and cannot control. In sacrificing himself in order to make amends for the sin committed by his father, Pierre is not merely displaying a noble idealism; he is also acting under the influence, without realizing it, of an incestuous desire. Yet in spite of Pierre's failure it is not suggested that he ought to have acted differently. For Pierre, as for Ahab and for Melville himself, man has a choice only between conquest and defeat. The argument for compromise is stated in the novel by the philosopher Plotinus Plinlimmon, who is represented as a thoroughly ignoble character; it is stated and rejected again, in symbolic terms, in Pierre's vision of Enceladus. Man must struggle to impose his moral will upon his own desires and upon his environment, even though he cannot hope to do so successfully.

Even though it is an æsthetic failure, *Pierre* goes more deeply into human psychology than any other writing of the period. It carries the doctrines of optimistic individualism and Emersonian self-reliance to their ultimate conclusions, and suggests that they may end in nihilism and despair. And since Melville was himself a self-reliant individualist and was projecting his own attitudes into Ahab and Pierre, he himself shared in their defeat.

In 1866 Melville abandoned the struggle to support himself and his family by writing, and buried himself for twenty years in the New York Customs House. Henceforth his silence was broken only by the publication of some mediocre poetry. Meanwhile the development of American society during these years was a testimony to the essential truth of his portrayal of the American spirit. This was an

age of men of strong will, who acknowledged no higher
law than their own purposes, who recognized no allegiance
to an ideal of social order, and who sought only conquest
and domination. Rockefeller and Morgan were in the materialistic world of economics what Ahab was in the
transcendental world of the spirit. But Melville was not
yet finished. During the last three years of his life he
worked on a story that was found among his manuscripts
after his death and not published until 1924, and which is
utterly different from his own earlier writings, and from any
other work in American literature. A parable rather than
a novel, *Billy Budd* is by no means a literary masterpiece;
but as an indication of Melville's spiritual development it
is of the greatest interest. It is infused with a spirit of
reconciliation to life and of religious acceptance that make
it comparable to the final works of the great Europeans.
Billy Budd is Melville's *Tempest* and his *Winter's Tale*.

The central figure in the story is a sailor in the English
navy during the period of the French Revolution. Falsely
accused of misconduct by an officer, Billy Budd responds
by striking his slanderer, and accidentally kills him. The
legal penalty for killing a superior officer is death, and
the captain of the ship, although recognizing Billy's innocence, decides (in view of recent mutinies) that the law
must be enforced. He argues that the maintenance of the
order of society is paramount, and that the individual, even
when unjustly treated, should submit to it. Man must accept the mystery of evil, which is an inextricable part of
human life; he must recognize that innocent men may
suffer, and that evildoers may flourish, and that to attempt
to impose a Utopian perfection upon the world can lead
only to anarchy. Billy Budd accepts the reasoning of the
captain and goes to his death, not merely willingly, but
gladly, in the conviction that he is serving a higher purpose. In the description of his death Melville introduces
symbolisms that suggest a parallel to the crucifixion; Billy
Budd is dying so that the order of society may be maintained, as Jesus died, according to some interpretations of
the atonement, to vindicate the sanctity of divine law.

The meaning of the fable is summarized in a saying of

the captain. "With mankind," he would say, "forms, measured forms, are everything; and that is the import couched in the story of Orpheus, with his lyre, spell-binding the wild denizens of the woods." [4] This profoundly un-American statement is the last word of the greatest of American writers. Having carried the drive of the individual will to its furthermost limits, Melville had found that it ended in the sinking of the *Pequod* and in the death of Pierre; but in his old age he passed beyond individualism and beyond its inevitable defeat. *Billy Budd,* unlike any other work by a major American writer, is based on the belief in an underlying social order and harmony that gives meaning to the lives of those who participate in it and that transcends the struggle between the will and the environment.

[4] Shorter Novels of Herman Melville (*1928*), *page 323.*

CHAPTER X

THE CIVIL WAR

★ ★ ★ ★ ★ ★ ★ ★ ★ ★ ★ ★ ★ ★

THE CIVIL WAR was the first major interruption in that process of material and social construction with which the Americans had been occupied since the founding of the first colonies. For the first time they had to turn aside from the task of building a new civilization and to deal with human problems of a more complex nature and on a profounder spiritual level. The main cause of the war was that North and South had developed deeply divergent social ideals; this divergency was too basic to be settled by the usual Anglo-Saxon methods of argument, compromise, and peaceful adjustment. Both Northerners and Southerners believed themselves to be justified in their own eyes and were unable to give way on doctrines they regarded as fundamental. Such a conflict of ideals was essentially tragic. It could be understood only in terms of the tragic imagination, and was so understood at the end of his life by one of the chief participants, President Lincoln, as he showed in his *Second Inaugural.* But it could not be accounted for and digested in terms of the usual American categories of thought, which visualized life as a battle between the will and the environment or between good and evil. The Civil War was not a conflict between good and evil but between rival conceptions of good. In consequence it was an experience the American mind was unable successfully to assimilate. For this reason it was not followed, like many wars in European countries, by an intellectual efflorescence; its results, in the victorious North as well as the conquered

South, were cynicism, corruption, and a sense of defeat. In some respects, in fact, American society never fully recovered from it. The Civil War abruptly cut short the cultural development of the 1840's and 1850's, and the intellectual activities of later periods had very little connection with what had gone before.

The divergencies between North and South dated back to the foundation of the earliest colonies. Massachusetts and Virginia had always represented different social and economic principles and different modes of living. In the nineteenth century these divergencies were carried over into the Mississippi Valley; Illinois and Ohio tended to imitate Massachusetts, while Alabama and Mississippi borrowed their social ideals from Virginia. The North was more dynamic, more progressive, more interested in commercial and industrial development and in schemes of social reform. The South was more static and more leisurely, and preferred to concentrate on agriculture and to preserve the way of life that landownership made possible. The drive of the American will, both externally in the conquest of nature and internally in the suppression of what was regarded as moral evil, was more conspicuous in the North, while the desire for individual economic independence was more fully exemplified in the South. Yet there is no good reason for supposing that the conflict of ideals would ever have ended in open warfare if the two sections had not also been divided by Negro slavery. An institution the North was learning to abhor had come to be regarded by the South as the very foundation of its social order. It was slavery, and slavery alone, that finally made it impossible for the two sections to remain peaceably within the same federal union.

The problem of slavery created for American democratic idealists an insurmountable dilemma. For while slavery itself was utterly contrary to the principles of American democracy, yet in some other respects those principles were more effectively safeguarded in the agrarian society of the South than in the new industrial society beginning to dominate the North. The heirs of the Jeffersonian tradition and the surviving followers of Jackson were compelled to work for the victory of the North in order that slavery might be abolished; yet in the final outcome that victory meant the triumph of Hamiltonian economics and, in large measure, the destruction of the agrarian way of life upon which American democracy had been founded. Only a man who saw life in terms of religion rather than of the Utopian optimism so characteristic of the Americans could accept the full tragic meaning of such a situation. Abraham Lincoln believed that Negro slavery was an offense against the absolute laws of justice and humanity. But although he condemned slavery he did not condemn the slaveowner. He believed (as he implied in his *Second Inaugural*) that since both North and South had participated in the enslavement of the Negro, so from both North and South a terrible recompense had to be exacted. But Lincoln did not live to see the full consequences of the Civil War. The price the Americans paid for their denial of the rights of humanity to the Negro race was not only the death of half a million men in the greatest civil war in history; it was also the frustration and debasement of the American ideal of a property owners' democracy that would maintain both freedom and equality.

During the Revolutionary period it was generally assumed that slavery would be abolished peacefully, although it was also assumed by most Southerners that white and black could not live side by side as equals and that the liberation of the Negroes must be accompanied by their removal to Africa or to some other part of America. Emancipation was accomplished in all the Northern states, and was favored by increasingly large minorities in Maryland and Virginia. The Constitution provided that the slave trade (by which many Northern merchants had profited) should be ended in the year 1808. Even in the lower South there was little disposition at this time to defend slavery or to do more than apologize for it as a temporary necessity. Unfortunately at this crucial point the cotton gin was invented, and as a result of the new need for labor the whole Southern attitude began to change. The Negro must remain, and the South believed that he could remain only as a slave. The cotton gin cheapened the cost of cotton production, for which slave labor was well adapted, and thereby made it a very remunerative occupation. This occurred in the year 1793 and was the work of Eli Whitney, a mechanical genius from Connecticut who was spending a few months with friends in Georgia. Whitney subsequently returned to Connecticut and began to manufacture firearms by a new method, making them from interchangeable parts. This became one of the basic principles of American mass production. Whitney thus helped both to cause the Civil War and to ensure that the North would win it.

English manufacturers were willing to buy all the cotton the South could produce, and from 1793 to the Civil War the cotton crop continued to double every ten or fifteen years, exceeding two billion pounds in the year 1860. For half a century it was not difficult for cotton growers to make a great deal of money, and the big plantation, manned by scores of Negro slaves, quickly became the dominant institution throughout large areas of the Deep South. Cotton production spread first through Georgia (which was still largely frontier country) and South Carolina. After the War of 1812 came the mass migration across the mountains into the lower Mississippi Valley, and many thousands of Negro slaves were transported into the West. Cotton spread through Alabama and Mississippi, and thence into Louisiana, Texas, and Arkansas. Meanwhile the older seaboard regions, particularly in Virginia and South Carolina, were suffering from soil erosion and from falling land values and a decreasing population. The new cotton kingdom, stretching for a thousand miles across the Deep South from Georgia into Texas and guided by a *nouveau riche* planter plutocracy, assumed the leadership of the entire South. By the 1840's and 1850's the most important part of the cotton kingdom, both economically and politically, was not the Atlantic seaboard but the newly settled region along the Gulf of Mexico.

Popular impressions of plantation life, both sentimental and hostile, still betray a tendency to confuse Alabama and Mississippi with colonial Virginia. Most of the cotton kingdom was a part of the Mississippi Valley and shared the

general characteristics of that region. A few of the planters came from seaboard aristocratic families, but a large
majority had begun their lives as small farmers; they had
been able to acquire more land, buy more slaves, and build
more impressive houses than their neighbors because of superior energy, shrewdness, and force of will. During the
same period and by the same qualities, similar men in Ohio
and Illinois were achieving wealth through speculation or
business enterprise. The cotton kingdom was too short-lived
to produce a genuine aristocracy. Down to the Civil War
it remained, in many ways, frontier country, and many of
those characteristics that so shocked New Englanders
should be attributed to the influence of the frontier rather
than of slavery. Its white inhabitants, like frontiersmen
elsewhere, were aggressively individualistic, accustomed to
violence, fond of celebrating their own achievements, addicted to a narrow and emotional Protestantism, and frequently illiterate. The Civil War was largely a conflict for
the control of the Mississippi Valley, fought between the
northern and the southern ends of it. It was appropriate
that the two Civil War Presidents should have been born
of similar small-farmer stock in similar log cabins within
a few miles of each other in Kentucky. The Lincolns had
subsequently gone north into Illinois, and the Davises south
into Mississippi.

And although the South accepted the political and social
leadership of the planters, it always retained much of the
frontier spirit of democracy. The typical Southern citizen
was not the planter but the small farmer. In 1860, out of
a total white population of over eight millions among whom
perhaps a million and a half were heads of families, less
than fifty thousand persons owned more than twenty slaves
apiece, and less than four hundred thousand persons owned
slaves at all. Three quarters of the white population did not
belong to the slaveowning classes, and a majority even of
the slaveowners were small farmers rather than planters
and were accustomed to work in the fields alongside their
Negroes. No part of the South, not even the rich black belt
in Alabama and Mississippi, became wholly plantation
country. Born from the same racial stocks and often closely

related to each other, the planter and the farmer lived
side by side in the same areas. The gulf between them,
economically and socially, was no greater than that between
the lawyer or business man and the small farmer in Ohio;
it was decidedly less than that dividing the capitalist of New
England from his factory operatives. In some degree the
small farmers of the South suffered from competition with
the planters, who were able to buy up the more fertile
lands; but they had plenty of vigor and independence.
Although they lived with little comfort or refinement and
often without benefit of education, they were very different
from the "poor whites" whose numbers and significance
were so exaggerated by antislavery propagandists. There
was no lack of strength and virility among the men who
served as private soldiers under Lee and Jackson. Genuine
"poor whites," degraded by poverty and devitalized by
hookworm or pellagra, existed only in a few areas and
were probably not much more numerous than their coun-
terparts in the cities and rural regions of the North.

Yet although the society of the Mississippi Valley,
whether along the Gulf of Mexico or beside the Great
Lakes, was built by men of the same type in response to
similar drives, sharp differences in direction and ultimate
objective quickly asserted themselves. Several factors combined to create a distinctively Southern attitude in the
states from Kentucky southward. The Southerner lived
alongside an alien and servile race, towards whom all white
men could feel superior. He lived in a hot climate, dis-
couraging to any sustained activity, and was accustomed to
storms of a tropic violence. And his view of life was
molded by an aristocratic social ideal derived from the
planters of tidewater Virginia, and indirectly from the
great landowners of rural England. The plantation South,
unlike other sections of the United States, retained the
sense of a fixed social order to which individuals should
conform. Unfortunately the social ideal of the South was
of European origin; and insofar as it was based on slavery,
it was hierarchical, undemocratic, and un-American.

An agrarian by temperament and preference as well as
from necessity, the Southern farmer valued his leisure and

his freedom, and did not care for a higher standard of living if it meant a loss of economic independence. If he was ambitious, he aspired to own slaves and a plantation and then to use his profits in lavish and generous living rather than to save them and reinvest them. He was usually unreflective, quick to take action and to resort to violence, guided mainly by prejudice and emotion rather than by calculation, fond of physical pleasures, hospitable and gregarious, and incurably loquacious. The Southerner contributed less than the Northerner to the advance of science, learning, and the arts; but he was also less likely to lose sight of the ends of human life by too exclusive a concentration upon the means.

Judged by all those standards that can be expressed statistically, the South appeared backward when contrasted with the North. But the more important aspects of human life elude statistical analysis. The Northerner built more industries and more schools, published more books and more newspapers, and made more money and enjoyed more comforts than the Southerner; but it is not certain that his life was richer or more satisfying. Nor was the backwardness of the South due merely to slavery as the North maintained. It is true that slavery was an inefficient labor system since the slaves lacked sufficient incentives and needed constant supervision; and the fact that the planter had to buy his labor supply, as well as his land and his raw materials, impeded economic mobility and flexibility. But the main reason for the backwardness of the South was that it was an agricultural section with few cities and little industry.

There seems to have been no sound economic reason why industry could not have developed more widely in the South. There was no lack of raw material or labor (even slave labor was occasionally used in Southern factories with good results). For forty years Southern leaders were proclaiming that the South ought to build its own factories and develop its own shipping instead of relying on Great Britain and the North. Yet their speeches and resolutions fell on deaf ears. The only sound conclusion is that the Southern population did not want to become urbanized and industrialized; it preferred to retain its agrarian independence, even at the cost of a low standard of living, a high rate of illiteracy, and a cultural inferiority to the rich urban areas in Massachusetts and New York. The South had a way of life that was valued by the farmer as well as by the planter; and although its growing population and the declining fertility of its soil caused it to become expansionist, its economic ideals were essentially static rather than dynamic and progressive. In their defense all classes of Southerners were willing, in the last resort, to fight.

But—tragically—all the virtues of the Southern way of life were counteracted by the primal evil of Negro slavery. Of the twelve and a quarter millions of human beings who lived in the South at the outbreak of the Civil War, about four millions were bondsmen who, in the words of Chief Justice Taney in the Dred Scott decision, had "no· rights which the white man was bound to respect." Slavery was not primarily an economic question. It was the sense of racial difference, and all the deep and complex fears and anxieties associated with it, rather than a mere desire for money, that prevented the South from emancipating the Negro. Not more than a quarter of the Southern white population shared in the profits of slavery; and it is probable that those profits would have been larger if the Negro had become a wage laborer and been given the incentives and the hope for advancement of the free citizen. Yet almost all Southerners, of whatever class, were agreed that he was congenitally inferior and must forever remain so. There is no good reason for supposing that the South, whether as a part of the Union or as an independent confederacy, would ever have abolished slavery voluntarily, except under the influence of some new and unpredictable factor, or that the North could ever have imposed abolition by any method except war.

For more than a hundred years Northerners and Southerners have been disputing with each other about the treatment of the Negro under slavery, one side insisting that cruelty was normal, and the other maintaining that the typical slaveowner was humane and paternalistic. Since it is possible to continue citing specific instances indefinitely in defense of either contention, the evidence is inconclusive. It is also irrelevant to the real issue.

There is no doubt that the dependent position of the Negro invited cruelty, and that there were slaveowners who took advantage of it. There is also no doubt that there were some Negroes who rebelled and many who attempted to run away. But the balance of the evidence supports the Southern belief that the majority of the slaveowners accepted responsibility for the welfare of their dependents and that the majority of the slaves submitted to servitude without conscious resentment. The South, unlike any other part of America, was evolving a pattern of social order; and this pattern, in spite of its reactionary tendencies, did actually work. The planter, as the heir of the aristocratic tradition, was expected to live by a code of behavior that inculcated self-restraint, paternalism, and a sense of *noblesse oblige*. The code was not always obeyed, particularly among the *nouveau riche* cotton growers of the Mississippi Valley; but violations of it met with social condemnation. The Negro was required to know his place and could be expected to be rewarded and protected in return for faithful service.

But the fact that this social pattern worked with little serious friction is no proof that it was good or that it deserved to survive. It was wholly contrary to the basic principles and ideals of American society and to the main trends of Western civilization. For this reason it could not be preserved except by violence. More important, it refused to take account of certain basic elements in human nature that sooner or later were bound to assert themselves. Four million human beings, possessed of all the normal human drives and aspirations and endowed with natural talents and capacities equal to those of the men and women of any other race, were denied the most elementary human rights and condemned to perpetual inferiority merely because of the color of their skins. During the period in which slavery existed most of the Negroes accepted this role of inferiority. Denied any hope of advancement or outlet for ambition, they remained easy-going and irresponsible; and these qualities, which were the necessary results of social conditions, were then declared by their owners to be congenital and used as a justification for the social system that had caused them. But since the Negro was human, it was inevitable that sooner or later he would begin to assert his humanity and to demand his rights to the fulfillment of his mental and emotional potentialities. In the last resort Negro servitude could be maintained only by the most brutal force and by the prostitution of truth and the suppression of free inquiry.

One should not blame the white men of the South too severely for their refusal to recognize their common bonds of humanity with the Negro. All branches of Anglo-Saxon society, even that of abolitionist New England, have been notorious for their inability to overcome differences of race and color. Destiny required of the South a wisdom and a generosity far in excess of the normal capacity of human beings. But because the white men of the South refused to recognize this requirement, their civilization was doomed to destruction.

2

The sectional conflict first showed itself in 1820 when the North objected to the admission of Missouri into the Union as a slave state and insisted that the spread of slavery into the Western territories should henceforth be limited by federal law. It began to dominate American politics in the 1840's.

Much of the conflict was caused by purely economic factors and had no connection with the rights and wrongs of slavery. Like most agricultural communities since the dawn of civilization the cotton kingdom was exploited by the centers of urban commerce and finance, and these happened to be located in the North. Southern planters paid tribute to Northern bankers, Northern merchants, Northern shipowners and Northern manufacturers. A large percentage of the profits of cotton production remained in the North. Making the mistake of interpreting the situation as a sectional rather than a class conflict, and at the same time failing to develop any considerable commerce or

finance of its own, the South complained that its just rights
under the federal Union were being violated and blamed
the policies of the federal government for what was happening. Southern spokesmen compiled statistics showing that
most of the federal revenues were collected in the South
(through the tariff) and that most of the proceeds were
spent in the North (on internal improvements). They
appealed to the economic philosophy of Thomas Jefferson
and John Taylor of Caroline in defense of their complaints.
Yet insofar as they thought in sectional rather than class
terms, they no longer adhered to strict agrarian principles;
and this abandonment of principle weakened their political
position and deprived them of possible Northern allies. The
political leader of the cotton kingdom, John C. Calhoun,
was no pure agrarian; he did not object to federal spending
and federal distributions of economic privilege when it
seemed likely that the South would benefit. Meanwhile the
spokesmen of the North wanted measures, such as a
higher tariff and more generous subsidies for internal
improvements, which were blocked by Southern opposition,
and were complaining of planter control over the federal
government.

But this economic conflict between agriculture and
business would never have split the Union. What caused
the South to secede was Northern hostility to slavery; and
here the propaganda of the abolitionists was of decisive
importance. It is impossible to attribute any economic
motive to these men. Northerners had economic reasons
for wishing to keep the South a minority section and hence
for preventing slavery from spreading; but they had none
for wishing to revolutionize the South itself. Abolitionism
was essentially a religious movement; it developed out of
the Protestant churches, particularly in the Middle West,
and it retained all the crusading fervor, the narrowness of
vision, and the mixture of idealism and intolerance that
have always characterized American Christianity. Like
their ultimate progenitors John Calvin and Jonathan Edwards, the abolitionists saw life in very simple terms, as
a battle between moral good and moral evil. Most of them
were fanatics on a number of other matters besides slavery,

particularly on the consumption of alcohol. Perceiving that slavery was wrong and that it ought to be abolished, they deduced that the slaveowners must be evil men who deserved no consideration. According to abolitionist propaganda the typical Southern plantation was a combination of torture chamber and brothel, and the planters were an arrogant and depraved aristocracy who domineered over a degraded mass of "poor white" farmers and spent most of their time beating their male slaves and begetting mulatto offspring on their female slaves. The propaganda of these righteous and violent men, continuing through the 1830's, 1840's, and 1850's, did not convert more than a small fraction of the Northern population to outright abolitionism, but it gradually changed the climate of opinion. Northerners came to recognize that slavery was a wrong that ought some day to be rectified, although they still believed that it should remain primarily a Southern problem. In one matter, however, they were willing to take positive action. As a result of the growing sympathy with slaves who succeeded in escaping into the North; many of the Northern states enacted personal liberty laws making it difficult for their owners to recapture them. The personal liberty laws represented a violation of the mutual obligations that all the states had assumed under the federal Constitution. Under the influence of the slavery issue the Northern states were beginning to break their ties with the South.

To the lurid and immoderate propaganda of the abolitionists the South reacted with an equally violent defense of their peculiar institution. The younger generation of Southerners—those born after 1800—no longer apologized for slavery. Instead they declared that it was a positive good; it was in accord with the laws of God and nature, and was both more stable and more humane than the system of wage labor in Northern factories. Terrified lest abolitionist ideas should reach the Negroes and lead to slave rebellions, they attempted to suppress all discussion of the question. After 1830, Southern opponents of slavery found it necessary either to remain quiet or to leave the South. Thus having denied justice to the Negro and resolved to keep him in servitude, the South was inexorably led to an abandonment of the democratic process itself, which is based on the maintenance of free discussion. And although the South based its main political defense on the theory of states rights, claiming that the federal system provided for local self-government and sectional diversity and for the protection of sectional minorities, it did not always concede to the North the rights it claimed for itself. It would have liked to suppress free speech on the slavery issue in the North also; it insisted on federal action to compel the North to restore fugitive slaves; and in the 1850's it began to maintain that slavery should be permitted in all the Western territories, whether the inhabitants wished it or not. Thus slavery became a problem that could no longer be settled by the methods of constitutional democracy. Men cannot live together under the same government, even if it is based on the federal principle and allows for sectional diversity, unless they are in agreement about first principles. But on the fundamental question whether all men, or only all white men, were endowed with rights North and South were no longer in agreement.

The conflict about slavery could not be settled by any kind of compromise. And because of this deep underlying conflict more superficial questions, which had little intrinsic importance, aroused the most bitter antagonisms. The immediate issue that occupied American politics during the twelve years before the Civil War was whether slavery should be legally permitted in the Western territories. Yet as the wiser men on both sides realized, this issue was essentially unreal. The limits of slavery were fixed by soil and climate; no matter what the federal government might do, the Great Plains and the Rocky Mountain regions could never accommodate slave plantations. It was therefore unnecessary for the North to insist on the legal prohibition of slavery in the West and useless for the South to protest. Nevertheless, politicians in both South and North stirred up violent emotions by inflating this issue into a real conflict.

Southern leaders played into the hand of the North by declaring that they had a legal right to take slaves into any territory; to deny this right was an insult to the South and to her peculiar institutions. Northerners replied that the South was planning to spread slave plantations through the entire West, in the hope of creating a majority of slave states and then imposing slavery upon the whole country. In order to check this aggressive and expansionist slave power, they declared, the free states must prohibit slavery in all the territories. This proposal appealed to many Northern citizens who wished to take some kind of action against slavery but who were not yet willing to support abolitionism. It also appealed to the economic interests of the North. Eastern business groups did not wish to interfere with slavery, but they were disturbed by the suggestion that the South might achieve political preponderance; and Western farmers were alarmed by the possibility that they might have to compete with slave plantations. The proposal to limit the spread of slavery by law thus appealed to all classes in the North; in particular, it made possible an alliance between Eastern capitalism and Western agriculture, in spite of the fact that these elements had been opposed to each other, and were still opposed to each other, on almost every other question. The suggestion that unless action was taken the whole West might become slave soil was, in fact, so cleverly designed to unite the North and to deprive the South of its Northern allies among the farmers and urban workers, and was at the same time so essentially untrue, that it is difficult to acquit the anti-slavery leaders who propounded it of deliberate dishonesty. Men who are most convinced of their own rectitude of purpose are often the most unscrupulous in their choice of means.

Yet although the coming of the Civil War was hastened by these political maneuverings, it does not follow that wiser and more forebearing statesmanship could have done more than postpone it. The North (apart from the abolitionists) was not yet willing to admit that it wished to interfere with slavery where it already existed; but such an intention was implicit in its political development. And whenever it became manifest, the South would fight.

The issue of slavery in the territories was settled temporarily by the Compromise of 1850. It was raised again by the Kansas-Nebraska Act of 1854. And the dispute as to whether slavery should be permitted in Kansas resulted in the formation of the new Republican Party, a fusion of Whigs and Jacksonian Democrats, dedicated to the prohibition of slavery in all territories. Representing both Eastern business interests and Western farming interests and led by politicians who were building careers on the slavery issue, this was the first purely sectional political party.

Meanwhile an increasing number of Southerners, recognizing that under no circumstances could they win control of the West, and foreseeing that Northern predominance would inevitably mean both increased exploitation of Southern agriculture and an attack on the South's peculiar institution, were thinking of secession. This idea had been advocated for a number of years by a small group of Southern radicals, headed by Rhett of South Carolina and Yancey of Alabama. The radicals believed that if the South formed a separate confederacy, she would be able to build an empire in the Caribbean, where land suitable for cotton was abundant; and some of them were beginning to talk of reopening the slave trade. These ideas appealed especially to those smaller planters and farmers who wanted more land and more slaves. It appears to have been this struggling and ambitious middle group, and not the richer planters, who responded to the radical program of the secessionists and carried the South out of the Union. It was not the Southern aristocrats, as the North believed, but men of a lower economic stratum, who were responsible for the Confederacy.

In 1860 Lincoln, as Republican candidate, was elected to the Presidency, and the secessionist group were then able to win over a majority of the Southern population. Before Lincoln took office in March 1861, seven of the cotton states had voted to secede and had joined each other in the Confederacy. In April, when it became obvious that the North was going to fight a war in order to prevent secession, four more slave states followed them out of the Union.

3

The reasons that caused the South to secede are not difficult to understand. But the reasons that caused the North to fight a Civil War in order to prevent secession are more intangible and less easily defined.

It is true that Southern secession would have meant economic losses for Northern merchants, shipowners and manufacturers; from which it can be argued that the war was fought in order to establish the domination of industrial capitalism. But it cannot be proved that this economic motive had any determining influence on Northern opinion. The strongest champions of the Union were not the Northeastern business groups but the nationalistic farmers of the upper Mississippi Valley, whose attitude cannot be adequately explained except in terms of sentiments and ideas. These Middle Westerners had learned to identify the federal Union with freedom and democracy; they believed that, by contrast with all other governments in the world, it represented a new and higher way of life. They believed secession to be illegal; and they believed that if a minority group, when defeated in an election, were allowed to violate constitutional procedure by seceding, then the American experiment in democracy would be proved a failure.

As Lincoln told Congress, the Civil War was "a struggle for maintaining in the world that form and substance of government whose leading object is to elevate the condition of man. . . . Our popular government has often been called an experiment. Two points in it our people have already settled—the successful establishing and the successful administering of it. One still remains—its successful maintenance against a formidable internal attempt to overthrow it. It is now for them to demonstrate to the world that those who can fairly carry an election can also suppress a rebellion; that ballots are the rightful and peaceful successors of bullets; and that when ballots have fairly and constitutionally decided, there can be no successful appeal back to bullets."

This attitude was undoubtedly correct. Whether or not secession was legally permissible—a question on which there were legitimate differences of opinion—it was certainly true that the democratic and peaceful American way of life could not have been preserved if the Union had been split into two mutually hostile sections. In recognizing that secession was a threat to all that America stood for, the Middle Westerners showed the same kind of intuitive wisdom that Americans displayed in 1917 and again in 1941.

Lincoln gave expression to these sentiments with a consummate clarity and sincerity. This Illinois politician had come to the Presidency with very little preparation for the tasks he had to assume. His previous speeches, although marked by a definite conviction that slavery was wrong, had been often fumbling and confused and not always candid. But once in office, he gradually rose to a moral stature unequaled by any other American before or since. Humble but courageous and deeply honest, he provided a perfect example of what leadership should mean in a democratic society. He regarded himself always as the instrument of the popular will, and consistently refused to take action unless he was convinced that the people desired it. But once he had decided that action was wanted, he could assume responsibility boldly and decisively, in defiance of the advice of all the men around him. At the outset of the war, for example, he refused to make slavery an issue in the conflict (in spite of his personal desire to see it abolished); but eighteen months later, when he felt that public opinion was ready for such a measure, he decreed the emancipation of all slaves in the Confederacy by his own authority. During the war years Lincoln acquired a sense of the tragic mystery and complexity of human life, to a degree that has been rare among Americans. He knew that slavery was an evil thing, and that evil breeds further evil until a full recompense had been made; but that did not lead him to regard the slaveowners as evil men who deserved no consideration or who were fundamentally different from other white men who did not happen to live in the South. And he knew that the course of events can never wholly be determined by human planning or design, and that men must learn submission and resignation. His *Second Inaugural,* delivered on March.4, 1865, when the war was almost concluded, exhibits a profounder understanding of human affairs than any other American utterance, spoken or written.

While Lincoln embodied the finest elements of the democratic ideal, the generals who won the war for the North were equally typical, in another fashion, of the American character. By materialistic standards the victory of the North may be considered as inevitable because of its superior manpower and economic resources; but this strength had to be mobilized and used. The North had to discover generals with a will to victory. After a number of failures it found them, in the American manner, among plain citizens with no social backing and little military experience. After the Northern army had been organized by a former railroad executive, McClellan, it found appropriate commanders in two Middle Westerners, Grant and Sherman. Both these men had been in civilian life at the outset of the war; both of them had previously appeared to be frustrated characters with a penchant for failure; and both of them emerged to leadership because they believed in taking the offensive and in concentrating all the force at their disposal, without mercy and without restraint, on the single object of crushing the South. By contrast, the Southern generals, most of whom were trained professionals and belonged to the planter class, were superb tacticians; but although they were able to win battles, they had too many professional and aristocratic inhibitions to make full and uncompromising use of their advantages.

Having the better army at the outset of the war, the South might have won its independence immediately if its leaders had been willing to take the offensive. Instead, they waited while the North mobilized its resources and was ready to strike. During 1862 and 1863, while spectacular but indecisive campaigns were occurring in the East, Grant and Sherman won complete control of the Mississippi Valley, thereby splitting the Confederacy in two. In 1864 Grant was transferred to the East and began to fight his

way southward into Virginia, while Sherman crossed the
Appalachians from the west and marched through Georgia,
deliberately laying waste the country in order to destroy
the Southern will to resist. By the spring of 1865 the South
knew that the war was lost, and the Southern generals
refused to continue fighting.

Meanwhile Northern industrial and financial interests
had taken advantage of the secession of the South to
establish a firm hold over the federal Congress. Although
Northern business men had not caused the war, their
aggrandizement was certainly the most conspicuous of its
results. A high protective tariff, lavish grants of money
and public land to the railroads, the right to import contract labor from Europe, banking legislation and a treasury
policy advantageous to creditor interests, and large-scale
and generous government contracts (accompanied by gross
corruption)—all these helped to transform the United
States from an agrarian into an industrial nation. Even
the one measure intended primarily for the benefit of the
farmers—the Homestead Act providing for the free distribution of public land—was taken advantage of by business
groups, who were able (through lax administration of the
act) to acquire ownership of the most valuable natural
resources in the West and of land that promised speculative
profits. There were many Northern leaders (like Lincoln)
who disliked much of this legislation, or who did not understand its implications; but they were powerless to prevent
the triumph of the moneyed interests. By attempting to
leave the Union in order to maintain Negro slavery, the
South had brought about the final and irreparable defeat of
agrarianism.

And just as the race issue had enabled the moneyed interests to win control of the government, so it made it
possible for them to consolidate their power after the war
ended. Those Northerners, such as Lincoln, who regarded
the war as primarily a struggle to maintain American democracy had proposed to restore constitutional rights to
the Southern states as quickly as possible, asking them
only to pledge allegiance to the Union and to accept the
abolition of slavery. After the assassination of Lincoln in

April 1865, this policy was put into effect by his successor, Andrew Johnson, a native of Tennessee and an exponent of old-fashioned Jacksonian democracy. Thus the agrarian South, chastened by defeat but by no means purged of its agrarianism, would regain its influence in Congress; and as Northern business men were quick to realize, the tariff, the railroad subsidies, and the payment of interest to government bondholders would be endangered. Such a prospect was intolerable both to the moneyed interests and to those Republican politicians who had used the sectional conflict as a device for achieving power. They decided that the South must be treated not as part of the Union but as conquered territory, and they were able to win the support of the most idealistic elements in the North for such a program by means of the race question. White Southerners had accepted the abolition of slavery, but it was obvious that they still proposed to keep the Negro in a subordinate position with no political and few civil rights. In 1867 the Republicans in Congress brushed aside Johnson's reconstruction program, imposed military rule on the South, decreed that the Negro should be enfranchised, deprived many of the Southern whites of political rights, and ordered the election of new Southern governments based on Negro suffrage. In this manner the predominance in the federal government of the Republican Party, and of the economic interests it represented, would be perpetuated. The leaders chiefly responsible for these measures, men such as Thad Stevens and Charles Sumner, were idealistically devoted to the cause of human equality; but their idealism had that bitter, fanatical, and self-righteous quality that is often a cloak for self-interest and greed for power. They were motivated more by a hatred for the Southern whites than by a love for the Southern Negroes.

If this radical reconstruction program could have succeeded, a major American problem would have been solved. Unfortunately deep-rooted human attitudes could not be changed in a few years by legislative action, particularly when the underlying motives for the action were so cynical. Thanks to the greed of Northern businessmen and the ambition of Northern politicians, the Southern Negro was given an opportunity; but the obstacles to effective use of it were overwhelming. Recently emancipated slaves, mostly illiterate, surrounded by a hostile white population, and guided by a small group of white Republican politicians who had moved into the South to supervise the program, were suddenly entrusted with political power. Reconstruction could have succeeded only if the Southern whites had been willing to adjust themselves to the idea of race equality, and this they were determined never to do. Actually the reconstruction governments put into effect much good legislation, especially in respect to public education, some of which has never been repealed; and some of their ablest and most honest leaders were men of Negro descent. But they failed to solve the economic problems of the Negroes by providing them with land; and they were guilty of much extravagance and corruption.

The faults of the reconstruction governments were loudly and persistently publicized by the Southern whites and were explained in terms of race. Yet in reality they proved nothing about the political capacity of the Negroes. If the Southern ex-slaves had been white and not Negro, they would have committed the same errors; political capacity and integrity cannot be acquired overnight. Nor is it certain that the Negro legislatures were actually worse than certain white legislatures in other parts of the country during the same period. None of the reconstruction governments indulged in as much stealing as the Tweed ring in New York or the whisky ring in Washington; and even in the South the worst offenders were white carpetbaggers and not Negroes. But where a white politician living in luxury at the expense of his constituents aroused only a cynical amusement, a Negro politician behaving in precisely the same manner was regarded as a symbol of the utmost infamy and degradation.

The Southern whites gradually regained control of their governments by intimidating the Negroes in order to prevent them from voting, and the Northern politicians gradually lost interest in the question. With the expansion of big business and the admission of new Western states, the Republican Party no longer needed votes from the

South in order to win elections. In 1877 the last federal troops were withdrawn from the South, and white supremacy was restored everywhere. The Negro was no longer a slave, but he still had few "rights which the white man was bound to respect."

But although the North no longer attempted to change the Southern pattern of racial relationships, the other results of the Civil War were more enduring. Henceforth the South was unable to protect herself from exploitation by Northern banking and business corporations or to maintain her agrarian way of life. Compelled to remain as a subordinate section in a Union which was now controlled by urban capitalism, the next generation of Southerners could see no solution to their problems except to imitate the North by adopting an industrial economy. A new South of textile factories and steel mills began to emerge, dominated by a new moneyed class of merchants, bankers, and landlords. Claiming that the South could not otherwise compete successfully with the North, this "Bourbon" ruling class insisted on the necessity of low wages and long hours, and became the most uncompromising opponents of trade unions and of social welfare legislation. In the 1890's the poorer classes in the South began to rebel against Bourbon control; but their leaders were usually demagogues and rabble-rousers who displayed little constructive leadership, and their resentment was easily diverted into the issue of white supremacy. The small white farmer of the South found that to denounce his Negro competitors and demand that they be kept in subjection was easier and more satisfying than to deal with the complex economic mechanisms that were the real causes of his poverty. As long as the South remained obsessed with the race question, any thoroughgoing solution to its economic and social problems seemed to be impossible. Through the twentieth century most Southern leaders were either Bourbons or demagogues, and an enlightened liberalism was rare.

If the South could have maintained and revitalized her traditional attitudes—her preference for human over material values and her belief in a code of manners and a concept of social order—and could have given them a meaningful relationship to twentieth-century conditions, she could have made a unique contribution to the emergent civilization of America. But to disentangle what was permanently valuable in the Southern way of life from the wreckage of the slave society destroyed in the Civil War seemed to be too difficult a task. The intellectual spokesmen of the South either regretted the defeat of the Confederacy or else accepted the values of the North and looked forward to the liquidation of whatever was distinctive in the entire Southern heritage.

Meanwhile the majority of the Negroes had subsided into a position of subordination to white landowners, although usually as tenant farmers rather than as wage laborers. The more restless and ambitious began to move from the country into the cities and from the South into the North, adopting those manual occupations not already pre-empted by members of the white race. But both in the South and in the North race discrimination continued to be an apparently indissoluble element in the American pattern of behavior. Any man with Negro blood was classified not by his personal qualities but by his race, all white men being automatically superior to him. In the South, insofar as the Negroes were willing to "know their place," the old pattern of racial relationships actually worked; in return for subordination, the Negro could expect some measure of protection. To this extent the South handled the problem more successfully than the North where there was no accepted pattern and where the Negro had more freedom but less protection and more isolation. But in the course of time an increasing number of Negroes became unwilling to "know their place" and began to demand the same rights as other human beings. In the twentieth century, with the growth of a Negro business and professional class serving the Negro urban population, Negro militancy and Negro resentment against their manifold economic, cultural, and social disabilities steadily increased. Yet beyond appealing to the white conscience and to such laws as white officials might be willing to enforce, the Negro could do little to improve his position. As long as white Americans continued to think

in racial and not in human terms, he could find no solution
to his problems; and there appeared to be no prospect of
such a solution within any visible period of time.

In twentieth-century world affairs the United States
claimed to stand for democracy, for freedom, and for the
equality of man. But at home more than twelve million
American citizens were exposed to continuous insult and
discrimination solely because of the color of their skins.
The harmful effects of race prejudice on the internal
development of America were deep and lasting. And in
a world approaching unification, in which the colored
races far outnumbered the white race, the international
results of color prejudice were likely to be even more far-
reaching and more damaging to the nation guilty of it.

CHAPTER XI

THE GROWTH
OF INDUSTRIALISM

★ ★ ★ ★ ★ ★ ★ ★ ★ ★ ★ ★ ★ ★

THE MOST IMPORTANT RESULT of the Civil War was to remove all obstacles to industrial expansion and to the growth of big business corporations. During the next two or three generations the United States became the richest and most powerful country in the world. At the same time she was transformed from a country in which the average citizen was an independent property owner to one in which there were extreme economic inequalities and most citizens were dependent for their livelihood on big corporations owned and controlled by a small minority of the population.

Whether industrial growth could have been promoted without giving such free rein to the predatory and acquisitive drives of the business class is a debatable question. In the early stages of the industrial revolution, government exercised more economic responsibilities than became customary after the Civil War, at least in the field of transportation; it both helped to provide new enterprises with capital and regulated their rates and services. The agrarian spokesman, Senator Benton, even suggested that the transcontinental railroads should be built and owned by the federal government. But effective government supervision of economic development ran counter to the national traditions of economic individualism and suspicion of government power that the agrarians themselves had helped to establish. And in an individualistic society there could be no industrial growth without inequality; industry required, on the one hand, large aggregations of capital and, on the other hand, a large class willing to work in factories. The American people, therefore, accepted inequality as necessary for economic progress. They allowed their industry to be organized by a small capitalist class, who acquired ownership of land, natural resources, and money, and whose property claims were protected by the state. And at the same time an industrial proletariat developed, composed mainly of new immigrant groups from Europe, who acquired no economic rights in America except the right to work for whatever wages the employing class chose to offer them.

The ideology of big business enterprise was essentially Hamiltonian. Its exponents believed in government aid for economic expansion; they believed (although they did not always say so in public) in the leadership of an elite; and they regarded the sanctity of contracts as the very foundation of civilization. They argued that if able and energetic individuals were encouraged to develop the country's resources and were permitted to enrich themselves in the process, then the whole of society would benefit. The unchecked drive of the will of ruthless men toward wealth and power was presented as a civilizing force. Attempts to interfere with them were attributed to the envy of the lazy and the inefficient, who deserved no protection or consideration. Yet the business classes also appropriated for their own purposes certain doctrines originally associated with agrarianism. When there were threats, not of government aid for business, but of government regulation of business, they could speak eloquently of the merits of private property, free enterprise, and individual liberty, thereby inviting the support of the farmer and the small owner. They could preach *laissez faire* as vigorously as Adam Smith (whose main argument had been that all government aid for business should be abolished, since it created special privileges and caused monopolies); and they could denounce the growth of government power as bitterly as Thomas Jefferson.

This ideology of business enterprise, originally justified partly by Calvinist theology and partly by the doctrine of natural rights, acquired added support from the Darwinian theory of evolution. According to Darwin's disciple Herbert Spencer, who acquired an enormous influence in America, progress came about through the competitive struggle of individuals. Such a struggle was represented as natural (and therefore good), whereas social action tending to limit it was denounced as artificial (and therefore bad). Yet in reality (as the agrarians had always insisted) there was nothing in the least natural about nineteenth-century American capitalism. It was an artificial man-made creation that had been brought into existence by government policies, by laws for the protection of contracts and corporate property rights, and by financial mechanisms tending to increase the wealth of creditor groups. It had, in fact, been deliberately and carefully planned, on models derived from Europe, by the makers of the Constitution and by such men as Alexander Hamilton and John Marshall.

After the Civil War this philosophy of business enterprise acquired for a period an almost complete domination over the American mind. It was taught in schools and colleges; it was propagated by the most reputable writers; it was accepted by the respectable and educated classes. Even those individuals who deplored the greed of business magnates and the degradation of the wage-earning class had no alternative social philosophy to propound. And until the twentieth century it determined both the policies of the federal government and the decisions of the federal judiciary.

The government aided business directly through a high tariff, through subsidies and grants of public land and natural resources, through patent laws that had the effect of protecting big corporations against competition, and through a financial policy designed to benefit creditors. The judiciary, abandoning the agrarianism of Taney and returning to the Federalism of John Marshall, maintained the sanctity of contracts and protected wealthy corporations both against state regulation and against trade-union activities. In particular, the Fourteenth Amendment, which had originally been adopted with the avowed purpose of protecting Negroes and which prohibited states from depriving persons of life, liberty or property except by due process of law, was gradually transformed into the Magna Carta of big business. In the latter part of the nineteenth century the Supreme Court adopted a new interpretation of the right of property. Property rights no longer referred merely to the ownership of tangible possessions (as in the agrarian eighteenth century); they now included the right to make money from one's possessions by selling them. And in accordance with this new definition the processes of capitalistic business were declared to be immune from government regulation. When a state attempted to limit the rates a railroad or a public utility might charge, the court declared that it was depriving corporations of their property. When a state attempted to protect workers by adopting a maximum-hour law, the court declared that it was depriving the worker of his right to work for as long as he might wish to contract for.

The masses of the American people accepted this process, partly because they had become enthralled by the hope of rapid industrial progress and of wealth for all, and partly because they were unable to see any relevant difference between the freedom and property rights of the small owner and those of the big corporation. As John Taylor had pointed out, "the grossest abuses" had been able to "artfully ally themselves with real and honest property." The post-Civil War generation ignored the warning of the agrarians against the use of political power to secure economic privilege; and they did not understand the agrarian distinction between the property of the farmer or mechanic and that of the banker or speculator. Discredited by its association with slavery and by the Civil War, and obliterated by the propaganda of the business classes, agrarian theory was almost completely forgotten. There was thus a curious lack of continuity in American political thinking. When opposition to big business revived near the end of the nineteenth century, it borrowed little from the American past. The economic doctrines of Franklin, of Jefferson and Taylor, and of the Jacksonians did not become a permanent part of the American intellectual tradition.

Yet throughout the entire period it is probable that most Americans still believed in a property owners' democracy, although they were not willing to take the kind of action needed to maintain it. The agrarian ideal was still the core of the American view of life. That ideal had, in fact, been restated at the beginning of the Civil War by the leader of the Republican Party, Abraham Lincoln. In a message to Congress in 1861 Lincoln had described America as a country where the large majority of the people were neither employers nor employees, and where the hired laborer was not "fixed to that condition for life. . . . Men with their families—wives, sons and daughters —work for themselves, on their farms, in their houses, and in their shops, taking the whole product to themselves, and asking no favors of capital on the one hand, nor of hired laborers or slaves on the other. . . . The prudent, penniless beginner in the world labors for wages awhile, saves a surplus with which to buy tools or land for himself, then labors on his own account another while, and at length hires another new beginner to help him. This is the just and generous and prosperous system which opens the way to all—gives hope to all, and consequent energy and progress and improvement of condition to all."

Even in the twentieth century most Americans wished for this kind of society; many of them, in fact, continued to insist, in defiance of all the evidence to the contrary, that America still was such a society.[1] But they were not prepared to act by agrarian principles. Attracted by the mirage of progress, and confused and misled by the exponents of business enterprise, they continued to hope that the growth of big industry would somehow prove to be

---

[1] *This is illustrated by the extraordinary popularity of the* Reader's Digest. *The* Reader's Digest *owes its circulation to the fact that its editorial point of view is identical with that of a vast number of middleclass Americans. It depicts America in early nineteenth-century terms, as a neighborly country filled with opportunities for small property owners.*

not incompatible with economic democracy and opportunity for all. In consequence, a kind of pathological schism, a lack of adaptation to realities, developed within the American mind.

And whatever the sacrifices may have been, the industrial achievement of America was, in fact, so remarkable that the optimism and the national pride it engendered were not surprising. When the national wealth was increasing so rapidly, it was easy to believe that in the long run all elements in the population would somehow benefit by it.

As a river may be traced back to its source in a tiny mountain spring, so the industrial revolution in America is usually traced back to a spinning machine constructed by an immigrant from Great Britain, Samuel Slater by name, at Pawtucket, Rhode Island, in the year 1791. This humble contrivance was housed in a shed and operated by the labor of a few small children. But a more significant landmark in the evolution of American industry was the formation of the Boston Manufacturing Company in 1813. Founded by a group of wealthy Boston merchants who had decided that more money was to be made from industry than from shipping, and who planned to establish a spinning and weaving factory on the most up-to-date English models at Waltham, Massachusetts, this was the first big business corporation in America. From this date the manufacturing of textiles by machinery increased rapidly, and the older handicraft methods were gradually eliminated.

During the next half-century mechanization spread to some other industries; occupations still carried on by the manual labor of skilled craftsmen passed under capitalistic control; coal and iron mining developed; a network of railroads covered the Eastern states; and Western farmers steadily increased their production of commercial crops for sale to the growing factory towns of the Northeast. By the outbreak of the Civil War thirty thousand miles of railroads were in operation; one million, three hundred thousand persons were employed in factories, and were turning out products worth close to two billion dollars a year; and nearly one fifth of the population were living in towns and cities. This industrial growth, however, was almost restricted to New England and to the Middle Atlantic states.

The generation following the Civil War was the great age of railroad building, during which the Eastern lines were improved and extended and the big transcontinental lines were built. By 1900 nearly two hundred thousand miles had been completed. Stimulated by the needs of the railroads, the mining of coal and the manufacturing of steel increased to enormous proportions. Meanwhile oil and other mineral resources were being exploited; mechanical methods were extended to the making or processing of most consumption goods; and agricultural production was expanded by the adoption of machinery. This rapid growth was facilitated by the import of European capital, in return for which the Americans exported foodstuffs, and by the immigration of millions of Irish, Germans, Scandinavians, Italians, and Slavs. Between 1840 and 1900 more than sixteen million immigrants entered the country, a number almost as large as the total population of the United States in the former year. By 1900 the total number of wage earners was about seventeen million. Four and a half million of them were employed in manufacturing, and the value of their products exceeded thirteen billion dollars a year. By this time forty per cent of the population were living in towns and cities.

Meanwhile, the use of electricity for power and light had been developed; new chemical industries were appearing; and such inventions as the telephone, the automobile, and the airplane were being made. In the twentieth century the American industrial system continued to grow, the greatest expansion occurring in the making of durable consumption goods, particularly the automobile. Oil and electricity began to replace steam as the principal sources of power; light metals and plastics began to replace iron and steel. Meanwhile, with the growth of technology, the rate of increase of factory workers became slower, but there was an enormous growth of new white-collar occupations. Between 1900 and 1930 no less than eighteen and a half million immigrants entered the country. By 1929 thirty-six million Americans were wage- or salary-earners, nearly eight and a half million of them being employed in factories; and industrial products were valued at seventy billion dollars. By this time the American people had become predominantly urban, fifty-six per cent of them living in towns and cities.

Industrialization was a world-wide process. The factory system and the use of machinery instead of hand labor, after being initiated in Great Britain in the eighteenth century, were gradually adopted, with varying degrees of enthusiasm or reluctance, voluntary choice or compulsion, by almost all other countries. But nowhere else (except in the Soviet Union in the 1930's) was their advance so rapid and so triumphant as in the United States. By 1929 the United States had achieved an industrial pre-eminence and supremacy over other countries that seemed scarcely credible. Since the American productive system never operated at anywhere near its full capacity (except in wartime), its astonishing potentialities were not fully realized until the Second World War. In the year 1944, with fourteen million of the most able-bodied citizens withdrawn from production into military service, the Americans turned out eighty-six billion dollars' worth of war materials in addition to producing ninety-seven billion dollars' worth of goods for civilian use. While fighting the greatest war in history and supplying their allies as well as themselves with war materials, they were actually able to increase civilian consumption and to raise the average civilian standard of living.

The industrial supremacy achieved by the Americans was due partly to material factors: to their natural resources and to the political unification of so wide an area and the lack of internal trade barriers. But material factors alone would not have produced such a result if the Americans had not developed the appropriate character and view of life. Rapid expansion was possible because the matrix out of which American industrialism developed was a democratic, pioneering, and agrarian society, and not a feudal society as in most other countries. From their pioneering and Calvinist past the Americans had acquired a special bent toward the domination of nature; they believed in conquest, self-control, and thrift, not in contemplation, enjoyment, or luxurious spending. They had always been an inventive people, and had always attached the greatest importance to pursuits of practical utility. Because of their freedom from class distinctions, their faith in the average man, and their belief in the duty of self-advancement, men of executive and technical ability from any social background were encouraged to assert themselves. Moreover, the American preference for mobility and versatility rather than for the development of specialized professional skills was in harmony with the new techniques of mass production developed by American engineers. In the new mechanized industries, which emphasized quantity rather than quality, the worker could often acquire a sufficient degree of skill in a few weeks, so that he need not bind himself for life to any particular occupation.

In pure science, which requires long professional training and disinterested intellectual curiosity and contemplation, the Americans lagged far behind the Europeans. But they were superior in technical inventiveness, as Franklin showed in the eighteenth century and Edison in the nineteenth. Of all the American technological triumphs the most significant, symbolically as well as actually, was the invention of flying. It was appropriate that a people who believed above all things in the domination of nature by the will should have been the first to achieve this most dramatic and spectacular of all human accomplishments —an accomplishment of which men had dreamed for thousands of years. And it was true to the spirit of American civilization that the men responsible for it should have been two obscure and unpretentious Middle Western bicycle mechanics who dared to set about it without professional or academic training and without official patronage or financial backing.

Thus the American genius for industrialization, like the American genius for war, was due to the fact that the Americans were a free, undisciplined, and unregimented people. Just as the Americans excelled in warfare because they were essentially a nonmilitary people, so they excelled in industry because they had originally been an agrarian people. Yet the tendency of industrial growth, of the kind that occurred after the Civil War, was to make the Americans less free, more disciplined, and more regimented, and thereby to weaken those qualities that had been responsible for that growth. The transformation of the average American from an independent property owner into the hired employee of a big corporation necessarily reduced his sense of responsibility and his capacity for initiative, while the growth of economic inequality made it more difficult for talent to assert itself.

The big corporations were built by entrepreneurs who were formerly known as captains of industry but whom a more irreverent age prefers to describe as robber barons. Some of the more important of them were Vanderbilt, Hill, and Harriman in railroads, Rockefeller in oil, Carnegie in steel, Duke in tobacco, Havemeyer in sugar, McCormick in agricultural machinery, and Morgan in investment banking. As Thorstein Veblen pointed out, these men should not be given credit for the achievements of American technology. It was the engineer and the mechanic, not the entrepreneur, who actually built American industry. And since most entrepreneurs were primarily motivated, not by a desire to contribute to human progress, but by a drive to make as much money and acquire as much power as possible, they sometimes preferred to sabotage technology, suppressing inventions that might reduce their earnings, making agreements with each other to limit production in order to keep prices high, and closing down factories when profits were too small. Yet in bringing together aggregates of capital and masses of workers and creating the administrative machinery for setting them in motion, the robber barons were performing a function that the society of their time considered to be desirable.

It would be unjust to condemn them too harshly. A few of them, such as Jay Gould, had no constructive impulses and were interested solely in making millions by any means whatever. But the majority genuinely believed that in organizing industry into large units that could more efficiently exploit the natural resources of America, they were doing God's work and promoting civilization. Yet one cannot acquit the robber barons without condemning the society that had produced them; for almost all of them were hard, ruthless, narrow, and uncivilized men. The ability to make a great deal of money is a specialized talent rarely accompanied by any broad understanding of social forces or by any cultural awareness. Unfortunately in the new industrial civilization money meant power. These men were not likely to use their power in any humane or disinterested fashion.

When the robber barons had finished their work, almost all the manufacturing and transportation of America was controlled by big corporations. A majority of the Americans worked for corporations, and the destinies of all of them were deeply affected by corporation practices. The twentieth century in America was the age of the corporation, as the twelfth in Europe had been the age of feudalism. And although corporations varied considerably in size, it was the two or three hundred largest, headed by vast billion-dollar monsters such as United States Steel and American Telephone and Telegraph, whose economic policies were of decisive importance.

By 1929 four fifths of all the profits of manufacturing were going to only 1,349 corporations, and the two hundred largest nonfinancial corporations had acquired ownership of nearly half of all corporate wealth and of twenty-two per cent of the total national wealth. As a result of this concentration of ownership and control the big corporations were largely able to evade the economic laws of supply and demand and to fix their own prices. Some branches of economic activity were dominated by single corporations; others were controlled by a small number of corporations which were able to make price agreements with each other. Big business was ceasing to be competitive, at least in the essential matter of prices, and was able to exploit the rest of the community by charging whatever the traffic would bear. And this growth of monopoly appeared to be, in large measure, the result of an inevitable economic development. In the Jacksonian period monopolies had been created by means of special privileges granted through state charters; and the Jacksonian remedy had been to

enact general incorporation laws making competition possible. But in the twentieth century, when most forms of
manufacturing required vast capital investments, corporations were able to establish monopolistic positions by
acquiring ownership of so much capital and capital equipment that newcomers could not hope to compete with
them. The result was that a relatively small group of men,
controlling the leading industrial and financial corporations
and to a large extent working in collaboration with each
other by means of interlocking directorates and common
association with the same New York firms of investment
bankers, were able to dominate the American economy and
to acquire the major share of the profits of industrial
enterprise.

Meanwhile the farmer and the small businessman were
still operating in a competitive market; and while the
prices they paid were largely fixed by big business, the
prices they received were dependent on supply and demand.
Even in the age of the big corporation there continued
to be a great number of small businesses in America; in
1929 the total number of corporations actively engaged in
business amounted to no less than 456,000. But the vast
majority of them earned small profits, even in periods of
prosperity, and were always close to bankruptcy. In an
economy dominated by big corporations, it was extremely
difficult for newcomers to establish themselves. As far as
the vast majority of the population was concerned, the
American creed of private enterprise and initiative had become a myth.

Legally, the big corporation had the same rights, although not the same obligations, as a person; and it had
inherited all the immunities the American constitution had
given to individual property owners. It could not be deprived of its property except by due process of law; and
for a long period its wage, hour, and price policies were
almost exempt from any kind of social control. The
managers of a corporation were not answerable to the
community for the use they made of the property under
their control, although their actions might have social re-
percussions unknown in the eighteenth century. The cor-

poration was, in fact, a kind of *imperium in imperio* claiming an economic sovereignty analogous to the political sovereignty of an independent state. Meanwhile, its employees had no legally enforceable rights in the institution upon which they depended for their livelihood, and could be dismissed at the pleasure of the management. When the employees of a corporation went on strike because their wages were too low, their behavior was generally regarded by the business classes as reprehensible. But when a corporation itself went on strike, closing down its factories and dismissing its men because its profits were too low, its behavior was believed to be sound and necessary business practice.

During the twentieth century few of the larger corporations remained under the ownership of one man or group of men. Ownership had a tendency to become more widely diffused among a large number of stockholders, who retained the right to be paid dividends but who ceased to exercise any of the powers and obligations traditionally associated with property. But this did not mean that any large proportion of the American people were sharing in the profits of ownership. In 1929 the total number of stockholders was probably about three or four million, and three fifths of all corporation dividends was paid to only 150,000 individuals. Meanwhile, effective control was being assumed by salaried executives, who were theoretically the agents of the stockholders but who appeared in practice to be almost independent of them. This divorce of ownership from control and development of a separate managerial class were regarded by some observers as developments of immense social importance, constituting a minor revolution. Actually, however, the corporation executives usually worked in close co-operation with investment bankers, who became the general custodians of stockholders' interests; and their main function was to produce profits. There was no good reason for expecting that their policies would be more humanitarian and broad-minded than those of the older owner-managers, whose main desire had been to make as much money as possible. At the same time, the growth of vast corporation bureaucracies, with scores of vice-presidents and minor executives hoping to work their way up by winning the favor of the men at the top, began to produce the evils traditionally associated with political bureaucracy: conservatism, timidity, and fear of initiative.

Meanwhile, the buying and selling of corporation stocks, by which purchasers acquired the right to share in the profits of ownership without incurring any corresponding responsibilities, became a major American occupation; and speculation in stock prices began to replace land speculation as the likeliest method of getting something for nothing. The manipulation of these claims to profits assumed the most intricate and fantastic forms, which no longer had any intelligible connection with the economic realities upon which they depended. Persons who were adept at this art of manipulation were able to extract millions of dollars' worth of real and tangible goods from the producing classes without having any direct contact themselves with any of the forces and techniques of production and without making any contribution of any kind to the welfare of the community. In an age in which genuine economic opportunities were restricted, but in which social prestige still depended upon financial success, stock speculation became the favorite activity of ambitious individuals who hoped to become rich quickly.

2

The growth of the big industrial and financial corporations was accompanied by most radical changes in the structure of American society. The "general happy mediocrity" of the eighteenth century disappeared. Gross economic inequalities developed and were followed by a marked sharpening of class differences. At the beginning of the twentieth century the Americans were less equal, socially and culturally as well as economically, than they had been at the beginning of the nineteenth century. And with the growth of the wage-earning class and the commercialization of agriculture, a smaller proportion of the Americans could regard themselves as economically secure and independent. Insofar as the average worker or farmer was dependent for his livelihood on the workings of a complex economic system, he was no longer free to determine his own destiny.

The most rapid growth of inequality occurred in the period after the Civil War, during which a small number of individuals were making fortunes from the new industries. It continued to increase during the first thirty years of the twentieth century. By the year 1929 there were six hundred and thirty-one thousand families who were receiving incomes of above ten thousand dollars a year; their combined income amounted to more than twenty-one billion dollars, constituting twenty-eight per cent of the total national income. At the same period more than eixteen million families, nearly sixty per cent of the total number of families, were earning less than two thousand dollars a year, and their combined income amounted to about eighteen billion dollars, constituting less than twenty-four per cent of the total national income. Thus the sixteen million poorest families were receiving a total income substantially smaller than that of the six hundred thousand richest families. Between these two extreme groups were ranged the remaining ten and a half million families receiving between two and ten thousand dollars a year, whose combined income amounted to thirty-seven billion dollars, forty-seven per cent of the total. At this period fifteen per cent of the working population belonged to the business and professional classes, and sixteen per cent were farmers, while the remaining sixty-nine per cent were wage earners of one kind or another.

It had formerly been an American theory that wealth did not remain permanently in the same families, but this ceased to be true after the Civil War. The enormous fortunes acquired by the robber barons were transmitted to their descendants, who became a hereditary leisure class. But unlike most European leisure classes they had no social function or sense of responsibility. Few of them remained active in business; and American society, having been organized on democratic and not on feudal principles, did not expect them to assume political leadership. They became, for the most part, a parasitical class of absentee owners, living on dividends and spending their money as conspicuously as possible, building themselves enormous houses modeled on Gothic castles or Renaissance palaces, aping the manners and attitudes of European aristocracies and frequently intermarrying with them, and introducing aristocratic customs into America.

The one social obligation expected of the millionaire families was that they give away a part of their money for philanthropic or cultural purposes. Some of them, such as the Rockefellers, showed genuine munificence and intelligence in their donations; but the philanthropic foundations that advertised the generosity of rich men or helped them to reduce their income taxes, were often of dubious value. Some robber-baron money promoted public health or popular education. And some of it went to universities, usually for the erection of expensive and ostentatious mock-Gothic buildings, although in a few instances a little of it helped to encourage learning and research. Little money, on the other hand, went to the arts. One of the most useful functions of a leisure class—intelligent patronage of writers, artists, and musicians—was beyond the capacity of most of the American rich. Some of them became collectors, thereby finding a new channel for the expression of their predatory and acquisitive drives, and in the course of time their collections enriched museums; but the presence of Italian primitives in American galleries did little to stimulate American culture. With a few notable exceptions, the millionaire class did more to debase than to encourage the growth of a living contemporary art.

Below the leisure class in the social structure of industrial America were the business, professional, and salaried classes. Insofar as America had now become a business civilization, these classes set the tone for its political and social thinking and determined its cultural standards. When one thought of a typical American, one thought of a businessman. American society did not wholly lose its mobility; and even in the 1940's an appreciable number of the business class, including some of the most successful, were men who had been born into the working class and worked their way upward. But although the line dividing the business class from the working class could be crossed, it was clearly defined. And within the business class itself a number of intricate and subtle distinctions developed, based chiefly on pecuniary standards, although ancestry and race were also of importance. Ability to spend money conspicuously (on an expensive house or a superior make of automobile) and success in securing admission to the more exclusive clubs and social milieus were indexes for determining an individual's status in any urban community. Yet since these social differentiations were copied from Europe and ran counter to the official American ideals, it was not often explicitly recognized that an embryo caste system was developing; in theory the Americans still believed in equality.

The mass of the urban population belonged to the working class, and this was composed predominantly of the more recent immigrant groups. Except in the South, most of the industrial workers were Irish, German, Italian, Slavic, and Jewish—and not Anglo-Saxon,—so that the basic class division of American urban society was also, in large measure, a race division.

The mass migration of Europeans across the Atlantic during the period of American industrial growth was the largest such movement in all history. Yet although it radically altered the racial composition of the American people so that by 1920 only about forty per cent of them were of Anglo-Saxon descent, it had remarkably little effect on their culture and mores. Regarding the United States as a higher civilization, the immigrants were anxious to become Americanized and assimilated as rapidly as possible. Their children spoke the American language and endeavored to live by American standards. Second- and third-generation Americans quickly became indistinguishable from Americans with pre-Revolutionary ancestors. This vast process of assimilation, by which many millions of individuals learnt to repudiate the traditions of their blood and ancestry and to assume for themselves the memories of the *Mayflower* and the Declaration of Independence, was carried through chiefly by the public schools. The welding of so many different groups into a national unity, and not the maintenance of high intellectual standards, was, in fact, the primary social function of the American educational system.

This capacity for successful assimilation was a remarkable proof of the vitality of the American tradition. Never before in history had a nation incorporated into itself, without undergoing any essential change, such a vast body of aliens. Yet insofar as the process of assimilation was successfully completed, to that extent would social unrest be stimulated. Workers who had themselves migrated from Europe usually accepted inequality and exploitation with considerable docility. They were accustomed to class privilege; they were afraid to assert themselves in an alien environment; and their earnings, low as they were, were usually higher than in Europe. As new immigrants arrived, moreover, earlier groups (such as the Irish) moved upward in the social scale. In consequence the building of the American industrial system was accompanied by relatively few labor disturbances. But since the immigrant groups were admitted to America not as second-class citizens but as full participants in the formative ideals of the American nation, with their promise of universal freedom and equality, they could be expected eventually to ask that those ideals should be fulfilled. The docility with which the American working class accepted the decrease of freedom and the growth of inequality would not continue indefinitely. It was possible for the robber barons to depart from the Jeffersonian tradition because the workers they exploited did not know what that tradition meant; but their children and their grandchildren learned to make that tradition their own.

For the peasants from Italy and Austria and Poland who manned the American steel plants and automobile factories, as for the indentured servants of the colonial period, America was still the land of opportunity, although they had to make homes for themselves in the tenements of enormous cities instead of in the solitude of the forest and had to do battle with a complex society rather than with the wilderness. America promised riches and independence, if not for the immigrants themselves, then at least for their descendants. A man might work for wages throughout his life, but he could hope that his children (in London's words) would not be permanently "fixed to that condition" but could rise to the status of independent property owners, free to make their own decisions and determine their own destinies. Unfortunately the city was less friendly than the forest; its rewards were far more dazzling; but they were reserved for the peculiarly gifted and the peculiarly lucky, and the struggle to attain them exacerbated every aggressive and acquisitive impulse. In the new America of the big industrial cities, men fought each other instead of assisting each other against the Indians and the wilderness.

Even in periods of economic expansion the spirit of the new America was violently competitive. But there were also periods of economic contraction when the whole process of increasing wealth, rising land and stock values, and upward social mobility went into reverse, and opportunities disappeared. Because of the unequal distribution of the national income there was a chronic tendency for the richer classes to accumulate savings they did not spend and could not profitably invest, and the result was that production was liable to exceed effective purchasing power. This gap between production and purchasing power was increased by the high price levels maintained by the big corporations. Since consumption thus lagged behind production, at fairly regular intervals the balance between had to be violently re-established. This was the underlying reason for the periodic crises that attacked the economic system. But while the farmer and the small producer had to maintain production and lower their prices during a time of crisis, thus making possible an increase in consumption, the managers of the big corporations were able to adopt other measures. Industrial production was sharply reduced, factories closed their doors, millions of wage-earners found themselves without employment, and the whole economic system sank into depression. Such a procedure was in accordance with the ideology of capitalism; since the wage earner was merely the hired employee of the corporation and had no legal rights, it was considered proper to dismiss him whenever it was no longer profitable to employ

him. The primary function of the corporation manager was
to maintain profits.

The docility with which industrial America accepted
these depressions, as though they were acts of God and
not due to the faulty workings of a man-made system, was
extraordinary. It was considered preferable that millions
of families should be condemned to starvation in the midst
of plenty rather than that corporations should be held
legally accountable for the welfare of their workers. Industrial America was incomparably richer and more powerful
than the agrarian America of the eighteenth century; but
whereas the average citizen of agrarian America, owning
the means of his own livelihood, had independence and a
considerable measure of security, the average citizen of
industrial America enjoyed neither.

3

As industrialization expanded, there was a growing discrepancy between the habits and beliefs of the American
people and the realities of their social environment. The
character of a people always changes more slowly than
their institutions, and the Americans carried over into the
more static and regimented society of the big corporations
the attitudes they had acquired while they were still
pioneers with all the vast resources of an empty wilderness
to conquer and exploit. They continued to insist that freedom and equality were actually realized in their society,
and to think and act on this assumption in the conduct of
their daily lives. This cultural lag produced a schism between idea and reality that may be described as a national
neurosis. To use such a word in this context is by no means
merely metaphorical. The neurotic individual is the individual who has failed to adjust himself to realities; and
when a whole culture exhibits such a failure of adjustment, the result is a growth of neurotic tendencies among
the men and women who have been conditioned by it.

The Americans believed that they were a free people.
But the wage earner was no longer his own master during
the most important part of his daily life—his working hours;

he was free only insofar as he could do and say what he liked during his leisure time, and (with considerable limitations) could choose his own form of employment. Unable to participate in making the decisions upon which his livelihood depended, he had become the victim of forces over which he had no control. The Americans believed in equality of opportunity. But the system of property and inheritance laws was creating class divisions as acute as those existing in the Europe from which they had come. Above all, the Americans believed that the individual should struggle to improve his condition and conquer his environment, that if he had energy, courage, and initiative he would surely succeed, and that if he failed it was because of some deficiency within himself. Yet in the new industrial system it was wholly impossible for more than a small minority of the total population to achieve what society regarded as success. The average wage earner must be "fixed to that condition for life." Even among the highly paid and responsible business men and salaried executives only a small fraction were actually able to reach the top. Thus insofar as the American people were committed to the American ideology of personal success, they were attempting to accomplish something that for most of them was impossible. Judged by the prevalent standards of American society, most Americans were compelled to regard themselves as having failed and to attribute their failure to some shortcoming within themselves. This attitude persisted even during periods of economic depression, when millions of men, through no fault of their own, found themselves unemployed. Instead of rebelling against a system that had denied them opportunity, most of the unemployed accepted their fate with a masochistic submissiveness.

Since the big corporations never achieved a total domination over the American economy, this disharmony between idea and reality was by no means universal. Rural and smalltown America retained much of the leisureliness and neighborliness of the agrarian past. There was still room for the exercise of initiative, and the Americans continued to be capable of an inventiveness and an adventurousness beyond any other nation. But in the big cities life became competitive, fast-moving, febrile, and neurotic; and to an increasing extent the cities tended to dictate fashions and beliefs and to determine the cultural tone for the rest of the country.

With the transformation of the pioneer into the businessman, money became the principal symbol of success and the main object of ambition. In the strict sense of the word, the Americans were not a materialistic people. They were less concerned with the mere accumulation of material possessions and less careful in their use than were most Europeans. They continued to be the most generous people in the world, and to be extravagantly lavish and wasteful in the spending of their resources. But the business classes sought to prove their strength by the conquest of money, as their ancestors had done by the conquest of the wilderness; and they judged each other in monetary terms. To believe that there might be forms of personal achievement not susceptible to pecuniary measurement was to be slightly eccentric. In the twentieth century, with the growth of the durable consumption-goods industries and the colossal expansion of advertising, the belief that all success was monetary was emphasized and played upon by almost every newspaper, magazine, motion picture, and radio program. The man who could not afford to buy a new car, a new refrigerator, and the most up-to-date plumbing was lacking in virility and had not done his duty by his wife and children.

Such an attitude was incompatible with strict standards of personal and political honesty. In the pursuit of money it was a mistake to be too scrupulous; and laws could usually be circumvented. The Americans had never been a law-abiding people. On the frontier individuals had always defended themselves without relying on any organized enforcement of justice. Outlaws, desperadoes, claim jumpers, cattle rustlers, and other "bad men" had played prominent roles in the legend of the early West. With so individualistic and exuberant a past, it was not to be expected that the Americans would suddenly change their habits when their society became more settled, although the social effects of lawlessness and chicanery were now much more deleterious. Most people kept their financial activities within the letter of the law, but they felt no compunction about twisting its spirit to suit their own convenience. Speculation in stocks and real estate in order to get something for nothing was a national pastime, and was not regarded as in any way reprehensible, in spite of its demonstrably harmful effects upon the economic system. And while a large proportion of the business class hoped to make fortunes by methods that might be unethical but were not illegal, an appreciable element among the poorer classes pursued the same goal by a more direct route. The "bad men" of the frontier and the early West were succeeded, in industrial America, by the big-city gangsters, Skillful criminals sometimes made fortunes, and the disapproval of their more cautious fellow citizens was not always unmixed with envy.

For the aggressive and ambitious individual who felt confident of his power to compete, the life of the big cities had an extraordinary glamor and intoxication. But the plain citizen, insofar as he accepted the standards of his society and regarded monetary success as the main gauge of individual merit, inevitably suffered from a sense of defeat. In this competitive world he could have little feeling of belonging to any social order that was more significant and more enduring than its individual members, and that gave meaning to their lives; such a conception had always been lacking among the Americans. And since he could not conquer his environment, he had to regard himself as its victim, as a man to whom things happened. Whereas the frontier had created culture heroes like Daniel Boone and Mike Fink who stood for physical prowess and mastery, industrial America developed a humor of a new kind, the humor of the little man who always expects defeat—an attitude most perfectly embodied in Charlie Chaplin.[2] Such

[2] *According to James West, Americans living in an old-fashioned agrarian community do not find Charlie Chaplin funny. Dr. Kardiner comments: "Most Plainvillers apparently consider Chaplin just silly. This observation is of considerable importance. It means that the unconscious appeal of Chaplin's bum is less powerful to Plainvillers than to city folks, and that*

conditions inevitably undermined self-esteem, dignity, and masculinity, and stimulated neuroticism. What proportion of urban Americans actually suffered from emotional disorders, nervous breakdowns, or outright insanity, it is impossible to say; but any investigation of the subject, such as that undertaken in the case of men of military age during the Second World War, produced startling results.[3] Even before industrialism had conquered the nation Tocqueville had commented on the high proportion of nervous disorders among the Americans, and had attributed it to the competitiveness of American life.[4]

Growth into psychological maturity requires a healthy self-assurance and self-esteem; and when self-esteem depends upon a competitive success difficult to achieve and always uncertain, then it becomes more difficult for individuals to assume the full emotional responsibilities of adulthood. They may prefer to remain permanently on an adolescent level. Such a prolongation of adolescence became a frequent characteristic of twentieth-century urban Americans, particularly among those business and professional classes who were most involved in the competitive struggle. Their perpetual boyishness was sometimes attributed to the fact that America was a young country in which an adolescent exuberance was somehow appropriate, yet it had by no means been characteristic of the men of the eighteenth century, who had lived at a time when America was even younger; it was a twentieth-century phenomenon. And the emotional immaturity of so many American men led to a further increase in the relative influence of American women. The frontier had already made women more powerful in America than in Europe; and industrial society intensified this tendency. European

the tensions which this strange vagabond purports to ease are less intense with Plainvillers. This would mean that the Plainviller is more secure and less troubled by the pursuit of goals approved in urban centers." Abram Kardiner: The Psychological Frontiers of Society, p. 369.

[3] During the Second World War psychoneurotic disorders were responsible for 1,825,000 draft rejections and for 600,000 discharges.

[4] Democracy in America, Vol. II, Second Book, Chap. XIII.

observers sometimes declared that American society was essentially matriarchal and that women had become the superior class. This development was hastened by the increase in the amount of property held by women and by the gradual abolition during the twentieth century of legal, political, and economic inequalities between the sexes; but its more fundamental causes were emotional. The man of the industrial age was apt to have a neurotic dependence, first upon his mother and afterwards upon his wife, owing to his own insecurity and lack of masculine self-assurance.

On the surface it seemed that this change in the relationship between the sexes could be described eulogistically in terms of feminine emancipation; women, it was often declared, were being liberated from their agelong subordination and were acquiring their own rights to life, liberty, and the pursuit of happiness. There were plenty of indications, however, that neither the American man nor the American woman was deriving full emotional satisfaction from the new order. For the first time in history, sex began to be regarded as a problem, not only in its social and theological implications, but also biologically; there was a rapid increase in the number of divorces; and there was an equally rapid decrease, at least in the cities, in the birth rate. Rural America continued to produce a surplus of children; among the farm population (according to the census of 1930) every ten adults had an average of fourteen children. But in cities with more than one hundred thousand inhabitants every ten adults had an average of only seven children, and among the professional classes, who presumably included the most gifted members of society, the deficit of children amounted to no less than forty per cent. This situation was due to various economic and social as well as emotional factors; but whatever its causes might be, it was an indication of serious maladjustments. A society that was failing to reproduce itself and in which the most talented stocks were steadily becoming extinct, could not be regarded as healthy.

And when sensitive Americans of the twentieth century contrasted their society with that of Europe, they could no longer feel assured that it represented any new and higher principles of social organization. The confidence in America which had been so characteristic of the great men of the eighteenth century had become less plausible. Jefferson's prediction that "when we get piled upon one another as in Europe, we shall become corrupt as in Europe, and go to eating one another as they do there" appeared to have been fulfilled, and with much greater rapidity than Jefferson had expected. This loss of faith in America was by no means characteristic of the nation as a whole. The average twentieth-century citizen continued to believe that men in America were more free and more nearly equal than in Europe, and to take pride in the material achievements of his civilization; and the average citizen did, in fact, continue to have wider opportunities and a higher standard of living in America than anywhere else in the world. But it was no longer possible to define with any clarity what American civilization stood for; liberal idealists in other countries were now inclined to see America, no longer as an inspiring example of freedom and equality, but as a horrifying specimen of capitalist domination. And among the Americans themselves the intellectual classes were increasingly inclined to feel that the hopes of the eighteenth century had somehow been frustrated, that the wealth and power of the industrial age had been purchased at too high a price, and that possibly American civilization from the beginning had been marred by some fatal flaw that would make it permanently inferior to the civilization of Europe.

In the eighteenth century the most gifted and widely cultured of the Americans had been the most convinced of the superiority of American society; but their twentieth-century successors felt no such certainty. The optimism of a Franklin and a Jefferson might be contrasted with the disillusionment of a Henry Adams, who was inclined to regard all Western history since the Middle Ages as a process of steady degeneration, with the tendency of so many American intellectuals to become expatriates, and with the sense of loneliness, of cynicism, and of defeat that pervaded so much of the American literature of the twentieth century.

CHAPTER XII

THE INDUSTRIAL MIND

★ ★ ★ ★ ★ ★ ★ ★ ★ ★ ★ ★ ★ ★ ★

THE CIVIL WAR and the triumph of industrial capitalism were followed by a cultural collapse from which America did not begin to recover until near the end of the century. The surviving intellectual leaders of the 1840's and 1850's retreated into a baffled silence; and for a generation no social critics of comparable importance took their places. The postwar period, which Mark Twain christened the "Gilded Age" and Parrington described as the "Age of the Great Barbecue," marked a kind of hiatus in the history of the American mind.

The cultural collapse was not due merely to the victory of forces inimical to social idealism and to disinterested intellectual activity. It is true that America had passed under the rule of barbarians who judged everything in predatory and acquisitive terms. But if the intellectuals of the period had inherited a sufficiently profound and well-integrated social philosophy, they would have been better capable of resisting the robber barons and their political henchmen. The real reason for their failure was their own lack of sound and relevant standards of judgment. For the task the men of the forties and fifties had undertaken— the formulation of an American and democratic view of life—had not been successfully completed. American thinking (except among the Virginians) had always been too naïve, too timid, and too derivative; the Americans had not acquired any coherent social and philosophical theory that matched their amazing achievements in practical activity.

And as a result of this intellectual backwardness, the economics of capitalism and the politics of Republicanism appeared, not as a denial of American ideals, but as their logical fulfillment. When Emerson and his associates had preached self-reliance, they had not intended to justify the activities of a Rockefeller or a Morgan; but they had not defined standards by which the self-reliance of the robber baron could be distinguished from that of the ideal American democrat. And when they had encouraged the abolitionists, they had not intended that an abhorrence of slavery should be used by the Republican Party as a device for perpetuating its own control over the federal Union; but they had been too Utopian and too unsophisticated to appreciate the tragic complexity—the mingling of good and evil—in all human affairs. In consequence their successors during the seventies and eighties found themselves adrift among forces they did not understand. They could not easily approve of the trend of affairs during the Gilded Age; yet at the same time they found it equally difficult to condemn it.

Unable to resolve this dilemma, the official exponents of culture and intelligence, particularly in New England, began to turn away altogether from American democratic aspirations and to lean for guidance and reassurance upon the British class tradition. They interpreted American history in conservative terms, glorifying Puritanism, the Constitution, and the Federalists, vilifying Jefferson and the agrarians, and denying the radical elements in the American past; and they preached social and æsthetic standards of gentility and decorum that had no relevance to the American scene. This revival of Federalism became known as the "Genteel Tradition." It was exemplified most completely in the writings of certain Bostonians, such as Barrett Wendell, Charles Eliot Norton, and James Russell Lowell, who inherited the attitude from Federalist and Unitarian forebears; but the trend was by no means restricted to New England. Both in the universities and among writers, editors, and publishers throughout the entire period from the Civil War to the First World War there was a tendency to propagate attitudes and ideas that were borrowed from Great Britain, and that had no vital relationship with life in America and could not fruitfully be applied there. American theory was in danger of becoming wholly an ivory-tower affair, divorced from American practice. These generalizations are true, in greater or less degree, of political writers like E. L. Godkin and G. W. Curtis, of economists like Amasa Walker and John Bates Clark, and of littérateurs like Thomas Bailey Aldrich, Richard Watson Gilder, and Hamilton Wright Mabie.

In economics, the most prominent scholars of the period adopted the ideology of the English classical school, which had been evolved to suit the special features of English capitalism and which provided no adequate interpretation of the American development from agrarian democracy to big-business monopoly. In politics, they were inclined to regard the English party system and the English ruling-class tradition as norms and to treat the peculiarities of the American form of government as reprehensible aberrations. And in literary criticism, they applauded pale imitations of Victorian poetry and fiction, and deplored anything too realistic, too original, or too native to America. They believed themselves to be good Americans; but their conception of America was carefully edited to conform with their borrowed standards of gentility and correct taste. In Barrett Wendell's *History of American Literature,* for example (in which Melville is dismissed in one sentence with the comment that his early books had been praised by Robert Louis Stevenson), Whitman's view of life and style of writing are condemned as un-American and more suited to the decadent tastes of the French.

In some degree, this sterile academicism can be regarded as the characteristic viewpoint of *rentier* groups who shared in the profits of big business but not in the processes by which they were acquired. And it is true that the men of the Gentell Tradition were profoundly conservative in their views on property; like their Federalist predecessors, they regarded the sanctity of contracts as the foundation of civilization, elevated property rights above human rights, denounced agrarian attacks on business corporations as criminal and anarchistic, and declared that individual self-restraint, rather than social reform, was the main remedy for injustice. This revived Federalism was particularly marked in two of the latest and most belligerent representatives of this mode of thought—Irving Babbitt and Paul Elmer More, who prolonged the genteel tradition into the 1920's. Yet the intellectual leaders of the post-Civil War period were by no means apologists for big business, although they were inclined to blame the politicians, and not the robber barons, for the degradation of American life. But their practical proposals were conceived in European rather than in American terms. Almost all of them, for example, denounced the tariff, but their arguments against it were derived from English economists and not from American agrarians. And their favorite social panacea was civil service reform. This proposal, which pointed towards the growth of a professional and privileged bureaucracy along European lines, had potentially authoritarian implications and was not in harmony with the spirit of American life. The spoils system, as it operated during the Gilded Age, was not a pretty spectacle; but the principle upon which it had been based—rotation in office—was an essential element of democracy.

Meanwhile, the millionaire families who were becoming the new owners of America were also turning toward Europe, although in the manner of barbarian conquerors seeking aggrandizement rather than of intellectuals looking for shelter. With the growth of capitalism American society was losing its unique characteristics and was developing class inequalities similar to those that had always prevailed in Europe; and it was to be expected that the *nouveau riche* capitalists, like their predecessors in the age of Alexander Hamilton, should seek to adopt a way of life modeled on that of European aristocracies. Social snobbery and the most wasteful and tasteless forms of conspicuous consumption were deliberately cultivated by millionaire society under the leadership of people like Mrs. Astor and Ward McAllister; and a similar barbaric ostentation characterized the artistic preferences of the American rich, who had none of the good taste occasionally developed by mercantile oligarchies of earlier periods. Architecture is the most socially significant of the arts; and American architecture after the Civil War was a vivid reflection of the changes in American society. With the decay of craft traditions, most American houses and factories were constructed without any artistic sense whatever. Meanwhile, the palaces of the rich and the homes of the business and professional classes were copied from different European styles, often mingling classical, medieval, and Renaissance motifs in an extraordinary confusion and emphasizing the most flamboyant ornamentation and display. Churches and university buildings, in keeping with their lack of any vital contact with the realities of American life, were frequently modeled on medieval Gothic. This vulgar eclecticism was most prominent during the 1870's and 1880's, although the vogue of the mock-Gothic and the mock-classical was not fully broken until after the First World War.

In view of the general degradation of standards, artistic integrity and originality were not likely to be encouraged; and much of the best writing and painting done in America during the forty years following the Civil War was the work of lonely individuals living in obscurity, whose importance was not recognized until the twentieth century. This was true, for example, of the poetry of Emily Dickinson, of the painting of Thomas Eakins and Albert Pinkham Ryder, and of a handful of novels that foreshadowed the realism of a later generation. On the other hand, two men—Mark Twain and Henry James—had enough vitality to become major writers, although the former was seriously handicapped by the lack of a discriminating audience and the latter became an expatriate.

Mark Twain summarized in his own person a century of American development. He grew up in the agrarian society of Missouri while it was still frontier country; he spent several years in the Far West during the pioneering period; and he settled finally in the industrial East, where he lived in close association with a number of big business magnates. His reactions to this varied experience were remarkably typical of the America of his time; being himself almost an embodiment of the American norm, he can be cited as a case study of how the agrarian American submitted to capitalism. He .had all the characteristic virtues of his agrarian background; a natural democrat, with the fundamental American respect for the rights of all human beings, he despised pretense and sham, and hated injustice and exploitation. At the same time, he had no coherent social philosophy; his political affirmations were instinctual rather than reasoned. He had no capacity for abstract thought and little respect for intellectual speculation, and his opinions, in spite of his homely and realistic common sense, were often remarkably naïve. Moreover, he was personally as eager as most other Americans to achieve material success and to discover some easy way of making a fortune. Transplanted from the frontier to the East, he could neither accept nor repudiate this new environment. He saw the dishonesty and the exploitation that accompanied the rise of capitalism; but he had no alternative social doctrine to propound, and he was too honest merely to condemn the robber barons without recognizing that they were doing what other Americans would have liked to do if they had had the opportunity. Human nature, and not the economic system, was to blame. Unable to formulate any coherent attitude towards the transformation of American life, he relieved his feelings in books denouncing feudal Europe, where the conflict between class privilege and the rights of man could be more clearly defined. In later life he succumbed to the blackest pessimism. Meanwhile, he allowed himself to be intimidated by the standards of gentility and decorum Eastern society imposed upon him, resenting them yet at the same time lacking sufficient self-assurance to reject them.

Mark Twain's one great book was *Huckleberry Finn.* This epic story of the Mississippi is written with an unlabored ease and spontaneity and a warmth of feeling which show that, for the first and last time, its author had found a release for his own deeper emotional drives. In the symbol of a little boy who ran away from home because he did not want to be civilized, Mark Twain was expressing his own dislike of social conformity. It is significant that he could give expression to his rebellion only through the medium of a child. All the sympathies of the author are with Huckleberry Finn, who can perceive right and wrong much more accurately than can any of the adults whom he meets; civilization, it appears, tends to corrupt man's natural sense of morality. Yet the whole framework of the book implies that civilization, with all its restraints and its hypocrisies, is an inevitable process, to which the individual must finally conform; to assert oneself against it is impossible, and to attempt to run away from it is infantile. And although the chief motivation of the book is Mark Twain's resentment against standards of gentility, it should also be remembered that it was written at a time when the old uninhibited freedom of the frontier was rapidly disappearing and agrarian Americans in general were submitting to a new kind of discipline. In its hidden implications *Huckleberry Finn* is a profoundly melancholy book that marks the point at which American individualism began to succumb to defeat. It represents the transition between the folk hero of agrarian and frontier America, who believes in self-reliance and seeks to assert his will against his environment, and the folk hero of industrial America, who is the victim of social forces he cannot hope to control Mike Fink is in process of being transformed into Charlie Chaplin.

In the development of American literature, however, Mark Twain has a different and more positive significance. He was the first American author of the first rank to write in American and not in English. Spoken American had long since diverged from the parent language; but American writers had not evolved a literary style in harmony with it. Lacking a style of their own, their writing had frequently become labored and unnatural—weaknesses that are particularly evident in Melville. It was in the frontier humor of the Mississippi Valley, first oral and afterwards journalistic, that an American style began to develop; and it was in Mark Twain, who was an oral storyteller and a newspaperman before he became a writer of books, that this style entered literature. Writing a prose that was always easy and quick-moving, filled with concrete American imagery, and close to the colloquial and living language, he set a pattern that had an immensely beneficial influence on the American novelists of the twentieth century.

While Mark Twain was, in a sense, broken by capitalist America, his great contemporary Henry James saved himself by looking for his subject matter, not at home, but in Europe. James's expatriation has been the theme of a prolonged and bitter controversy; and hostile critics persistently alleged that he was motivated by social snobbery. Yet it is impossible to read his books with any discernment without recognizing that throughout his life he remained an American—much more profoundly American than the Anglophiles of the Genteel Tradition who remained on the other side of the Atlantic. There have been some American expatriates who have repudiated their native heritage and endeavored to reshape themselves into Europeans; but James was not one of them. He preferred to live in Europe because, as he himself explained, European society provided him with the kind of material best suited to his special talents. He felt himself unequipped to deal with the turbulent and chaotic America of the Gilded Age; as he told Charles Eliot Norton, the American scene would "yield its secrets only to a really *grasping* imagination." [1] But his approach to the European social order was always from outside. His subject was the difference between the American and the European—as significant and fruitful a subject as any novelist has ever chosen —and if he can be accused of partiality, it is because his sympathies were too often weighted on the side of the American.

Most of James's books deal with the impact of the European social order upon the American visitor. The European character is presented as more complex, more sophisticated, more worldly-wise, and at the same time more corrupt, with a much greater potentiality for evil. The American is narrower and more naïve, but more honest and virtuous. Sometimes (as in *The Ambassadors*) the American is intellectually and emotionally enriched by his contact with European sophistication. More often (as in *The American*,

[1] Letters of Henry James (*1920*), *Vol. I, p. 30.*

The Portarait of a Lady, The Wings of the Dove, and *The Golden Bowl*), he (or she) must fight for self-preservation against European corruption. On the surface James appears to be presenting his Europeans admiringly; yet he rarely credits them with any honesty or capacity for self-sacrifice, and their motives are usually coarsely materialistic. Although James was fascinated by European aristocracy, his real attitude to it (as revealed in his private letters as well as in his novels) was decidedly hostile. Looking at it from outside, he was well aware of its essential selfishness and of the crudely economic basis beneath its idealistic pretenses. He saw in it, he said, the "accommodation of the theory of a noble indifference to the practise of a deep avidity." [2] A large number of his upper-class European characters are motivated solely by the desire to acquire money (usually by marrying an American) in order that they may be able to maintain their positions in society. Like Madison and other American political theorists of the eighteenth century, James could see the economic foundations of social order with much more clarity than could most Europeans.

James's Americans are not always plausible, if one considers the background from which they are alleged to have emerged. It is incredible that Christopher Newman of *The American* and Adam Verver of *The Golden Bowl* could have made fortunes in the Gilded Age and at the same time remained so innocent and so benevolent. But that James grasped the essential psychological differences between the American and the European cannot be denied; he was really dealing with typical and average middle-class Americans, not with robber barons, although for the purposes of plot he found it necessary to endow them with a great deal of money. And if his presentation can be criticized, it is because he frequently exaggerates both the virtue of his Americans and the wickedness of his Europeans— a favorite propensity of American commentators from the eighteenth century down to the present day. At times, in fact, he seems to be unaware of all the implications of the behavior of his American characters. In *The Golden Bowl*,

---

[2] *Preface to* The American (*edition of 1907*), *p. xx.*

for example, his admiration for his two American protagonists, Adam Verver and his daughter Maggie, prevents him
from recognizing that their attitude towards the Italian
prince whom Maggie has married is essentially acquisitive
and possessive; they have bought him as though he were
a work of art, and they mean to keep him. Another aspect
of American psychology which James introduces into his
books without full awareness of its importance is that his
women are usually stronger than his men; in the typical
Jamesian plot the woman pulls the strings and the man is
a puppet (although, like Strether in *The Ambassadors* and
Densher in *The Wings of the Dove,* he may finally assert
his independence). This view of the relationship between
the sexes (which James extends to his European characters)
is more true of America than of Europe, and rarely appears in novels by European writers.

James was an American, moreover, in a deeper sense—
not only in his attitude towards his characters but also in
his general view of life. He .was primarily concerned with
moral questions, and what he regarded as ultimately valuable was the attainment of moral awareness and enlightenment—such enlightenment as Strether acquires at the end
of *The Ambassadors,* Densher at the end of *The Wings of
the Dove,* and Maggie at the end of *The Golden Bowl.* The
Jamesian moral sense is not associated with any particular
notion of social order, and does not necessarily lead to any
particular mode of activity; it is presented as one of the
fundamental elements in human experience, and its importance is intrinsic. This profoundly individualistic conception of morality is not exclusively American; but it is
easier for an American, than for a European, to arrive at it.
When the individual is regarded as subordinate to a hierarchical social order, in accordance with the European tradition, his morality is determined by society and consists
in doing the duties appropriate to his station. For the European, moral attitudes usually have some social reference.
But James had been born into the American world, which
lacked the concept of social order. In his novels the moral
sense is presented as an innate and fundamental element

in the human personality, which every individual must discover for himself. Moral awareness means a realization that the individual has his own sense of good and evil (in the same way that he has an æsthetic sense), and that moral values are an essential and intrinsic aspect of all inter-personal relationships.

2

At the end of the nineteenth century what Americans most obviously needed was a more honest appreciation of the divorce between their principles and their practice. At this period their intellectual and æsthetic attitudes, some of them inherited from the agrarian culture of the eighteenth century and others borrowed from Great Britain, had very little relevance to contemporary conditions. As Van Wyck Brooks, a generation later, declared of the average American, "the theoretical atmosphere in which he has lived bears no relation to society, the practical atmosphere in which he has lived bears no relation to ideals. . . . Human nature itself exists in America on two irreconcilable planes, the plane of stark theory and the plane of stark business." [3]

Most Americans, especially those of the most educated class, continued to profess a belief in economic individualism, independence, and self-reliance, in spite of the growth of monopolistic corporations. They interpreted the industrial economy in terms of *laissez faire,* free competition, and the rights of private property, ignoring the fact that it had been built up so largely by state intervention. They upheld the sanctity of certain ethical laws and insisted that sin was always followed by retribution, although the country was filled with flourishing evildoers. They liked to believe that progress was inevitable and that America was a prime example of it, evading the truth of Henry Adams's suggestion that the change from President Washington to President Grant seemed more like a degeneration. And

[3] *Van Wyck Brooks:* America's Coming of Age (*1915*), *pp. 24, 27.*

they preferred a genteel and sentimentalized literature and art that would shield them from a recognition of unpleasant realities.

In order that these illusions might be exposed, theory and practice must be brought into closer relationship with each other; principles must be contrasted with actualities and tested in terms of their practical efficacy. When American thinkers and writers began to recover from their retreat from reality during the Gilded Age, this was the task they undertook. The result was the emergence of new tendencies in philosophy, in social and economic theory, and in literature and the arts. The merit of these intellectual and æsthetic movements was that they served to expose illusions; their weakness was that they failed to put forward new positive affirmations.

This was particularly true of the most important of the new intellectual attitudes, the philosophy that William James called pragmatism and that John Dewey preferred to describe as instrumentalism. James, Dewey, and their disciples insisted that the sole function of theory was to serve as a guide for action, that the meaning of any theory consisted in its practical consequences, and that its truth should be judged by those consequences. The universal validity of these propositions was questionable. Both James and Dewey often spoke as though they were denying the value of disinterested intellectual curiosity, and they did not always explain with sufficient care in what sense the truth of a principle should be determined by its results; insofar as this meant merely that any hypothesis must be tested by experiment, it was unexceptionable, but some members of the school were inclined to argue that any belief should be considered "true" if it had "good" effects on the behavior of the believer. As a weapon for destroying principles that had lost their efficacy, however, the pragmatist-instrumentalist philosophy was of the greatest value. Applied, for example, to legal theory (by such men as Justice Brandeis) and to the principles of ethics (in Dewey's *Human Nature and Conduct*), it suggested that the interests of true justice and true virtue were not served by applying traditional formulas without regard for consequences. On the other hand, the adherents of such a philosophy could not explain with sufficient clarity what kind of consequences should be regarded as good or why, nor could they develop new standards of social justice and personal virtue. The importance of the movement was primarily destructive; it lacked positive ideals.

If this fact was not always apparent to the readers of James and Dewey, it was because both men had positive beliefs, which they derived, not from their epistemology, but from the American democratic tradition. This was particularly true of William James, whose view of life, like that of his brother in a different field, seemed almost a quintessence of the whole American attitude. No other thinker has been so deeply or so characteristically American in his intellectual preconceptions and habits of thought, or has reflected so clearly both the virtues and the deficiencies of the American mind. And no other thinker, it should be added, has been so honest and courageous in his efforts to arrive at truth or so charming and unpretentious as a human being.

It was from the American past that James acquired the distrust of abstract theory that pervaded his pragmatist epistemology, deriving it partly from the suspicion of dogmas and intellectual absolutes that had always been characteristic of the Anglo-Saxon mentality, and partly from the added emphasis on practical utility the Americans had acquired during the pioneering experience. It was from the American past that he acquired the faith in individualism and in freedom, and the realization that every person and every event were in some way unique and could never be wholly explained by general laws, which were perhaps the most deeply ingrained of his intellectual characteristics. Above all, it was from the American past that he acquired his vision of the universe not as a cosmic order in which everything had its appointed place but as the scene of a battle between good and evil in which nothing was predetermined and the future was always uncertain. James was most deeply an American when he saw life as an adventure in which there was no ideal harmony and in which struggle and insecurity were the ultimate realities.

When James was a young man he suffered for several years from a paralyzing "sense of the insecurity of life." For a long period he was unable to go into the dark alone; he dreaded to be left alone, and could not imagine "how other people could live, how I myself had ever lived, so unconscious of that pit of insecurity beneath the surface of life." According to James's account of his experience it is apparent that both his neurotic anxiety and the methods by which he finally cured himself were in conformity with the American psychological pattern. His anxiety, as he described it, was due to a feeling that he was too weak to struggle with an external world he regarded as alien and hostile; he did not have that sense of inner division and of conflict between universal moral law and private impulse that has usually been the most important element in the spiritual experience of Europeans. James succeeded in curing himself of his anxiety by learning to assert his will and discovering that, in spite of his fears, he could do so successfully. Where a European would have sought salvation through submission to some conception of cosmic or social order, James determined to "posit life (the real, the good) in the self-governing resistance of the ego to the world. . . . Hitherto, when I have felt like taking a free initiative, like daring to act originally, without carefully waiting for contemplation of the external world to determine all for me, suicide seemed the most manly form to put my daring into; now, I will go a step further with my will, not only act with it, but believe as well; believe in my individual reality and creative power." This mode of salvation proved to be successful. James never afterwards suffered from any serious emotional problem, and this assertion of his moral self became his habitual method of reacting upon the world. Some years later he told his wife that he felt "most deeply and intensely active and alive" when he felt "an element of active tension, of holding my own, as it were, and trusting outward things to perform their part so as to make it a full harmony; but without any *guaranty* that they will." On such occasions he felt "a sort of deep enthusiastic bliss, of bitter willingness to do and suffer any-

thing which translates itself physically by a kind of sting-
ing pain inside my breastbone." [4]

James's cure was genuine because he learnt to accept,
and even to rejoice in, insecurity. Unlike some earlier
Americans he did not demand omnipotence. But his initial
experience was similar to that which had expressed itself in
the Edwardean theology and in the writings of Poe and
Melville. When he spoke of "the self-governing resistance
of the ego to the world" he was defining not only his own
conviction but the whole American view of life.

It was because James was a voluntarist, believing that
the will was the center of the human personality, that he
found it so easy to regard theory as always a guide to
action; his pragmatism was closely associated with his
belief in struggle between the "ego" and the "world." And
in later life he went on to propound a whole voluntarist
cosmology. He castigated those European and Asiatic philosophers who had believed in a universal and rational
world order to which the individual must submit, declaring
that they were "simply afraid, afraid of more experience,
afraid of life." Instead, he suggested that the whole universe was involved in a cosmic Armageddon between good
and evil; God was not omnipotent, and his creation had
"only a fighting chance of safety." Men should participate
in the battle for goodness in the belief that it was "a real adventure, with real danger, yet it may win through." [5]

Such a view of life was American both in its emphasis
on struggle and in its adolescent exuberance. And James's
failure to explain in any clear terms what he meant by
goodness was also American. Like his brother Henry, he
had an individualistic conception of morality; and like his
brother, he believed that the moral sense was a primary
and fundamental element in human experience. "The feeling of the innate dignity of certain spiritual attitudes and
of the essential vulgarity of others," he declared, "is quite

[4] Letters of William James (1920), Vol. I, pp. 146, 147,
152, 199.
[5] William James: The Will to Believe (1897), pp. 178, 210.

inexplicable except by an innate preference of the more ideal attitude for its own pure sake. The nobler thing *tastes* better, and that is all that we can say." [6] This belief—that moral feelings were innate—was, as Thomas Jefferson had recognized, one of the essential foundations of American democracy; for if moral feelings were not innate, then men needed indoctrination and discipline, and could not be trusted with freedom. But simply to state the doctrine, with the comment that "that is all that we can say," was not sufficient, as the whole American experience had demonstrated. With other Americans, James believed in struggle between the human will and its environment; and with other Americans, he was inclined to equate the will with positive good. Like Emerson, he assumed much too naïvely that the will would respond to the moral sense; and he was too ready to identify "the real, the good" with "the self-governing resistance of the ego to the world." But it was apparent from the whole development of America, with its transition from agrarian democracy to a capitalism dominated by power-hungry business magnates, that men could not always be trusted to respond to their moral feelings, that conceptions of good and standards of value (even though they might be innate) needed to be clarified, defined, and rationalized, and that the perpetual drive and tension of the American will would end in the destruction of ideals rather than in their fulfillment. And because James (who was himself a man of great moral sensitivity) failed to recognize these facts, his philosophy, in spite of its value as a destructive instrument, must be considered primarily as a mere reflection, not a clarification, of the weaknesses in the American view of life. What America needed was, not only a dissolvent analysis of principles that had lost their relevance, but also an affirmation of new positive standards (in terms appropriate to the democratic experience and not borrowed from the European class system) and an assertion of the values of contemplation and enjoy-

---

[6] *Ibid., p. 187. Cf.* Principles of Psychology (*1890*), *Vol. II, p. 672.*

ment and of relaxation of moral tension. But these needs were not met by the pragmatist philosophy.

There was a similar deficiency in the other new intellectual trends of the late nineteenth and early twentieth centuries. In economics, for example, this period saw the growth of institutionalism. The institutionalists concentrated on describing conditions as they actually were, without inquiring into what they ought to be. They collected statistics and made detailed studies of specific trends, thereby demonstrating how far the actual operations of the American economy failed to conform with the laissez-faire theory of the English classical school. But the institutionalists were reluctant to put forward any alternative general theories of their own. For synthetic interpretations of economic processes, combining analyses of what was with statements of what ought to be, American economists were still dependent upon the Europeans. American conservatives continued to uphold the validity of English classicism. Its opponents borrowed their theory from Karl Marx or, at a later date, from J. M. Keynes.

The most radical and the most original of the institutionalists was Thorstein Veblen. Veblen's distinction between industry and business was an important clue to the understanding of the American economy. Industry made goods, while business was a series of devices enabling financiers and other absentee owners to make money by collecting tribute from the "underlying population." Industry was an expression of the creative "instinct of workmanship," while business was predatory and acquisitive. Analyzing the growth of business, Veblen concluded that it would eventually become incompatible with the existing political and social structure. Either the American people must expropriate the absentee owners, or else they must pass under the rule of some kind of business dictatorship. But although Veblen's faith in the "instinct of workmanship" was affirmative, at least by implication, there was little positive affirmation in his mordant and sardonic style or in his gloomy analyses of the power of the business classes. He appeared to have little hope in human nature or in the American future.

Meanwhile the younger writers and artists were turning to realism. The decade of the 1890's saw the advent of the first fully realistic novelists (Stephen Crane, Frank Norris, and Theodore Dreiser), the beginning of a more realistic painting (in the work of Robert Henri, John Sloan, and the so-called Philadelphia Group), and the growth of a more realistic trend in poetry (exemplified by Edwin Arlington Robinson). Realism meant a concentration on social conditions as they actually were, emphasizing their more sordid and gloomy aspects and demonstrating, at least by implication, the inapplicability of the accepted economic, political, and moral dogmas. The trend towards literary realism had been initiated earlier by William Dean Howells, a mediocre novelist although an admirable human being, and by certain Middle Westerners, such as Hamlin Garland, who had voiced the grievances of the farmers against Eastern plutocracy. It had also been stimulated by influences from continental Europe, particularly by the examples of Tolstoi and Zola. But it was not until the twentieth century that it began to dominate the American literary scene. Like the other movements of the time, it was essentially a protest against illusory beliefs. Confessing themselves bewildered and defeated by industrial society, the realists could make no positive affirmations, either æsthetically or morally. Their duty, they believed, was to tell the truth; and the truth, as they saw it, did not give much encouragement to any faith in spiritual or ideal values.

The architectural equivalent of pragmatism and realism was functionalism. First expounded by the Chicago architect, Louis Sullivan, during the 1880's, functionalism was a demand for architectural honesty. Instead of designing a public library that looked like a Roman temple, a bank that imitated a Byzantine church, and an office building that recalled the Parthenon, the architect should consider first the purposes of the building he was planning and the material out of which it was to be constructed; the form and decoration of a building should develop out of its function and should be in harmony with it. Functionalism had a slow growth in the United States; but it was adopted more quickly in certain European countries, whence it eventually returned to the land of its origin. The best functional buildings had an admirable grace and simplicity; but it was not one of the great architectural styles. Modes like the Gothic and the baroque had been the expression of certain positive beliefs about the nature of the universe and the destiny of man. Functionalism (except perhaps in the work of Frank Lloyd Wright, whose architectural theories were combined with an Emersonian and Whitmanesque faith in American democracy) made no spiritual affirmations. It was the handmaid of technology, and in the best known (although far from the best) of its manifestations, the New York skyscrapers, it expressed only the drive toward wealth and power. To express that drive sincerely was better, both æsthetically and morally, than to disguise it and sentimentalize it by a barbaric plundering from the styles of the past; but it was also a confession of spiritual poverty.

Much of American intellectual activity during the twentieth century might be summarized as a conflict between a traditionalism that lacked relevance to contemporary conditions and a realism that put forward no positive standards. On the one side were conservatives who preached moral, political, philosophical, and æsthetic beliefs that could not fruitfully be applied to the exigencies of daily living and that often, at least by implication, were undemocratic and un-American. On the other side were radicals who emphasized this discrepancy between belief and actuality, and who were usually fond of professing their loyalty to democracy but had no coherent system of principles. The task Emerson and Whitman had started—the elaboration of the American democratic faith into a general view of life having the power of a religion—remained unfinished. And the underlying reason for this failure was that, with the rise of industrialism, faith in democracy had lost its economic and social foundations. There was no longer harmony between the ideals most Americans professed and the manner in which most of them lived.

The principal storm center of the conflict was in the field of education, particularly in the colleges. Early American higher education had been predominantly classical and theological, and had never broken away from the influence of the European humanistic tradition. In the latter part of the nineteenth century, under the leadership of such men as President Eliot of Harvard, the colleges began to destroy the supremacy of the classics by introducing a great variety of scientific, technological, and other modern courses, and by adopting the elective system. Students were thus enabled to learn more about the contemporary world, but, at the same time, they no longer acquired any coherent view of life or any sufficient grasp of their cultural heritage. Meanwhile, educators imbued with the pragmatist-instrumentalist philosophy under the leadership of John Dewey were making similar changes in the school system, bringing the curriculum into closer contact with social realities, reducing the emphasis on discipline, and encouraging free self-expression. Controversy between the educational traditionalists and the progressives continued through the twentieth century, becoming increasingly bitter during the 1930's and 1940's. Traditionalists (such as President Hutchins of Chicago) insisted that education ought to provide a philosophy and a system of values and not merely a mass of unrelated facts; progressives replied that the philosophy and the values the traditionalists wished to inculcate were potentially authoritarian and undemocratic. There was much justice in the contentions of both parties. What America needed was a philosophy and a system of values, but of a kind that would support, instead of weakening, democratic aspirations.

3

Meanwhile an increasing number of individuals were devoting themselves to the practice of the arts, and critical standards were becoming more discerning, more sophisticated, and less moralistic. The twentieth century, and particularly the decade following the First World War, was unquestionably the period when the higher culture of the Americans lost any trace of colonialism or provincialism, and the nation had its æsthetic coming-of-age. It can plausibly be argued that a larger quantity of good work in litera-

ture, painting, and music was done in the United States
between 1919 and 1929 than in the whole of the previous
three hundred years. Yet although the work of this period
was remarkable for its richness, variety, and vitality, most
of it was imbued with a profound sense of bewilderment
and defeat. The product of a society which was largely permeated with commercial and pecuniary standards and no
longer had any clear grasp of spiritual values, the American
artist of the twentieth century felt that he was lost in an
alien world. In conference, much of the best work of the
time had a tortured and neurotic quality, and lacked that
note of serenity and spiritual certainty which had been
achieved by some of the pre-Civil War writers. The personal history of most of the leading artists of industrial
America was one of frustration and maladjustment; having
little sense of organic harmony with their environment,
none of them grew into that full maturity that produces
the greatest masterpieces.

This mood of disillusion did not fully show itself until
after the First World War, although it had been foreshadowed by the realists of the 1890's. The first decade of the
twentieth century was a more hopeful period, during which
American intellectuals were appraising their national traditions in a critical spirit. They were also beginning to digest
new revolutionary ideas from continental Europe that ran
counter to the conventions of the Genteel Tradition. The
prevalent spirit of liberation was exemplified in the emergence of certain creative personalities who combined an
American optimism and Utopianism with a bold self-affir-
mation derived from Emerson and Whitman: such were the
dancer Isadora Duncan, the architect Frank Lloyd Wright,
and the photographer Alfred Stieglitz. Meanwhile, most of
the writers of the time devoted themselves, on a decidedly
superficial level, to the problems of politics. Two women,
Edith Wharton and Ellen Glasgow, were producing work
of finer quality; but each of them dealt with a fragment
of ordered society, imbued with traditional standards of
manners and morals, in no way typical of the American
scene. Mrs. Wharton found her material among the old
families of New York, and Miss Glasgow, among those of

Virginia. Their achievement, like that of Henry James, was an object lesson in the literary utility of fixed social reference points. But their example could not be followed by novelists who proposed to handle the central themes of American development.

The most prolific period in American æsthetic history began about 1912 or 1913. During the next few years an unusual number of new figures emerged, while older men, such as Theodore Dreiser, began for the first time to win wide recognition. Noncommercial "little" magazines for the publication of experimental writing began to appear in all parts of the country; and critical battles were fought between the survivors of the Genteel Tradition and the exponents of æsthetic radicalism. Most of the younger men shared certain common ideas expressed most clearly.by a group of critics of whom Van Wyck Brooks was probably the most influential. According to this group, American society was both too acquisitive and too puritanical, and had never had sufficient respect for the spiritual development of the individual or for æsthetic values. For a period an attitude of hostility to almost every aspect of American life and an equally exaggerated admiration for continental Europe became almost universal among writers and artists. But although Brooks and his disciples could point out what was wrong with America with considerable insight and acuteness, it was not easy to discover what positive values they wished to assert. Beyond a vague belief in some kind of economic change, apparently in the direction of socialism, they made few affirmative proposals. And the hopefulness that animated their early work changed to disillusion after the First World War.

But it was in the novel that the mind of industrial America expressed itself most fully and achieved its highest level of self-awareness. The novelists of the twenties and thirties depicted almost every aspect of national life with an extraordinary vividness and fertility. And although they borrowed ideas and techniques from the Europeans, particularly from the exponents of sociological realism, their work was altogether American both in style and in spirit. Like Mark Twain, they wrote in American and not in English, with a colloquial vigor and richness of sensuous impact; and like Poe and Melville, they saw life as a battle between the will and the environment. But this battle was now presented with a different emphasis. The individual of industrial society was more helpless and more quickly defeated than the individual of agrarian society; he was more frequently a puppet of forces he could not control; and when he achieved success, it was often by sacrificing his spiritual integrity. Unlike Ahab, whose destiny had been tragic, he was likely to appear pathetic or ignoble, and could achieve dignity only by a stoical endurance or by some act of defiance. Frustration and defeat were the normal experience of the twentieth-century American as exhibited in fiction. For the novelists of the twentieth century, as for those of the nineteenth, American society in general lacked that sense of order in terms of which the life of the individual, even when unsuccessful, can acquire value and significance.

These generalizations can be applied, in one form or another, to all the major novelists of the period: to the older generation represented by Dreiser, Lewis, Anderson, and Willa Cather; and to the younger men who first appeared in the twenties.

Dreiser's massive integrity, his sense of reality, and his refusal to accept any easy or merely conventional solution to the problems he encountered made him a leader in the revolt against the Genteel Tradition; and his insistence on his right to tell the truth as he saw it cleared the way for his successors. The main theme of his books was the struggle of the individual to achieve wealth, power, and social prestige. His heroes were sometimes successful, like Cowperwood of *The Financier* and *The Titan,* and sometimes defeated, like Clyde Griffiths of *An American Tragedy;* but either way Dreiser was too honest to pretend that he knew of any spiritual resolution of such a struggle. Seeing life as a product of chemical and biological forces, he communicated a brooding sense of pity for the endeavors of the human race, and frankly confessed that its destiny bewildered and dismayed him.

Sinclair Lewis, whose special talent was for conveying

Essentially similar attitudes were presented by the writers of this generation whose interests were more exclusively æsthetic and who were less concerned with the social background of their characters. Ernest Hemingway was the most affirmative of the major novelists of the period; but he found value primarily in simple physical pleasures and in the stoical courage of men and women willing to confront inevitable defeat without cringing. Hemingway's heroes were usually ordinary men who were the victims of blind natural or social forces against which there could be no defense. And although F. Scott Fitzgerald, like Hemingway, was interested mainly in the individual, two of his novels gave perhaps the clearest statement of the malaise of twentieth-century urban society. Unlike most other writers, Fitzgerald knew from his own experience the life of that leisured wealthy class which dominated the new America of urban capitalism, setting its standards and making itself the focus of envy and ambition. He had felt the glamor of great riches, and had learned how hollow and meretricious it was. All this was set forth in *The Great Gatsby*, a novel that captured the essential spirit of the 1920's. Gatsby had dreamed of becoming a rich man because of his sentimental adoration of a girl from a rich family and of the milieu to which she belonged; yet when the wealth which he had acquired by bootlegging admitted him to the society of the very rich, he found that they were callous, brutal, egotistic, and dishonest.[9] Fitzgerald's other important book, *Tender Is*

and founding a family, in imitation of the planters of tidewater Virginia. When he fails in this "great design" (chiefly as a result of the Civil War), he is convinced that he has made some mistake, but is unable to discover what it is. The structure of the novel makes it evident that his real mistakes were his lust for power and his attitude towards the Negroes. At the end of the book the only surviving member of the family which Sutpen had hoped to found is a mulatto.

[9] Gatsby, the poor boy from Dakota whose simple-minded goodness is frustrated by the corruption of a sophisticated society, is an embodiment of the American myth. He is the successor of Leatherstocking, Huckleberry Finn, and a long series of Henry James heroines. His lack of reality is the novel's

the Night, may be regarded as the sequel of *The Great Gatsby*, in the same sense that the great depression of the 1930's was the logical sequel of the false values and the wild acquisitiveness of the 1920's. *Tender Is the Night* dealt with the psychic weakness of the American man of the wealthy and well-educated class, with his liability to apparently unmotivated defeat and collapse, and with the domineering and devouring propensities of the American upper-class woman.[1]

All in all, the world depicted by the novelists of the 1920's was probably the most gloomy in the whole of literary history. American fiction had moved a long way from William Dean Howells, who had once declared that "the more smiling aspects of life" were the more American. More positive and affirmative attitudes were to be found only in writers who (like Elizabeth Madox Roberts) produced relatively little and remained outside the main stream, or (like Thornton Wilder) were synthetic and imitative rather than genuinely creative. Nor did the writers of the next generation portray American life in more optimistic terms. During the 1930's and 1940's the universal domination of politics and the extension of political criteria to moral and æsthetic problems made it impossible for the arts to flourish. Most of the younger writers were captured by the European ideology of Marxism, and set out to allegorize American experience in Marxist terms. But insofar as their work passed beyond allegory and became an honest rendering of experience (as in Farrell and Caldwell), it presented only decay and degeneration; it did not successfully communicate the positives of the Marxist creed. The most vigorous and fertile novelist of this

---

major weakness (the fact that he is actually engaged in the criminal activity of bootlegging is barely mentioned and never made plausible). Fitzgerald, as he showed in his letters, was well aware of this weakness, and described himself as writing much fine prose in order to cover up his inability to achieve a full imaginative realization of his central character.

[1] *Two other minor masterpieces of the period dealt with similar subjects: Hemingway's* The Short Happy Life of Francis Macomber; *and John O'Hara's* Appointment in Samarra.

of a total revolt against all those social restrictions and responsibilities men were compelled to obey in their real lives. This peculiarly anarchical kind of screwball humor (best exemplified by the Marx brothers) was perhaps the most effective and the most characteristic aspect of twentieth-century American popular culture.

That a people who had always prided themselves on their optimism, and who had on the whole more substantial reasons for optimism than the people of any other country, should produce an art so largely concerned with frustration and maladjustment, was a phenomenon that required explanation. And plenty of commentators blamed the artists for it and complained that they had become obsessed with the more sordid aspects of American life and were deliberately ignoring its virtues. According to the surviving representatives of the Genteel Tradition, such as Irving Babbitt and Paul Elmer More, it was the duty of the artist to preach affirmative beliefs and to inculcate a sound morality. Other critics (such as Van Wyck Brooks in his later period) thought that writers, particularly in America, ought to be elevating and inspiring, and that the Americans had been corrupted by European decadence. Yet it remained an undeniable fact that optimism and elevation were, with few exceptions, to be found only among the mediocre and the imitative, and that the most genuinely creative of the Americans were usually the most tormented and the most pessimistic.

And although European society was much more corrupt and much more deeply infected with the germs of decay than was the society of the United States, European literature never lost the capacity for spiritual affirmation. Much of the European writing of the twentieth century was concerned with the same themes as the American—with the loneliness and the neuroticism of the little man who was the victim of urban capitalism. But this mood did not dominate the literature of Europe as it did that of America. The greater European writers of the same period (like Thomas Mann and even—in spite of his morbid tendencies —Marcel Proust) still found it possible to regard the emotional and intellectual development of the individual as inherently valuable, and to convey a sense of man's essential dignity and significance; and they were capable of achieving a wisdom and a serenity by which evil was not evaded but was seen as merely one element in the total pattern of human existence. Except in Melville's *Billy Budd,* this kind of serenity was not presented in any novel by any major American writer.

The pessimism of American literature was probably due in some measure to the anomalous position of the artist in American culture. American society, with its practical and egalitarian propensities, had never shown sufficient friendliness or respect for æsthetic activities; and the artist was likely to feel a sense of isolation and a maladjustment that were, in part, peculiar to himself. But there were also broader and more significant reasons for this state of mind.

The Americans were a people who had believed that evil could be overcome and that the method of overcoming it was the assertion and tension of the will. America from the beginning had been a Utopian and a Messianic nation. But after the disintegration of agrarian society and the triumph of industrial capitalism, the disparity between the original ideal and the reality grew wider, and the possibility of a successful assertion of the will diminished. Yet American culture offered only the alternatives of success and failure. As a nation, the Americans must achieve an ideal social order or (in Whitman's words) "prove the most tremendous failure of time"; as individuals, they must conquer their environment or be conquered by it. For the American, there was no middle ground, so that the acceptance of failure could lead only to cynicism or despair, not to a profounder wisdom.

From one point of view, the æsthetic manifestations of the industrial mind may be regarded as a necessary and salutory reminder of the discrepancy between ideal and actuality; urban capitalism was not a fulfillment of the American dream. And it should be remarked that although the twentieth-century novelists found little to admire in the society of their time, their condemnation was usually derived, either directly or by implication, from and become the victims of a complicated economic system in which the controls were held elsewhere. As small producers, unable to combine with each other, they were subject to the mechanisms of supply and demand; whereas the big corporations with whom they had to do business were able to determine their own price policies. As usual, the section of the community that produced raw materials was being exploited by the centers of industry and finance.

Between 1860 and 1900 the acreage of American farms more than doubled, while during the same period their productivity was greatly improved by technological improvements and by the introduction of machinery. The result was a vast increase in total farm production. A large part of it was exported, which meant that the American farmers were competing, not only with each other, but also with those of Europe and South America. The inevitable consequence was a steady decrease in the prices the farmers received. This process was intensified by the deflationary policies, beneficial to bankers and creditors, that were being pursued by the federal government. But there was no corresponding decrease in the prices the farmers paid. They continued to pay high rates to the railroads that shipped their produce, to the elevator owners who stored it, to the industrial corporations from which they bought their equipment, and to the bankers from whom they borrowed money. By 1900, thirty-one per cent of all American farms carried mortgages, and thirty-five per cent of all farm operators were tenants and not owners. By 1930 each of these figures had risen to about forty-two per cent.

American statesmen continued to insist that the small independent farm owner was the healthiest element in the nation and therefore deserved special consideration. This was true, not only insofar as the farmers had always been the chief representatives of American ideals, but also because the American nation so largely depended on them for survival; whereas urban America failed to reproduce itself, agrarian America continued to produce a surplus of children. But it was evident that, without some fundamental change in public policy, the farmers could not maintain their traditional place in the community. If the needs of the nation were judged solely in terms of economics, then it followed that a considerable part of the farm population was becoming superfluous. Improvements in agricultural technique were making it possible for a relatively small number of farmers to satisfy all domestic needs. And as foreign nations began to buy American manufactured goods, they could no longer buy American farm products also (except during periods of world war and world starvation), so that the farmers were losing their foreign markets. In the twentieth century a relatively small number of efficient commercial farmers located on good land were receiving most of the total farm income, while the growing number of tenant farmers, many of them migratory, incompetent, and miserably poor, had become a national liability. In 1929 half of the farm families were producing less than one thousand dollars' worth of products a year each, while there were three-quarters of a million families who produced less than four hundred dollars' worth a year each.

This agricultural decline was hastened by the progress of soil erosion. The Americans had always used their natural resources with an incredible wastefulness, and in the twentieth century they began to discover the extent of the damage. Before the coming of the white man there had been more than six hundred million acres of fertile land in the area of the United States. By 1934 no less than fifty million acres had completely lost their topsoil as a result of careless farming; another fifty million had been almost ruined; and another two hundred million had been seriously damaged. These facts were dramatized by a series of catastrophic floods and dust storms; but the effect on the American farmer was even more serious. In large areas of the country it was becoming impossible for the farm population, however efficient and industrious, to make an adequate living.

One twentieth-century economist concluded that the American farmer was doomed. But the farmers were by no means willing to accept the fate for which (according to the rules of capitalist economics) they were apparently group, with a policy of supporting its friends and opposing its enemies in both political parties, it worked for legal recognition of the right to organize and to bargain collectively, and for legislation that would raise wages, reduce hours of labor, and provide for accident and unemployment insurance. And as the representative of that section of the community most exposed to economic insecurity, it was interested in any kind of government action that would maintain full employment and prevent depressions. Although it accepted the capitalist system, it wanted the powers of big business magnates to be limited and controlled by the state.

The farm organizations and the trade unions were the most vigorous advocates of reform; but they were not the only ones. Small businessmen and professional men throughout the country were alarmed by the trend towards monopoly. And the sectional issue was by no means unimportant. After the Civil War ownership and control of most of the wealth in the country had become concentrated in the Northeast. Factories, mines, and railroads in all parts of America were the property of corporations with offices in downtown Manhattan. The South and the West were becoming, in large measure, colonial areas exploited for the benefit of wealthy stockholders in New York and New England. There was, in consequence, a very considerable disparity in the living standards of the different sections. In the South, in particular, which was handicapped by a vicious agricultural system and by its racial problems as well as by Northern economic domination, a large part of the population suffered from a crushing poverty comparable to that of the peasants of South America or of the Orient. Those Southerners and Westerners who thought in sectional rather than in class terms wished to see a development of locally owned industries, the profits from which would stay where they were earned instead of flowing toward New York. And they wanted government action in order to break the Northeastern control of capital, transportation, and natural resources. For this reason Southern landowners and businessmen, in spite of their hostility to trade unionism and their illiberal racial attitudes, frequently found themselves politically allied with the farmer and labor organizations of the North and Middle West.

Although these different movements against big business were by no means fighting for identical objectives, almost all of them professed allegiance to the traditional American ideals of individual freedom and equality of opportunity. Few Americans wished to abolish private property in the means of production or regarded the growth of the power of the state (although accepting its necessity) with full approval. Essentially, the demand for reform represented an agrarian counterattack against the big corporations. There can be no doubt that a large proportion of the American people were still predisposed towards agrarian principles, even though they also wished to preserve the economic benefits of large-scale industry. The American ideal was still a society in which most people owned property or could hope to acquire it and in which individual initiative was not restricted either by monopolistic corporations or by an authoritarian state, however benevolent. Americans in the twentieth century, as in the eighteenth, continued to dislike coercion and to fear bureaucracy.

On account of this agrarian background the attack on capitalism in America assumed a form not paralleled in the larger European countries. Most European reformers thought in class terms and were accustomed to regard the state as the embodiment of social order and as a positive force for social betterment. In consequence, most European opponents of capitalism advocated some form of socialism, declaring that political power must be transferred from the employing class to the working class and that big corporations must become the property of the state. But European socialist doctrines never had any strong appeal to Americans (except among the intelligentsia, who were professionally interested in ideas). The United States was the only large capitalist country in which there was never any strong socialist or communist movement. The earliest (and at all times, the favorite) American panacea for the abuses committed by the big corporations was not socialism but the enforcement of to secure economic advantages, the reformers were compelled to support them. Some of them (Justice Brandeis being a notable example) laid most of the emphasis on the abolition of the privileges of big business and the restoration of a regime of genuine economic freedom. There were others, however, who made a complete break with the whole agrarian tradition and who, like the Europeans, regarded the growth of a strong and positive state with full approval. The most notable intellectual exponent of this latter point of view was Herbert Croly, whose *Promise of American Life* appeared in 1909. Croly praised Hamilton, condemned Jefferson, and argued that the twentieth-century liberal should aim, not at destroying special privilege, but at extending some form of privilege to every section of the community. On the whole, most of the leaders of the agrarian counterattack preferred to speak in the manner of Brandeis; but their actions, in their concrete effects, usually conformed more closely with the program of Croly. The political dynamics of the situation, in fact, made such a result almost inevitable. Twentieth-century Americans, like those of the early nineteenth century, were opposed to the special privileges of other people; but they preferred to seek privileges for themselves rather than to see all forms of privilege abolished.

2

Politics in a democracy takes its direction from public opinion; and during the period when the American people were not yet sufficiently aroused to demand action against the abuses of big business, their political representatives were not disposed to anticipate them. The agrarian counterattack, although slowly gathering strength during the three decades after the Civil War, did not become the dominant force in American politics until the twentieth century. Prior to the Progressive Era politicians were usually willing to give big business the legislation for which it asked, knowing that they would not thereby lose the votes of the majority of the electorate. Even during these years certain antibusiness measures were enacted. The Interstate Com-

merce Act for the regulation of railroad rates and practices
was passed in 1887, and the Sherman Antitrust Act prohibiting combinations in restraint of trade was passed in
1890, although enforcement of both measures was ineffec-
tive until the Progressive Era. But on such basic questions
as the tariff and the currency, big business could usually
count on political support.

The general level of American political life has, in fact,
never been lower than during the period between the Civil
War and the end of the century. An uninspiring succession
of dull, dreary, and mediocre men occupied the Presidency;
the issues in most of the electoral campaigns were unimportant or fictitious; and corrupt party bosses and party
machines assumed control of many of the city and state
governments. It should always be remembered, however,
that the function of the American government is to reflect
the will of the people; and when the activities of politicians
become trivial and dishonest, it is because they are no
longer receiving any vital and healthy impulse from the
people whom they represent. The American political
leaders of the seventies and eighties were reduced to
shadowboxing because the American public mind was
not stirred by any vital issue. Some of them, such as
James G. Blaine and Roscoe Conkling, were probably
equal in ability and force of personality to the greatest of
their predecessors; but they had no adequate opportunity
to prove their quality. They were actors equipped for
tragic roles who were condemned to perform in vaudeville.
And although they usually responded to the wishes of big
business, they should not be regarded merely as the political agents of the capitalist class. Business could get political
protection because it was the best organized and financed of
pressure groups, while the opposition was disorganized
and often apathetic. The corruption of post-Civil War
politics, however deplorable, is, in fact, an indication that
big business had no absolute control over the American
government. Businessmen were frequently compelled to
pay for legislative favors, particularly in the city and state
governments; and although this process has often been
interpreted as showing that they had bought a decisive in-

fluence over the political organizations, the businessmen themselves never regarded it in this light. They resented the independence of the politicians, and complained of being blackmailed and held to ransom.

Meanwhile, a series of insurgent movements was sweeping across the Western farming regions, and the votes recorded for candidates who attacked big business were increasing. During the 1870's and 1880's the grievances of the farmers were voiced by the Granger and Greenbacker movements; in the early nineties the People's Party had a rapid growth, winning a popular vote of nearly a million and a half in the election of 1894; and in 1896 the Democratic Party, repudiating the conservative leadership represented by Grover Cleveland, absorbed most of the People's Party and adopted a large part of the agrarian program. William Jennings Bryan of Nebraska, as Democratic candidate, was defeated by McKinley in one of the bitterest of all American presidential campaigns, but he won forty-seven per cent of the popular vote.

To these attacks on organized wealth and privilege, the upper-class Easterners, including not merely the business magnates but many who liked to regard themselves as liberals, reformers, and spokesmen of culture, reacted in the same manner as the Federalists a hundred years earlier. In the same mood of unreasoning panic they drew parallels with Robespierre and the French Revolution, spoke darkly of the end of civilization, and predicted anarchy, mob rule, and terror. It was, in fact, true that most of the farm leaders were relatively uneducated men with no profound understanding of economic forces. The American agrarian tradition had been broken by the Civil War. The insurgents of the late nineteenth century were reacting against immediate grievances, and the movement had no philosophical foundation and no comprehensive program. Bryan was honest but, unlike Jefferson and the Jacksonians, he was also naïve, narrow-minded, and provincial. Yet in spite of the intellectual deficiencies of the insurgents, they were the genuine representative of the American democratic tradition; and although they failed to win political power, they performed the essential service of educating American public opinion.

By the turn of the century the American people were ready for reform. An acceleration of the trend towards monopoly, exemplified particularly in the formation of *United States Steel* in 1901, strengthened the case of the agrarians, and their arguments were confirmed by the exposés of big-business practices and of its corrupt connections with politics, written by the group of journalists who became known as the muckrakers. For the next dozen years Progressivism, which meant, in general, control of big business in the interests of the average citizen and the revitalization of political democracy, was in the ascendant.

The best work of Progressivism was done in local government, and its ablest representatives were municipal leaders like Tom Johnson of Cleveland and state leaders like Robert La Follette of Wisconsin. Essentially a middle-class movement with a strongly moralistic bias, it was too inclined to crusade against symptoms rather than to remove causes. Campaigning on behalf of virtue and against evil, the Progressives denounced corruption, and concentrated on ejecting rascals and electing honest men to office; and their reform programs frequently had a strongly puritanical flavor. Yet although the evils they attacked frequently reappeared in new forms, they did succeed in making government more directly responsive to public sentiment, in limiting the powers of public utilities and other business corporations, and in raising the moral and intellectual standards of American public life.

But any thorough-going reformation of the American economic system could be accomplished only by the federal government, and the leaders of the Progressive movement in federal politics moved much more cautiously. The first president to speak the language of Progressivism was Theodore Roosevelt, who entered the White House as a result of the death of McKinley in 1901. Roosevelt's reputation has passed through various phases, and he remains one of the most controversial characters in American history. His main importance was that he was the first

president since the rise of the big corporations to insist
on the principle of government supremacy over business.
He was also the first Republican president since Lincoln
to assert strong executive leadership. The infectious gusto
with which he went about his duties, his superb show-
manship, and his talent for coining pungent phrases did
much to stimulate popular interest in politics, while his
varied intellectual enthusiasms elevated the whole tone
of national life. No other president except Jefferson has
been so keenly interested in learning and the arts. But
in spite of his propensity for making radical speeches, he
was essentially a conservative. He was shocked by the
apparent conviction of businessmen that they were independent of the laws and the government, and believed
that they must be compelled to conform to higher ethical
standards, but he had no desire to make any fundamental
changes in the economic system. In consequence, his seven
and a half years in office were considerably more fruitful
in speeches than in deeds. His concrete achievements in
domestic affairs were meager, and the most publicized of
his activities, his enforcement of the Sherman Act against
some of the big corporations, had little positive effect.
Meanwhile Roosevelt also conducted a vigorous foreign
policy; and though he displayed a refreshingly realistic
understanding of the role of power in international affairs,
he had a tendency to believe in the therapeutic value of
war and the moral nobility of imperialism which could not
be reconciled with Progressive ideals.

Retiring in 1909, Roosevelt bequeathed the Presidency
to Taft, an amiable and honest conservative who was willing to support mild reforms. Actually, Taft accomplished
more in four years, although with considerably less pub-
licity, than Roosevelt in seven and a half; the Sherman
Act was enforced more frequently, the Interstate Commerce Commission was for the first time given effective
power over railroad rates, and the Constitution was
amended to allow the income tax and the popular election
of Senators; but none of these measures could be considered radical. Meanwhile the Republican Party was
splitting into conservative and Progressive wings, and in

1912, when the conservatives nominated Taft for reelection, the Progressives seceded from the party. But instead of rallying about some genuine exponent of Progressive ideals, such as La Follette, they allowed themselves to be captured by Roosevelt, who wanted to run for the Presidency again and whose speeches had become even more fiery and more radical. Roosevelt was nominated for a third term by a strangely assorted gathering of Western liberals who liked his speeches, Eastern business men who liked his practices, and political emotionalists who liked the glamor of his personality; after hearing him declare that "we stand at Armageddon and we battle for the Lord," they concluded by singing *Onward, Christian Soldiers*. This division among the Republicans resulted in the election of the Democratic candidate, Woodrow Wilson.

The last of the three Progressive Presidents had grown up in the South and was more nearly an agrarian than any of his predecessors since the Civil War period. The main theme of his speeches was opposition to special privilege and protection for the economic rights of the small property owner. But in spite of these echoes of John Taylor, Wilson had spent most of his adult life in the decidedly conservative atmosphere of Princeton University, and until shortly before his election to the Presidency had shown little appreciation of the need for economic reforms. The measures he sponsored, therefore, although agrarian in tendency, were mild. They consisted of a reduction of the tariff, of the establishment of the Federal Trade Commission to police big business and check monopoly, and of the creation of the Federal Reserve System with the intention of providing a more elastic currency and preventing the concentration of financial power by the New York bankers. These reforms were adopted in 1913 and 1914. The outbreak of the First World War then brought the Progressive Era to an end.

The most conspicuous result of the Progressive Era was an increase in the responsibilities of government. Through the Interstate Commerce Commission, the Federal Trade Commission, and the Federal Reserve Board, officials of the federal government were entrusted with far-reaching powers over the national economy. Numerous minor laws, both federal and state, provided for government regulation of business practices and conditions of labor in different industries. But how these powers would be used depended on the character of the officials who exercised them. American liberals were adopting the Hamiltonian doctrine of a strong state in the hope that it could be used for Jeffersonian purposes; but they could have no guarantee that the state would always be used for such purposes. It was possible that the representatives of special privilege would win control of the new administrative machinery and use it to promote their own interests. The new liberalism might lead towards social democracy; on the other hand, it might also end in the dictatorship of big business.

Meanwhile, no essential change had been made in the existing system of property relations. Under the three Progressive Presidents the Sherman Act had been applied on two hundred and twenty-six different occasions, and many of the big corporations had been dissolved into smaller units. But it was impossible to compel these smaller units to engage in any genuine price competition with each other. Corporation directors were forbidden to make outright combinations with each other, but they could achieve the same purpose by means of unofficial price-fixing agreements beyond the reach of the law. The control big business had acquired over the economy of the nation remained unbroken. And although business magnates were dismayed and alarmed by the popular denunciations to which they were subjected and by their temporary loss of political influence, they soon adopted new techniques of self-defense. No longer able to depend on the protection afforded by the Constitution and its judicial interpreters and on their capacity to bribe politicians, they began to discover that the attitudes of the American people themselves could be swayed and manipulated by propaganda. This change in business attitudes may conveniently be dated from 1914 when the Rockefellers hired Ivy Lee as their "public relations counsellor." Corporations began to spend large sums on winning good will, public relations developed into a skilled profession, and deliberate efforts were made to control all the instrumentalities that influenced public opinion. Business was depicted as a form of "service," and any movement that threatened to limit its profits was depicted as an attack on American freedom and the American way of life. This growth of propaganda for special privilege was not the least important, and certainly the most ironical, of the results of the Progressive Era.

3

For a decade after the First World War the new techniques of public relations were conspicuously successful. The war itself, with its disillusioning aftermath, caused a general deflation of ideals, and the American people were very willing to believe that the pursuit of wealth was the only objective that had any reality. They were easily convinced that the big corporations were engaged in serving the community, that the antisocial practices that had been denounced by the Progressives had been genuinely reformed, and that if the business magnates were free from political interference they would establish a universal and an enduring prosperity. Through most of the 1920's economic trends were, in fact, conducive to optimism. Production increased rapidly, average wages (which had risen sharply during the war) remained high, and it seemed easy to make a great deal of money. And encouraged by the propaganda of prosperity, a larger proportion of the American people than ever before engaged in speculation. The national propensity to look for a quick and easy way of acquiring a fortune, which had been stimulated ever since the founding of the first colonies by rising land values and which had been the main reason for the failure of the agrarian ideal, was never more widely displayed than during the 1920's. Millions of middle-class citizens used their savings to buy real estate or stocks in the hope, not of finding sound investments, but of being able to sell at some dizzy rate of profit.

The Republicans regained control of the federal government in the election of 1920, and its leaders no longer displayed any Progressive inclinations. The Progressive Party, which had been launched with such enthusiasm in 1912, had been killed by its leader Theodore Roosevelt a few years later; and its members had been compelled to return to the Republican fold and to submit to conservative control of the party machinery. Presidents Harding, Coolidge, and Hoover and their supporters in Congress believed that their chief function was to assist business in earning profits, for which reason they raised the tariff to unprecedented heights and lowered income-tax rates, particularly in the upper brackets. The mechanisms of government control that had been established during the Progressive Era were not abolished, but they were now used primarily to help the big corporations rather than to police them.

The decade of the twenties was indeed an extraordinary period, in which the American people seemed to be engaged in a collective effort to evade realities and return to the golden illusions of infancy. During the latter part of the nineteenth century an epoch in American development had ended; the frontier had been closed, the big corporations had destroyed the economic bases of agrarian democracy, and the rise of aggressive imperialisms in Europe and Asia had ended the possibility of isolation. But in their initial attempts to deal with these new problems—by the reforms of the Progressive Era, and by participation in the First World War—the American people had not succeeded in solving them. So for a few delirious years they insisted that these problems did not really exist and had been maliciously invented by the enemies of the American way of life. Whatever happened in other parts of the world, the United States need assume no international responsibilities and could safely remain isolated. And in spite of the growth of the big corporations, the United States was still the land of freedom, equality, and opportunity for all. Anybody who denied these comforting assumptions was cynical, un-American, subversive, and probably in the pay of Moscow. The representative figure of the period was President Coolidge, who—with complete sincerity—voiced the individualistic sentiments which he had acquired from his

Yankee ancestors and which would have been relevant to
the social conditions of the eighteenth century. Perhaps
the most revealing expression of the national refusal to face
realities was the maintenance of the prohibition amendment. After generations of campaigning and much decidedly unscrupulous pressure politics, the enemies of
alcohol had induced American legislators to vote against
what they believed to be vice and to attempt to make the
nation virtuous by legislation. For thirteen years, from
1920 until 1933, this grotesque violation of individual
rights and liberties remained a part of the American constitution, although it was openly evaded by a large part
of the population and although its most obvious results
were to encourage disrespect for the law and to increase
the power and earnings of organized groups of criminals;
and for thirteen years many politicians, businessmen, and
other leaders of opinion continued to patronize boot-
leggers in private, while insisting in public that prohibition
was an idealistic experiment that deserved national support. It is not surprising that most of the American writers
and artists of the period, being sensitive to those underlying
realities that the American people were trying to evade,
felt a deep bitterness and sense of frustration sharply in
contrast with the complacency of the popular mind.

Actually the prosperity of the twenties was far from
universal and was not based on any secure foundation,
although scarcely anybody, even among professional economists and sociologists, can claim to have foreseen the
inevitable collapse. Most of the profits of industry went
to the big corporations, and the mortality rate among
small businesses continued to be high; agriculture was
suffering from a chronic depression; and although average
wages had risen, there were millions of workers who had
not shared in the increase. A country in which (as in
1929) forty-two per cent of all families were still earning
less than fifteen hundred dollars a year could not legitimately pride itself on having a high general standard of
living. And the result of such inequalities was that effective
purchasing power lagged behind productive capacity; the
American economy could produce more goods than it

could sell. That the crisis was averted until 1929 was due chiefly to three compensating but temporary factors: to spending on public works by states and municipalities at the rate of about three billion dollars a year, the money being raised largely through borrowing; to installment buying and the borrowing of money by people who could not afford to pay for what they needed in cash; and to the investment of some thirteen billion dollars of American capital in foreign countries, thereby enabling those countries to increase their purchases of American goods. Big business, in other words, enlarged the market for its goods by lending to other people, at substantial rates of interest, the money with which to buy them. Obviously this process could not continue indefinitely.

This era of illusion ended abruptly in October 1929. Stock market prices, which had been pushed upward by a fantastic orgy of speculation, suddenly collapsed, and by November the American people were some thirty billion dollars poorer in paper values than they had supposed themselves to be in September. The structure of prosperity was too fragile to withstand such a shock. Businessmen stopped investing money in industrial expansion; middle-class citizens curtailed their purchases of all but articles of immediate necessity; the production of capital goods and of durable consumption goods therefore declined; factories began to close their doors; the growth of unemployment led to further contractions of purchasing power and further closings of factories; and for three long years the American economy spiraled down into the whirlpool of the great depression. By 1932 the national income had dropped from eighty-two billion dollars a year to forty billion; the total income of labor had decreased from nearly eleven billions to about four and a half billions; total farm incomes had decreased from twelve and a half billions to five and a half; and the total output of goods had decreased by thirty-seven per cent. Between twelve and fifteen million workers were unemployed and dependent mainly on charity. A vast number had become homeless migrants, while others were living in huts they had built for themselves out of refuse timber on vacant city lots. These extraordinary events occurred in the richest country in the world, and were not brought about by any natural catastrophe or act of God or by any deliberate perversity of human beings. They were due solely to the weakness of a man-made economic system.

The American people, allowing the drive of the individual will towards wealth and power to frustrate the democratic ideals of freedom and equality and solidarity, had chosen the way of capitalism rather than that of agrarianism; and capitalism had failed them. They had rejected the America of Jefferson; and now the America of Hamilton had ended in catastrophe. Their first reaction was one of total incredulity. In his opening speech in the election campaign of 1928 President Hoover had declared that "we in America today are nearer to the final triumph over poverty than ever before in the history of any land"; and it was not easy for a nation which had believed this assurance to recognize how deeply it had gone astray. During the first two years the administration did little but make reassuring statements, in the belief that all that was needed was a revival of confidence; and when it finally took action, it adopted the Hamiltonian method of lending money to business corporations in the hope of checking bankruptcies and encouraging a revival of production. President Hoover sternly refused to allow any spending of federal money for the relief of the unemployed, declaring that to do so "would have injured the spiritual responses of the American people," and insisted that the economic structure was essentially sound. Meanwhile, most of the unemployed, faithful to the myth that America was the land of opportunity and that individuals who failed to prosper had only themselves to blame, accepted starvation with a remarkable docility. Western farmers, believing like their eighteenth-century ancestors that the property rights of the man who had mixed his labor with the wilderness should have precedence over the obligations of contracts, resorted to violence in order to stop the foreclosure of mortgages. But in the cities the victims of the depression displayed an

amazing respect for established law and order. They waited
for the next election and for the promised upturn of the
business cycle.

Presumably the mechanisms of the economic system, if
left to themselves, would eventually have brought recovery,
but the price in human suffering and loss of self-respect
would have been incalculably great. The Democratic administration of Franklin Roosevelt, elected in 1932, insisted
that men were not the helpless victims of a system they had
themselves created, and promised action; and during the
next seven years, until the outbreak of the Second World
War, the agrarian counterattack against the economy of
big business was resumed. Whatever may be the ultimate
verdict on the measures taken by the Roosevelt administration, one all-important achievement must always be set to
its credit: that it restored the faith of the American people
in their capacity to control their own destiny, in their form
of government, and in their future.

The New Deal was essentially a continuation of the Progressive Movement, although on a broader scale and with
more intellectual sophistication. Like Progressivism it had
no coherent program or philosophy, but was based on the
pragmatic belief that wherever there was a maladjustment
in the economic system the government should intervene
in order to remedy it. The favorite idea of the New Dealers
was the idea of balance; they declared that the American
economy had lost its balance, chiefly because big business
had acquired too much power, and that the government
must redress the balance, chiefly by enlarging the earnings
of agriculture and labor and by expanding the total effective
purchasing power of the community. They believed in
the virtues of private enterprise and initiative, but argued
that a free economy could no longer be maintained without positive government intervention and supervision.
In the long run such an attitude may have created almost
as many problems as it solved. Yet it would be unfair to
blame only the New Dealers for its deficiencies. The government had to act, and any action that tended to restore
public confidence was better than none. Unfortunately the
American people were neither intellectually nor psycho-

logically prepared for any long-range program of economic reconstruction. No such program had, in fact, been formulated, except by the socialists and communists; and most Americans continued to dislike collectivism, believing that the maintenance of freedom depended on the maintenance of private property and on the decentralization of control.

Whatever may be said in criticism of the New Deal, it should always be recognized that it drew into the service of the government many men of unusual vision, idealism, and broad social understanding, and that its leader was perhaps better qualified to fulfill the peculiar requirements of the presidential office than any of his predecessors. It must be admitted that Franklin Roosevelt lacked the integrity of Washington and the spiritual depth of Lincoln, and that he sometimes let himself be carried into tricky and devious courses by the boyish zest with which he played the game of politics. He was not the greatest of American Presidents. Yet he was second to none in his capacity for understanding popular sentiment, responding to it, and giving it direction; he was sufficiently bold, generous, and imaginative in mind and heart to recognize that civilization was in crisis, and to meet the challenge in appropriately large terms; he had a superlative courage; and although he could be supple and opportunistic, often to excess, in his choice of means, his ultimate objective was always the preservation and fuller realization of American ideals.

In general, what the New Deal set out to accomplish was to counteract the privileges of big business by giving similar privileges to other elements in the community. Through the AAA the farmers were enabled to restrict agricultural production and thereby to raise farm prices, while wage earners acquired a legal right to form trade unions and to bargain collectively, by which means they could raise their wages and reduce their hours of labor. Social security legislation, moreover, provided wage earners with unemployment and old age insurance. At first the New Dealers hoped that the business classes, appreciating the need for increasing purchasing power, would agree to this program; but a large majority of American businessmen was unwilling to make such concessions, and quickly began to denounce the administration as the enemy of free enterprise and the traditional American way of life. Meanwhile the government directly increased purchasing power by spending money on unemployment relief and on public works and by enlarging the Hoover program of making loans to business; and it extended its control over the currency and adopted various methods of increasing the quantity of money in circulation.

These major measures of reform were accompanied by a great variety of other innovations, some of which were perhaps more interesting than the central program. Among these peripheral activities of the New Deal, the most creative and imaginative was the TVA. Insofar as this was a publicly owned corporation engaged in the production and sale of electrical power with the purpose of forcing down private utility rates, in the manufacture of fertilizers, in flood control, and in other activities through the Tennessee Valley, it may be regarded as an experiment in socialism. Yet it was a form of socialism which avoided all the evils associated with bureaucratic control. It exercised no coercive powers, seeking voluntary public cooperation for all its activities and assisting private business and agricultural expansion throughout the region in which it operated. The TVA, moreover, represented a new departure in its attitude to nature. A vast region of the United States was treated as a unity, and it was recognized that men could maintain an enduring civilization only by co-operating with nature and conserving her resources, not by plundering her until the land became a desert. "For the first time since the trees fell before the settlers' axe," declared the chairman of the TVA, David Lilienthal, with some exaggeration but with a pardonable enthusiasm, "America set out to command nature not by defying her, as in that wasteful past, but by understanding and acting upon her first law—the oneness of men and natural resources." [1] In its philosophical meaning, which marked a break with the whole American background of conquest

[1] David E. Lilienthal: *TVA: Democracy on the March* (1944). p. 46.

and exploitation and the coming to consciousness of a new and more humane attitude, the TVA was even more significant than in its social implications. How far its principles could be extended was uncertain. But here at least was something new: a way of using the advantages of modern technology that did not restrict any legitimate form of individual freedom, political or economic, and that was neither capitalism nor bureaucracy.

Whether because of the New Deal program or because of the mechanisms of the business cycle, there was a considerable economic recovery; and by the summer of 1937 production was not far below the level of 1929. Yet there were still seven and a half million persons unemployed, most of whom were now being supported by the government; and the recovery was not sustained into 1938. Apparently the New Deal had failed to restore prosperity because it had retained too many inhibitions about borrowing and spending money on a sufficiently bold and generous scale. But in 1939 further attempts to solve the nation's economic problems were rendered unnecessary by the outbreak of the European war. During the next few years all restrictions on government spending were forgotten, the national debt was allowed to shoot up to an astronomical figure, and the nation's manpower and equipment were fully employed in making war materials.

Postwar economic movements seemed to justify the New Deal approach. By legislating directly for the benefit of agriculture and labor it had brought about a considerable redistribution of the national income. The result was a great increase in the effective purchasing power of the mass of the people, thus maintaining a broad foundation for postwar prosperity. Between 1929 and 1948 the share of the national income going to the richest one per cent of the population dropped from 16 to 8 per cent, and that going to the next highest 6 per cent dropped from 15 to 13 per cent. Nor did these figures allow for income tax payments, which reduced still farther the share of the richer classes. Between 1939 and 1948 the proportion of families earning less than $2,500 a year sank from 75 to 25 per cent. Another significant change was the movement, mainly

during the war years, of millions of impoverished farm
families from agriculture into industry, the result being a
sharp drop in the number and proportion of tenant farmers. Thus the United States had made a considerable advance toward a more equitable system of distribution, and
the economy had a much wider and more stable market for
its products. Although conservative businessmen continued
to complain about the powers acquired by labor unions and
by government officials, the New Deal legislation was
gradually accepted as a permanent part of the American
system. When the Republicans took office in 1953, all its
essential measures were retained and some of them were
actually extended. As the economist J. K. Galbraith suggested, American capitalism was now operating by the principle of countervailing power. Big industry was balanced
by big agriculture and big labor. Checks and balances
functioned, moreover, between different branches of business; for example, between the manufacturing corporations and the chain stores, the latter being able, unlike
individual storekeepers, to enforce lower prices and hence
protect the public interest.

Stimulated by continuous high government spending for
defense and foreign aid and enjoying a wide domestic
market, the postwar economy moved fairly steadily toward
higher levels in production and employment. Occasional
recessions were neither so prolonged nor so severe as before the New Deal. Under such conditions there was little
popular support for further reforms. The Truman administration advocated extensions of the New Deal, but had
little success in persuading Congress to adopt its proposals.
The Eisenhower period was characterized by a reduction
of domestic tensions and controversies. Only issues of
foreign policy and the perennial problem of race relations
continued to cause any strong emotions.

But while the more urgent problems of the industrial
economy seemed largely to have been solved, at least for
the immediate future, questions of much deeper import
were being ignored. The Americans of the 1950's, like
their pioneer ancestors, continued to regard the conquest
of nature and the transformation of natural resources into

articles for human consumption as intrinsically desirable goals. With their memories of the great depression, they were not inclined to question the necessity of full employment and full production, regardless of the purposes for which men were kept at work and the ultimate value of what was produced. The productive process, which should have been regarded as a means for better living, had, in fact, become transformed into an end. In prosperity, as in depression, the Americans were still the victims of the economic system they had created.

Continued prosperity required uninterrupted production and consumption, with a growing emphasis on durable goods rather than on articles of immediate necessity. The pace could be maintained only by speeding up the rate of obsolescence, constantly introducing new styles and constructing nothing to last more than a few years. Through most of the 1950's the American economy maintained a stupendous flow of new goods and services, accompanied by a vast expenditure on advertising and on the entertainment industries associated with it. Meanwhile farm overproduction had again become chronic, and the government was obligated to store billions of dollars' worth of unsalable foodstuffs. Relatively few persons inquired what values were served by the plethora of automobiles with their megalomaniac exaggeration of size and power, the network of new highways enabling people to move more rapidly across the continent without noticing the landscape, the constant demolition and rebuilding of office and apartment buildings, the proliferation of new articles of household equipment, the unending flow of commercialized entertainment over the airwaves, the rapidly accelerating consumption of the world's shrinking mineral and gasoline resources. But if this was the meaning of full employment, then the prospects of continued prosperity seemed almost as disturbing as those of prolonged depression.

Meanwhile many services essential not only for the improvement of American civilization, but even for its survival, received only the most grudging support. The American system of private enterprise apparently required the wildest extravagance in all forms of private spending, combined with the most rigid economy in all activities supported by public taxation. Government spending beyond the necessary minimum was justified only as a pump-priming measure during depression, which meant that during prosperity all public services were handicapped by severe budgetary restrictions and failed to keep pace with the growth of wealth and population. Thus the distribution of the nation's productive resources was marked by a growing imbalance. While the economy was producing all the new automobiles and television sets that high-pressure advertising and salesmanship could dispose of, schoolteachers were underpaid and the decline of educational standards approached catastrophic proportions; the inhabitants of every large city were endangered by inadequate police protection and public health services; and the national government was even reluctant to spend adequate sums on national defense.

Such an imbalance required a fundamental reappraisal of economic values. The traditional attack on capitalism, which had stressed the prevalence of depressions and the poverty of the mass of the working population, lost most of its force during the prosperity of the 1950's. After the New Deal reforms, the system displayed a renewed vitality which took its critics by surprise. Yet it was increasingly obvious that the maintenance of full production and the diffusion of high living standards could no longer be regarded as the only goals of a healthy economy. The American people during the 1950's, however, were not disposed to raise radical questions. On all economic levels and in all age-groups the nation was in a conservative mood, preferring to enjoy the goods it had acquired rather than risk losing them by demanding something better. There was a growing emphasis on social conformity and group affiliation. This manifested itself in such phenomena as the rapid rise in church membership, which reflected a fear of individual isolation more than any revival of vital belief. The temper of the time could not, in fact, be described as genuinely confident or optimistic. If Americans during the Eisenhower period were reluctant to concern themselves with fundamental problems, it was not from a conviction that such problems had been solved, but from a suspicion that they might prove to be insoluble.

Thus the agrarian counterattack had led to somewhat paradoxical results. The drive of the farming and wage-earning classes for more freedom and equality had improved the workings of the capitalist system, but had not changed its essential nature. The main lesson of agrarian thought—that economic factors were subordinate to moral, political and cultural values—was remembered only under the impact of depression and forgotten in times of prosperity.

★ ☆ ☆ ☆ ☆ ☆ ☆ ☆ ☆ ☆ ★ ☆ ☆ ☆

THE UNITED STATES
IN WORLD AFFAIRS

★ ★ ★ ★ ★ ★ ★ ★ ★ ★ ★ ★ ★ ★

EFFECTIVE AMERICAN PARTICIPATION in world affairs began during the 1890's. For the previous three quarters of
a century the Americans had been in the singularly fortunate position of not needing a foreign policy. They had become the dominant power in the western hemisphere, and
for a variety of reasons they had been in no danger of
attack from either Europe or Asia. The British navy had
policed the seas, and no other power or group of powers
had threatened the British maritime hegemony. Under such
conditions the Americans had been able to maintain their
peaceful way of life and their democratic institutions, and
had not required a strong army or navy or an authoritarian
government. Unfortunately this happy isolation could not
endure.

The abandonment of isolation was due in some measure
to internal factors. Before the end of the nineteenth century, American industrialists were beginning to look for
new foreign markets, and to ask for political assistance in
securing them. Meanwhile American politicians (most notably Theodore Roosevelt) were becoming infected with
European imperialist attitudes and acquiring an ambition
to play power politics, while American newspaper owners
(like William Randolph Hearst) found it profitable to stir
up nationalistic excitements and propagate hatred of for-

eign countries. The internal tensions caused by the maladjustments of the industrial economy were becoming more acute, and opponents of reform preferred that they find an outlet in foreign war rather than in class conflict. It was also important that the West was now settled; with the closing of the frontier Americans began to look to Latin America and across the Pacific for new worlds to conquer.

For a few years the United States became interested in acquiring colonial possessions and had a tendency to threaten the independence of her smaller neighbors. Yet the American people as a whole were never converted to imperialism and were never willing to support an aggressive foreign policy. The more important causes for their involvement in world politics during the twentieth century were always external and not internal. American security was now endangered by the growth of imperialist rivalries in other parts of the world and, in particular, by the rise of two strong and expansionist powers, Germany and Japan, that threatened to put an end to the British naval supremacy. This was the primary reason why the Americans could no longer remain aloof from international affairs.

The underlying objectives of American foreign policy in the twentieth century (as indicated, not in the public statements of American statesmen, but in their actions) were identical with those that had been pursued by Washington, Jefferson, and Monroe. In the first place, the Americans sought security against any possible aggression. They were not afraid of being conquered; but they knew that if they lost their security they would be compelled to devote a large part of their energies to defense instead of to the arts of peace, and must abandon their democratic institutions and allow the growth of a strong authoritarian government. But whereas the statesmen of the early republic had been concerned only with the North American continent, their twentieth-century successors had to extend their interests to the further shores of the two oceans. Technology had decreased the size of the world; and British sea power was no longer invincible. The first principle of American policy, therefore, was to prevent any aggressive power from acquiring control either of the eastern end of the Atlantic or of the western end of the Pacific. It was primarily in order to maintain this principle that the United States participated in the two world wars.

In the second place, the Americans continued to seek access to markets in other parts of the world, on terms of equality with other countries. In spite of their tariff policies they believed, in general, in the Open Door, and did not resort to state action in order to acquire exclusive control of foreign or colonial markets. As in the early days of the republic, they were hostile to closed monopolistic empires and systems of autarchy, which they regarded as oppressive and conducive to war.

In the third place, the Americans wished to see democratic institutions extended throughout the world. They believed that democratic governments were inherently more peaceful and more law-abiding than were autocracies. They regarded the conflict between the principles of freedom and those of dictatorship as world-wide, transcending all national and continental boundaries. And since they felt their own institutions to be superior to those of any other people, they were eager that other nations should adopt them. When they engaged in war they always declared that they were fighting to defend democracy and to destroy autocracy or dictatorship.

These principles did not involve any threat to the legitimate rights of other peoples and could be universalized into a new world order of peace and freedom. The national interests and ideals of the United States, unlike those of any other great power, in no way conflicted with the general interests of humanity. Unfortunately the Americans were frequently slow, fumbling, and confused in taking action in defense of their interests and ideals. Their leaders no longer displayed the boldness and certainty of touch which had characterized their eighteenth-century predecessors.

This was partly because the American government was democratic. Despite all allegations to the contrary, the major outlines of American policy were determined by public sentiment; and no decisive action could be taken— in particular, there could be no declaration of war or commitment that might lead to such declaration—unless it had the support of a large majority of the electorate. But inevitably the electorate was unable to decide upon such issues with any rapidity. A democratic foreign policy necessarily seemed slow by contrast with that of a dictatorship, since fifty million voters could not make up their minds as quickly as could one man. This is one of the reasons why, under twentieth-century conditions, democracy and dictatorship cannot easily coexist side-by-side in one world. And while all democratic nations were handicapped by their inability to make decisions quickly, the United States was likely to be even slower than were the European democracies. For her population was more heterogeneous and less imbued with a spirit of national unity, and it included large immigrant groups who (ignoring the advice given in Washington's Farewell Address) retained hereditary attachments to some European countries and equally strong antipathies to others.

But it was not merely because the United States was democratic that her foreign policy often seemed ineffectual; it was also because the American people lacked a sufficiently clear understanding of the issues that confronted them. Unlike the peoples of the European countries, they had not acquired habits and traditions which were relevant to the situation in which they now found themselves. For three quarters of a century, except during a few brief periods, they had been able to forget about world affairs, and during this long stretch of time they had acquired a belief in the virtues of isolation. Plenty of twentieth-century Americans continued to insist that isolation was still possible, in spite of the changes in world affairs, and attributed its abandonment not to external dangers but to the ambitions or the weaknesses of American leaders. And even those Americans who were most convinced of the need for a vigorous foreign policy were often unable to see the situation in realistic terms; instead of recognizing that in a world of competing imperialisms the United States must act to maintain her security and her peaceful way of life, they were always inclined—in accordance with the general preconceptions of the American character— to interpret international affairs in terms of a battle between good and evil. Without such an interpretation the Americans were, in fact, unable to resort to force in defense of their own way of life and vital interests. For this reason, as so often in the past, the actions of the Americans showed more boldness and farsightedness than the public statements of their policy. This was notably true of their intervention in the two world wars. In each instance an intuitive sense of their own vital interests caused them to abandon neutrality soon after the outbreak of the conflict; but in each instance they were unable to become full belligerents without insisting that they had been the victims of an unprovoked attack. They could take positive and necessary actions, but they always preferred to believe that their actions had been forced upon them by others.

This lack of conscious understanding did not prevent the Americans from defending their interests in war; but it made it more difficult for them to deal realistically with the problems of peacemaking. Obviously it was to their interest, not only to defeat aggressive imperialisms, but also to work for the creation of some kind of world order in which no new imperialism would be permitted to develop. After each of the two world wars American statesmen took the lead in making plans for such a world order. But having visualized the conflict in which they had recently been engaged as a battle between white and black, the Americans were too inclined to assume that virtue was now triumphant, and to see the new world order in Utopian terms. Failing to take account of the complexity of all human affairs, they were then startled to discover that the allies who had shared their triumph were not white but various shades of gray and were continuing, after the war as before, to think chiefly of their own interests. The resultant disillusionment of the Americans might lead, as in 1919, to a retreat into a self-righteous isolationism.

These adolescent traits of the American character were most conspicuous in their dealings with Europe. In the Pacific, which for generations had seemed destined for American control, they acted with more assurance, though not always with more wisdom; the Americans had always felt happiest when they faced the west. But when they turned back towards the continent from which their ancestors had come, they were inclined to feel bewildered and to become suspicious and resentful. They displayed, in fact, the attitudes that had been explored in the novels of Henry James. Like James's heroines they were genuinely more generous and more idealistic than the Europeans, but had less worldly wisdom. And like James himself they were disposed to exaggerate both their own purity of motive and the corruption of Europe. They visualized themselves in the role of a Milly Theale, taken advantage of by European fortune hunters. Their actual behavior more often resembled that of Maggie Verver, who had a real purity and simplicity but who had also a drive to impose her will upon her European husband.

In their diplomatic relations with Europe twentieth-century Americans were therefore less successful than the men of the eighteenth century; they could neither defend their own interests and ideals nor appreciate the European point of view with the adult self-confidence that had been so remarkably displayed by Franklin and Washington and Jefferson. And the reasons for this failure were not merely intellectual. Twentieth-century America had less faith in itself. The men of the eighteenth century had believed that the United States represented a new and higher way of life; but the men of the twentieth century could not feel the same certainty. They still felt that their country stood for certain ideals that might be of world-wide application and that ought to be the salvation of humanity; but they no longer knew with sufficient clarity what those ideals were or how they could be embodied in institutions. The Americans were confused in their dealings with the rest of the world because they were confused in the handling of their own internal affairs. So when they were called upon to draw a blueprint for a new world order, they could enunciate principles but could not show how they could be made effective. In their foreign policy, as in their social organization and their intellectual life, ideal and practice had become divorced from each other. This fundamental moral weakness was apparent during the First World War, when the American government formulated a general program for world reconstruction that could not be translated into concrete actualities. It was still more apparent after the Second World War, when the United States was confronted by a power whose leaders were the spokesmen of a new and rival ideal for world order and who knew very clearly what that ideal was and how it might be carried into effect.

2

The brief infection of the Americans with imperialist attitudes showed itself most conspicuously in the Spanish-American War of 1898, as a result of which they annexed Puerto Rico, the Philippines, and Guam and established a protectorate over the newly liberated Cubans. In the same year they also acquired the Hawaiian Islands. There was no genuine necessity for the war, but the American government was pushed into it by popular excitement, in which a desire for nationalistic aggrandizement and a crusading urge to assist the Cubans in their struggle for independence were curiously mingled. Throughout the whole decade the Americans were, in fact, in a bellicose mood; they had already threatened to go to war with the Chileans in 1891 (as a result of the killing of some American sailors in a Chilean port) and with the British in 1895 (about the boundary line between Venezuela and British Guiana). This was no doubt due chiefly to the exacerbation of their internal political conflicts, although it may also have been a reflection of some kind of psychological rhythm. It can hardly have been accidental that each of the three minor (and unnecessary) wars in which the Americans have been engaged began a little more than thirty years after the ending of the previous war.[1]

[1] *The War of 1812 began thirty-one years after the Battle of Yorktown. The War with Mexico began thirty-one years after the Battle of New Orleans. The War with Spain began thirty-three years after Lee's surrender at Appomattox. Each of these wars began as a result of American actions, and was not precipitated by the other nations involved.*

After the war with Spain the Caribbean began to become an American sphere of influence. This process seemed at first to be a minifestation of outright imperialism. In 1903 Theodore Roosevelt violated the legitimate claims of Colombia in order to secure the right to build the Panama Canal; and in 1905 he enunciated the Roosevelt Corollary, by which he declared his intention of intervening in the internal affairs of Latin American nations that failed to maintain order and protect the rights of foreign citizens. Before the end of the First World War, American armed forces had assumed partial or complete control over Cuba, Haiti, the Dominican Republic, and Nicaragua, and had also intervened in Mexico. This extension of American political power was accompanied by a considerable increase of American economic interests, such as the investment of capital, throughout the Caribbean countries and in South America.

But in spite of the aggressive attitudes of certain American statesmen, the most important underlying motive for American policy was at all times security and not the desire for aggrandizement, either political or economic. The Caribbean was a part of the American defense system, particularly after the building of the Panama Canal; and although Great Britain accepted American supremacy in this region at the beginning of the twentieth century, other European powers, particularly Germany, seemed less amenable. It was primarily in order to forestall the Europeans, and not in order to enrich themselves, that the Americans moved into the Caribbean. Provided that their vital interests were safeguarded, they were willing in using their power to show a restraint that cannot be paralleled in the history of any of the European imperialist powers. After the First World War the United States gradually withdrew her armed forces from the countries she had occupied and repudiated the Roosevelt Corollary. It was assumed that the Caribbean and Central American peoples would continue to follow United States leadership in foreign affairs, but they were no longer disturbed in the conduct of their internal affairs. This mutual recognition of what was implied by a sphere of influence set a new and admirable pattern in relations between a great power and its smaller neighbors.

Meanwhile the stronger and more advanced Latin American countries further to the south were alarmed by this expansion of United States interests. Hitherto the two sections of the American world had had very little contact with each other. In the twentieth century the growth of trade and capital investments and the new developments in world politics began to draw them together; and it seemed to the Latin Americans that this process was a threat to their independence. Journalists like the Argentinian Ugarte insisted that the United States was consciously planning to control the entire hemisphere, while intellectuals like Rodó of Uruguay urged their fellow citizens to preserve their own way of life, with its rich Catholic and Latin cultural traditions, and not to be seduced by the more materialistic and utilitarian standards of the Yankees. For Rodó, the United States, in spite of its technological achievements, was a country of barbarians who were dominated by the drive towards power and material success and who had no understanding of æsthetic and spiritual values. The Yankee differed from the Latin, he declared, as Sparta differed from Athens. No doubt it was chiefly in order to compensate for its material weakness that Latin America was so insistent on its spiritual superiority; yet such comparisons indicated also that the United States, as seen by her southern neighbors, no longer represented any noble ideal. The Latin Americans knew the United States as the country, not of a democratic way of life, but of big business. It was not until the administration of Franklin Roosevelt that they began to see her in a more favorable light.

Meanwhile in the Open Door notes of 1899 and 1900 the American government had tried to lay the foundations of a Far Eastern policy. In declaring that China must remain independent, instead of being carved into colonies and spheres of influence controlled by imperialist powers, the American officials were initially motivated by a desire to keep Chinese markets open for American traders and investors. It was largely in order to secure a base for economic expansion in the Far East that the Philippines had been annexed. But Americans never developed any important economic connections with China; and the Open Door policy gradually lost its expansionist implications and became a measure of defense. China must be protected in order to check the growth of any aggressive imperialism in the Far East. After the Russo-Japanese War of 1904 it became evident that Japan was potentially the most dangerous of the various powers with Far Eastern interests; and henceforth the policy of the United States was to oppose Japanese penetration into China. But the American people were not yet willing to support a vigorous Far Eastern policy, and their government had to limit itself to verbal protests and declarations of principle. As long as the Japanese did not threaten to seize the Philippines and the East Indies and to acquire control of the whole of the western Pacific, they did not constitute any obvious threat to American security. While they contented themselves with seizing pieces of China, the United States, although expressing strong disapproval of the process, did not resort to action.

3

The American intervention in the First World War and the subsequent controversy about its causes provide an illuminating case study of the weaknesses in the American attitude toward foreign affairs. The real reasons for the intervention should be sufficiently plain. The American government and a majority of the American people came to the conclusion that Germany was a dangerously aggressive power and that German control of the eastern Atlantic would be a threat to American security. As Woodrow Wilson said in September 1914, a German victory would compel the United States to "give up its present ideals and devote all its energies to defense, which would mean the end of its present system of government. . . . England," he declared, "is fighting our fight." For this reason the Americans abandoned strict neutrality early in the war, giving diplomatic and economic assistance to the British and French, and in 1917 they became full belligerents. It is possible that they exaggerated the German menace and that their entry into the war was therefore unnecessary; but to take chances on a German victory seemed foolhardy.

But the Americans were unable to interpret their own behavior in these simple and rational terms. Instead, they insisted that they had obeyed all the rules of neutrality; and when they finally entered the war, they believed that they had been the victims of an unprovoked attack. Actually, they took of their own volition the steps that led up to full belligerency; yet they insisted that they had been dragged into the conflict by forces outside their control. It was this curious reluctance to accept responsibility for their own behavior that caused so many Americans during the 1920's and 1930's to decide that they had somehow become involved in a conflict with which they had no concern and that the United States must therefore adopt legislation by which her neutrality in any future conflict would be made inviolable.

According to the accepted doctrine of neutral rights in wartime (in the formulation of which the United States had played a leading part), the Americans had a right to trade freely with the civilian populations of all the warring powers. These rules were violated both by the British and by the Germans: the British by imposing a blockade of Germany and of all northern Europe; the Germans by using their submarines to sink British ships, some of which carried American goods or passengers. Toward the British President Wilson and his advisors confined themselves to purely verbal protests; and when these protests brought no results, they never threatened to resort to action. Toward the Germans, on the other hand, their attitude was much more severe. They insisted, moreover, on two points, neither of which had any sufficient basis in international law. They declared, firstly, that American citizens who chose to travel on British passenger ships should be immune from danger and were still under the protection of the American government; and, secondly, that British merchant ships (in spite of the fact that they were armed with offensive weapons, and should therefore be classified as warships) might not be sunk without warning. After a long controversy Wilson threatened to break off diplomatic relations unless Germany gave way; and the Germans then agreed that no more passenger ships should be attacked and that other ships should not be sunk without warning. In compelling the Germans to abandon unrestricted submarine warfare Wilson had made a considerable contribution to Allied victory. The British were dependent for their survival on the shipment of food and munitions from abroad (largely from the United States), and unrestricted use of the submarine might have starved them into submission. Although the American government claimed to be concerned only with American rights, it was actually interpreting those rights in such a way as to give diplomatic and economic assistance to Great Britain.

In the spring of 1917 the Germans revoked their previous agreement and resumed their attempt to starve out the British by sinking ships without warning; and they now began to sink American as well as British ships. The United States then became a full belligerent. Wilson's previous refusal to tolerate unrestricted submarine warfare made a declaration of war on Germany unavoidable. At the same time there can be no question that a majority of the American people wanted to ensure an Allied victory and welcomed the final decision; German attacks on American ships provided them with a pretext, rather than a reason, for taking an action they believed to be necessary for their own security. Their underlying motive was a fear of the possible consequences of a German victory. And although they may have been influenced by the economic ties with Great Britain developed during the first three years of the war, we need not assume that economic motives were paramount; if the Americans had not been initially sympathetic to the British, they would not have engaged in shipping them goods and lending them money on such an extensive scale.

American military participation in the war was relatively unimportant; Germany surrendered before the Americans were ready to undertake large-scale military operations. But Americam economic aid to the Allies was of decisive effect. And at the end of the war the United States was unquestionably the strongest world power, and apparently in a position to determine the nature of the peace settlement. In the conferences that drafted the Treaty of Versailles America confronted Europe in a conflict that had the quality of a tragic drama and that illuminated all the divergencies in the spiritual atmosphere of the two continents.

While Clemenceau, with his worldly wisdom and his distrust of Utopianism, was an appropriate representative of Europe, Woodrow Wilson was remarkably typical of America. Descended from a line of Presbyterian ministers, he saw life as a battle between good and evil, in which the champion of righteousness, although he might finally be broken by defeat, must never compromise or surrender. He dreamed of creating a new world order in which war might be made forever impossible; and he believed that it was the peculiar mission of the United States to lead mankind towards this new order. He succeeded in communicating this faith to the masses of the people in war-torn Europe, who received him during the early months after the German surrender as though he were a semidivine savior and liberator. Yet although Wilson could enunciate the general principles of freedom and justice with a moving eloquence and simplicity, he could not show how they might be made effective. He had no practical solution for the tangled problems of Europe, with its agelong fears and hatreds. Neither the League of Nations nor the other idealistic proposals in Wilson's Fourteen Points could maintain peace unless all the great powers were genuinely willing to repudiate the past and abandon the use of force. But as the European statesmen well knew, there was no such willingness. In reality, as Clemenceau insisted, peace could be maintained only by a settlement that would keep Germany permanently weaker than her victorious opponents.

The result was a battle of wills between the two men, ending in a treaty that fully satisfied neither of them and that was neither genuinely idealistic nor effectively realistic.

The peace conference was a novel by Henry James, translated into actual life and weighted with tragic implications for the entire human race. And while Wilson, when confronted by the Europeans, displayed all the naïve idealism and the moral determination of a Jamesian heroine, he recalled also, in the drive of his will, an earlier symbol of the American character. He was Ahab doing battle with the white whale.

In the final outcome, what defeated Wilson (like Melville's Pierre as well as his Ahab) was his own lack of realism and his own spiritual pride. He had dramatized the American participation in the war, not as a necessary measure of security for the American way of life, but as a crusade for righteousness on a world scale. When it became apparent that the peace settlement had not created any new world order, the American people rapidly succumbed to disillusion and resolved to forget about the apparently insoluble problems of Europe. Yet in spite of the reaction to isolationism the Senate might still have agreed to American membership in the League of Nations if Wilson had been willing to accept reservations safeguarding American sovereignty. It is unlikely that such reservations would have weakened the League, but Wilson stubbornly and self-righteously refused to compromise. And after neither the Wilsonians nor the reservationists had succeeded in obtaining the necessary majority in the Senate, the question was dropped and the United States remained outside the League. For the next two decades the Americans refused to recognize that what happened on the other side of the Atlantic might vitally concern them and that they should therefore use their influence to maintain the settlement which their entry into the war had made possible. Until 1940 they left European affairs to the Europeans.

4

During the twenty years between the two wars it was increasingly apparent that the world was approaching unity, that the destinies of the different nations were becoming inextricably entangled with each other, and that what happened anywhere might alter the lives of all men everywhere. But for a long time the Americans did not face the political implications of these facts or assume responsibilities in keeping with their power and their national idealism.

The United States government was officially against war, in the same way that it was officially against sin; and in 1928 it sponsored the Kellogg Pact, by which all the nations of the world solemnly pledged themselves to renounce war forever. But the Americans would not commit themselves to take any kind of action against warmakers. In the Far East, by the Washington Treaties of 1922, Japan was induced to promise that the *status quo* should be maintained; but when she violated her promises, first by seizing Manchukuo in 1931 and afterwards by going to war with China in 1937, the United States confined herself to verbal protests. In Europe conditions remained relatively stable through the twenties, partly because of the flow of American loans. When the stream of American money ran dry and the American economy plunged into the great depression, the political and economic structure of Europe began to crumble; and during several depression years the Nazis rose to power in Germany. The primary responsibility for failing to stop Hitler before Germany was ready for war rested with the British and French; but the American attitude was far from helpful. The initial American reaction to the threat of another war was to pass a series of neutrality acts designed to prevent America's natural allies from receiving economic assistance. Only in Latin America, where successive administrations, Republican and Democratic, worked to remove suspicions and to transform the Monroe Doctrine into a joint Pan American obligation, did the Americans during these years adopt a constructive policy. Toward Europe and the Far East they acted as though the United States, instead of being incomparably the richest and strongest power in the world, were some second-rate country too weak to influence the course of events.

During the thirties the powers who wished to overthrow

the *status quo* formed agreements with each other, and made their plans for expansion. The ambitions of the Axis presented a triple threat to the United States. German control of the eastern Atlantic and Japanese control of the western Pacific would destroy American security and compel the Americans to devote most of their energies to defense, and might make it necessary for the American government to assume dictatorial powers. The autarchical economic policies pursued by both Germany and Japan would enable the German and Japanese governments to dictate their own terms to American traders and exclude them from foreign markets. Finally, by taking advantage of all the internal weaknesses of the United States, by propaganda, by fifth-column activities, and by the example of their success, the Axis powers would undermine American democracy from within. It was therefore imperative that the United States should prevent Germany and Japan from destroying their opponents in Europe and Asia.

After the outbreak of the Second World War the United States gradually moved towards belligerency in the same wavering fashion as in the previous war, but more quickly and with more conscious awareness of what was at stake. After the fall of France the American people engaged in a great debate, and a large majority of them came to the conclusion that Germany must not be allowed to win control of Europe. The American government continued to insist that the first purpose of its foreign policy was to keep the United States out of war, apparently in order to reassure voters who were not yet willing to face all the implications of American policy. But it undertook to supply the British and their allies with foodstuffs and munitions, and subsequently it began to assist the British in guarding the convoys by which these goods were carried to their destination. By the autumn of 1941 the United States was engaged in an undeclared naval war with German submarines in the North Atlantic. Meanwhile, no action was taken against the Japanese as long as they restricted their aggressions to Chinese territory; but when they began to move southward, in preparation for the seizure of the East Indies, the American government embargoed sales of war material and adopted other measures of economic warfare. The Roosevelt cabinet was agreed that if Japan actually attacked the East Indies, the United States must go to war. How large a proportion of the American people would have supported them is an interesting question; but fortunately for American morale it was unnecessary to answer it. Rather than take her chances on the American decision, Japan decided to cripple the United States Pacific fleet before proceeding with her plans of expansion; and on December 7, 1941, the Pearl Harbor raid put the Americans fully into the war.

The American achievement in the Second World War, in both its industrial and its military aspects, was of stupendous proportions.

During peacetime, as a result of internal conflicts and faulty economic mechanisms, the Americans had never realized the potentialities of their industrial system; and although they produced goods on a vast scale during the First World War, Germany surrendered before their strength became fully effective. But in the Second World War the national energies over a period of three and a half years were co-ordinated toward a single objective. Inevitably there were cases of error, confusion, and fraud. One of the great virtues of a democracy, by contrast with a dictatorship, is that mistakes are fully publicized; and this often causes them to assume a magnified importance. A blunder or an act of corruption is news, whereas competence attracts little attention. But the shortcomings in the American performance should not obscure its magnitude. While they were fighting major wars both in Europe and in the Pacific, and while they were employing fourteen millions of their most able-bodied citizens in the armed forces, the Americans produced war materials valued at nearly ninety billion dollars a year, creating incomparably the strongest navy and the strongest air force and one of the strongest armies in human experience, and at the same time supplying a large part of the needs of their allies. And during this same period they actually raised their average civilian standard of living and increased the volume of civilian consumption.

In the arts of warfare the Americans, as a democratic people, have always shown the greatest ingenuity and capacity for initiative. A large number of both the weapons and the techniques of modern war were originally invented by Americans, most of the remainder being the work of the British.[2] Peoples (like the Germans and the Japanese) who have never acquired the habit of freedom rarely make innovations, even in warfare, although they may make themselves formidable by adopting and organizing innovations that have been made by others. In the Second World War the Americans showed that their democratic qualities had not been seriously impaired by the growth of their industrial society and their failure to solve the problems it had created. The American war record, considered in detail, was filled with extraordinary examples, not only of courage and endurance, but also of more peculiarly American traits; men accustomed to civilian life, when exposed to the novel conditions of warfare and suddenly required to assume unexpected responsibilities, displayed the same kind of adaptability and resourcefulness as their pioneering ancestors. Meanwhile, scientists and engineers evolved a long series of new weapons and instruments of communication and transpor-

[2] *Americans invented the submarine and the airplane, and have been responsible for many of the improvements in small arms during the past two hundred years (the machine gun, for example, was developed mainly by two Americans, Gatling and Maxim). The British invented the tank and were mainly responsible for the evolution of the battleship (with some assistance from American experiments during the Civil War). The first aircraft carrier was British, and the second was American. The atomic bomb was a joint British and American product. The Americans were the first to experiment with paratroopers. The technique of the blitzkrieg was first worked out by the British General Fuller at the end of the First World War. The Nazis declared that their methods of economic mobilization were copied from American policies during 1917 and 1918, and that they learned both the importance and the specific techniques of war propaganda partly from Lloyd George and partly from Woodrow Wilson. Even the German rocket bomb was based on experiments made by American inventors during the 1930's.*

tation. Although the most formidable of the new implements of warfare, the atomic bomb, was an international enterprise insofar as scientists from several different countries co-operated in the research that made it possible, the actual construction of the bomb was done in America and financed by the American government, and it was the American air force which first employed it.

The industrial and technological achievements of the Americans and the quality of their fighting men were the chief factors in their victories; but they were effective because they were directed by leaders who understood how to make full use of them. Both in Europe and (after the disasters of the first five months) in the Pacific the American high command conducted the war with a remarkably clear comprehension of the means at their disposal and the ends they proposed to achieve. The American method of warfare was to plan an offensive action, and then to accumulate such an overwhelming mass of weapons and supplies that the expenditure of human lives was held to a minimum. War, in other words, became a series of engineering problems, and lost much of its uncertainty. Behind this approach were three hundred years of history, during which the Americans had acquired the habit of approaching problems in a severely practical spirit, unimpeded by irrelevant notions of honor, glory, or adherence to traditional rules and conventions.

Obviously the winning of the war was a co-operative enterprise, in which each of the leading United Nations played an indispensable role; but it was American resources, American ingenuity, and American élan that conquered the Pacific and won the most spectacular and possibly the most important of the victories in Europe. At the end of the war, with a navy surpassing that of all other nations combined, with the world's strongest air force, with one of its two strongest armies, and with control of a secret weapon of unparalleled destructivity, the United States had a global military supremacy that had never been equaled by any other country in history. Such a power necessarily carried with it equally extraordinary responsibilities. It was incumbent upon the United States to assume a position of world leadership.

All the earlier history of the American people, at least when superficially considered, seemed to have prepared them for such a role. Whereas each of the nations of western Europe was organized around a community of race and tradition from which other peoples were necessarily excluded, the unifying principles of the American nationality were certain common social ideals and hopes for the future that were capable of world-wide extension. The United States had always been a Messianic nation, and its greatest leaders had always seen it as an experiment in a new way of living and declared that its destiny would affect the whole human race. According to Washington the maintenance of liberty had been mainly, if not solely, entrusted to American safekeeping, while Lincoln had called the American republic "the last best hope of earth." And in spite of fears of American imperialism, there can be no doubt that during the Second World War a large proportion of the human race, not only in Europe, but also in the East, looked to the United States with hope and good will.

The Americans did not wholly disappoint these expectations. Most of them recognized that any retreat into isolation was now impossible, and they continued to display an extraordinary generosity toward other peoples and a genuine reluctance to use their power for selfish or coercive purposes. But whether they could acquire a more realistic understanding of world affairs fast enough to prevent catastrophe remained a doubtful question. During the war years they concentrated all their energies on the single objective of crushing the enemy, regarding victory not as one step in a continuing struggle but as a final triumph over evil. While their government took the lead in the drafting of elaborate plans for international security and economic cooperation, these plans were predicated on the naïve assumption that all the countries allied against the Axis had a common devotion to peace and democracy and would respond to demonstrations of friendship. At Yalta and other conferences damaging concessions were made to the Russians under the illusion that they would result in lasting co-operation. Only slowly and reluctantly did the Americans come to recognize that the Soviet Union was dominated by such wholly different beliefs and principles of government that no agreement was possible, that the world for an indefinite period to come would necessarily be divided into two hostile spheres, and that the United States could achieve security for herself and her ideals only by carrying out a long-range program of containing Communist expansion and strengthening and unifying the sphere of freedom. Such a situation demanded a patience, a self-restraint, a capacity for choosing realistically not between good and evil but between different degrees of evil, that the Americans had never been required to develop in their earlier history.

As soon as the war ended, the United States began to demobilize her armed forces on the assumption that they were no longer needed, while the Russians, already violating the Yalta agreements, began to impose satellite governments in eastern Europe and give help to the Communists in China. It was not until the spring of 1947 that the Americans fully abandoned the illusions about Soviet objectives that had developed during the war years, and recognized that one kind of world crisis had been succeeded by another. During the next few years they undertook commitments that marked an irrevocable abandonment of their traditional hostility to entangling alliances. By the Truman Doctrine, the Marshall Plan, and the North Atlantic Treaty Organization the United States began to assume the responsibilities of leadership in Western civilization and gave explicit recognition to that need for preventing any hostile power from controlling western Europe that had been the main underlying reason for her entry into the two world wars.

In Asia, on the other hand, the problem of containing Communism was much more difficult, since the forces opposed to it consisted in most countries not of well-established democratic organizations but of corrupt and reactionary ruling classes or of European imperialisms, while the Communists could appeal to the resentment of the peasant masses against economic exploitation and foreign privilege. Communism could be defeated only by some more dynamic and constructive movement of democratic reform. This was the main lesson of the Chinese catastrophe, where the Nationalists were defeated primarily because of their loss of popular support, while the United States remained hesitant, giving military supplies to the Chiang regime but refusing to intervene on a sufficient scale either to insist on a more liberal program or to prevent the Communist victory. The subsequent Communist attempt to conquer South Korea was defeated, though at a heavy cost in American lives, and the United States began to build a defense system among the non-Communist states in southeastern Asia and the western Pacific. But without bold and imaginative American leadership for the implementation of democratic ideals in terms applicable to Asiatic peoples, there was no guarantee that the Chinese experience would not be repeated in other countries.

With the loss of China, followed by the dreary and protracted Korean War, the American people began to display symptoms of a failure of nerve. Why, in spite of such an expenditure of blood and wealth, had the United States failed to achieve her World War Two objectives? Why was her government apparently so reluctant to crush the forces of evil, allowing them to win control of China and fighting only a limited and defensive war in Korea? The apparent revelation that certain individuals in the Roosevelt administration had been secret agents of the Communist Party suggested a possible explanation, and anti-New Deal politicians began to insist that all the victories of Communism had been made possible by treason in the American State Department. Such an interpretation was a fantastic falsification of history; for although the Roosevelt administration, together with most of the American people, had undeniably developed illusions about Soviet policy, the victories of Communism were due mainly not to the wartime agreements with the Soviet Union but to violations of those agreements during the period of American demobilization after the war and, in China, to the weakness and corruption of the Nationalists. The early fifties, nevertheless, saw a wave of anti-Communist hysteria, resulting in security regulations for all public employees and in a general pressure for conformity which did more damage both to the efficiency of the government and to America's reputation abroad than the Communists could ever have hoped to accomplish. Senator McCarthy, who succeeded in making himself the chief symbol of the hysteria, was too arrogant and brutal to acquire leadership of a major political organization; but McCarthyism, as a manifestation of certain characteristic weaknesses in the American temperament, was more significant than McCarthy. It displayed the American anti-intellectualism, the American tendency to resort to lynch law against supposed public enemies, and, above all, the American illusion of omnipotence and the resultant assumption that treachery was the only possible explanation for failure.

This recrudescence of frontier attitudes was an alarming indication of immaturity, for in the world of the 1950's neither total security nor total victory was a possible objective. The pursuit of the former could lead only to the suppression of freedom at home; and after both sides had acquired atomic weapons, any attempt to achieve the latter could result only in common destruction. The Americans had therefore to learn how to coexist in the same world with forces which they regarded as evil and could no longer hope to eliminate by military conquest. While the free nations must be continually ready to defend each other against possible Communist aggression, the ultimate destiny of the human race would be determined mainly by spiritual rather than by material factors. Communism spread because it proclaimed the equality of man and promised to abolish poverty, class oppression, and race discrimination. It could be permanently contained only by a convincing demonstration that these ideals could be genuinely achieved not by the political methods of totalitarianism but by those of democracy. The final decision between the two systems would depend on which had more to offer to the mass of the people, not only in Europe and

America but also in Asia and Africa, and which could release for constructive purposes the greater fund of energy, initiative, and resourcefulness.

For this reason the example set by the American people in the conduct of their internal affairs was fully as influential in the struggle against Communism as their diplomatic and military decisions. Whenever they failed to live up to their professed beliefs by maintaining economic privilege, by tolerating lawlessness, by displaying race and color prejudice, or by showing a fear of free inquiry, they were giving aid and comfort to the enemy. The principles upon which American society had been founded were more profoundly and constructively revolutionary than those of Communism; but the Americans could not win support for them among oppressed peoples in other countries unless they could show that they understood them and practiced them at home. In certain directions, most notably in the decrease of race discrimination, the postwar years saw real progress. At the same time the American people were reacting to the Communist threat by displaying a growing intolerance of dissent and a tendency to identify the American ideal with narrow loyalty to political and religious tradition. Such developments recalled words written a century and a quarter earlier by John Taylor of Caroline: "If our system of government produces these bitter fruits naturally, it is substantially European; and the world, after having contemplated with intense interest and eager solicitude the experiment of the United States, will be surprised to find, that no experiment at all has been made."

★ ☆ ☆ ☆ ☆ ☆ ☆ ☆ ☆ ☆ ☆ ☆ ★

CHAPTER XV

CONCLUSION

★ ★ ★ ★ ★ ★ ★ ★ ★ ★ ★ ★ ★ ★ ★

THE NATIONALISTIC CONFLICTS of Europe have thrust upon the American people the unwelcome responsibilities of leadership in the Western World during a period when they have also been confronted by far-reaching internal readjustments. During the twentieth century the Americans have been faced by three major new developments, each of which has necessitated profound modifications in their traditional mores and institutions. The conquest of the continent, which absorbed so much of the national energy and determined so much of the national view of life for nearly three hundred years, has been substantially completed. The growth of industrial capitalism has caused a widespread economic insecurity, which has led to a vast expansion of the powers and responsibilities of government, and has resulted also in a serious curtailment of the personal liberty and equality of opportunity that had formerly been the chief characteristics of American society. And the growth of imperialist and ideological conflicts in a rapidly shrinking world has put an end to the possibility of isolation and threatened to destroy the whole heritage of Western civilization. These problems can be met only by conscious and deliberate effort; they cannot be solved by allowing events to take their course.

As long as there was an open frontier and an unsettled West, material conditions in themselves promoted equality and provided opportunity. What was chiefly required of the government was that it should give men access to public land without discrimination and should refrain from creating systems of privilege. In the age of Jefferson and Jackson democracy was best served by a state that took as little positive action as possible. But after the closing of the frontier and the growth of the big corporations, material conditions no longer favored freedom and equality. In the twentieth century it has become necessary to work out some kind of deliberate and constructive program guided by an awareness of ultimate principles and values as well as by a consideration of the available means. For though the immediate problems have been practical, their implications are spiritual and philosophical; and without a full consideration of these implications they cannot be solved successfully. Freedom can no longer be preserved by a piecemeal and pragmatic approach. As Whitman declared, the preservation of American ideals depends on the growth of the appropriate "religious and moral character beneath the political and productive and intellectual bases of the States." Without this "religious and moral character" no merely practical proposals can be effective.

The main animating principle of American nationality has been the belief that the average man can be trusted with freedom, that he does not require the guidance of an authoritarian church or of a privileged aristocracy or bureaucracy, and that whenever he finds adequate opportunity for exercising initiative, hidden talents and energies will be released for constructive purposes. This belief, derived from European religious and philosophical sources, but brought for the first time to full fruition in the open spaces of the American continent, has justified itself again and again in American history from the first settlements in Virginia and Massachusetts down to the Second World War. Throughout the history of America, moreover, it has exercised a magnetic influence upon the development of Europe. The revolutionary doctrine of equality, preached by European radicals but most fully exemplified in the American world, has been the chief provocation of European internal conflicts; and the inability of some European countries to make the necessary adaptation of their institutions has been the main underlying cause of twentieth-century totalitarianism.

But while the Americans have believed in the right of all men to freedom and opportunity, they have also exalted the drive of the individual will toward wealth and power; they have adopted a morality of personal (and largely material) success; and as a result of both their economic system and their Calvinist heritage, they have exalted activity above contemplation and material accumulation above æsthetic, intellectual, and spiritual development. The animating standards of American civilization have been predominantly acquisitive and competitive, while more important values have received little social sanction or encouragement. This emphasis on the will, on conquest, and on a kind of materialistic asceticism was the natural and appropriate accompaniment of the pioneering process; and as long as there was still empty land to be settled, it was possible to reconcile it with democratic ideals. Yet there has always been conflict between the ideal of freedom for all and the drive of power-hungry individuals for privilege and success. And since the settlement of the West and the growth of capitalism, the continued emphasis on material conquest has become a cultural lag that is no longer appropriate to the social environment. It is a main cause of the sense of frustration and maladjustment that is so pervasive a characteristic of the American mind in the twentieth century.

In the last resort, as all the early spokesmen of American democracy recognized, faith in the human capacity for freedom depends on religious and philosophical affirmations. It is derived, as Jefferson declared, from the belief in an innate moral sense and, as Emerson proclaimed, from the belief that man has the lawgiver within himself and can trust his own deepest intuitions. But while the history of America confirms in many ways this trust in human nature, it also suggests that confidence in the individual is not enough. Man's moral sense and spiritual intuitions require the objective support of a general view of life and of appropriate social institutions. And the creation of spiritual values and social forms that will give support to

American democratic aspirations is a task that has remained unfinished. There is still much truth in Whitman's gloomy suggestion that Americans were "somehow being endowed with a vast and more and more thoroughly-appointed body, and then left with little or no soul."

Every high civilization is imbued with a sense of form, style, and order. The individual feels himself to be part of a social unity and harmony, which is regarded as the embodiment of universal and objective ideals and as a reflection of an ultimate harmony in nature. He finds emotional security and personal fulfilment, not through the assertion of his will against the natural and social environment, but through participation in the processes of nature and in the collective enterprise of society. Yet in subordinating himself to the social order, he does not deify it or endow it with absolute and final authority (as in the totalitarian states). He is loyal to it only because, and insofar as, it is an attempt to realize ideals to which he himself gives spontaneous allegiance and by which he himself can achieve the full development of his own personality; and he recognizes that evil is an inherent element in human life, that concrete social institutions must always fall short of ideals, and that the struggle to realize them more fully is unending. It is only in these terms that the apparent polarity of freedom and order can be transcended. The synthesis of individual will and social discipline, without which there can be no high civilization, is to be found not in intellectual formulas, but in the sentiment of patriotism, in moral and religious idealism, and (as Whitman declared) in "the manly love of comrades."

American civilization has never sufficiently developed this sense of form, order, and underlying harmony, as its literature, its philosophy, and its economic development abundantly make manifest. Without a deeper and more comprehensive sense of order, the United States cannot become a high and stable civilization, nor can the Americans as individuals find emotional security and fulfilment. But this sense cannot be borrowed from elsewhere, as American intellectuals have sometimes been tempted to

believe. As Whitman insisted, any American order must be
a native product, accepting the concept of human equality
and developed through a deeper understanding of American society and the needs and aspirations of American
man.

This growth of a more vital sense of order is indispensable if the Americans are to retain their freedom. The
United States was able to flourish without it for three
hundred years chiefly because of its unique situation—its
open frontier and rapidly expanding economy. But when its
society became less mobile and more static, both a greater
restraint on individual ambition and a fuller individual
participation in social enterprises became necessary. If
this problem is not solved through the growth of a genuine
social idealism, then it can be predicted that America will
finally become totalitarian. For totalitarianism is a method
of enforcing order upon a people who have lost any
genuine sense of unity. Either the Americans will achieve
an organic order based on the free participation of individuals or they will succumb to a mechanistic order imposed by an absolute state. Either they will give a free
allegiance to their society as an attempt to realize common rational values and liberal ideals, or they will become merged on a subhuman level in a mass movement of
emotionalism and fanaticism.

Ever since the time of Alexander Hamilton, Americans
who have felt a need for order have often turned back to
European traditions of authority and class hierarchy in
the belief that a democracy must necessarily be anarchical
and hostile to cultural standards. But according to the
evidence of history there is no necessary connection between high civilization and any particular political and
social system. Civilization flourishes when society is permeated with humane values, and at different periods this
has occurred under the rule of kings, of aristocracies, and
of popular majorities. If the American faith in the possibilities of a democratic civilization has not so far come to full
fruition, it is not because of any inherent incompatibility
between high cultural attainment and popular government,
but because, as a result of certain specific factors in their

historical experience, Americans have been too narrowly intent on the production and consumption of goods. But there are other resources in the American heritage which have been insufficiently explored. In particular, there is the whole agrarian tradition of the eighteenth and early nineteenth centuries. The spokesmen of agrarianism believed that the proper standard for judging an economic system was not whether it produced as much wealth as possible, but how far it maintained the freedom of individuals and promoted their moral and cultural development. In spite of their fears of strong government they were by no means averse to legislation designed to bring about a wide distribution of private property, maintain economic security, and prevent that "accumulation of wealth by law without industry" which John Taylor regarded as the essence of aristocracy. The agrarian economy has now disappeared, but the underlying principles of agrarian thought have not lost their validity. Thomas Jefferson and John Taylor can be quoted on both sides of virtually every current controversy, but their lasting importance is that they judged political and economic questions by humane standards combined with a faith in the possibilities of popular government.

A nation's foreign policy is always a reflection of its internal institutions; and if American policy during the postwar years has too often seemed to have only negative objectives, being motivated by the fear of Communism rather than by any positive ideals (as shown particularly by its willingness to give military aid to any dictator who is sufficiently anti-Communist), it is because Americans have been uncertain and confused about their own values and beliefs. The preservation and extension of the American heritage of freedom in the twentieth-century world require a clearer sense of direction and a deeper appreciation of intellectual and spiritual values. Otherwise there can be no happy answer to the question raised by Whitman as to whether the United States would "surmount the gorgeous history of feudalism" or "prove the most tremendous failure of time."

Index

HENRY BAMFORD PARKES was born in Sheffield, England, in 1904. After attending Oxford (B.A.), he came to the United States, doing his graduate work at the University of Michigan, where he received his Ph.D. in 1929. Since 1930 he has been on the faculty of New York University, at which he is now a Professor of History. Mr. Parkes has also taught at Barnard College, the University of Wyoming, and the University of Washington, has lectured at the New School (New York), and has been an editorial writer for the Baltimore *Sun.* He has contributed widely to periodicals. During the 1956–7 academic year he was Fulbright professor in Greece, at the University of Athens. His published books include *Jonathan Edwards* (1930), *A History of Mexico* (1938), *The Pragmatic Test* (1942), *Recent America* (1942), *The World after War* (1942), *The American Experience* (1947), *The United States of America* (1953), and *Gods and Men: The Origins of Western Culture* (1959). Mr. Parkes is married and has two daughters.